EROS
BREAKING
FREE

INTERPRETING SEXUAL THEO-ETHICS

ANNE BATHURST GILSON

The Pilgrim Press
Cleveland, Ohio

The Pilgrim Press, Cleveland, Ohio 44115
© 1995 by Anne Bathurst Gilson

Printed in the United States of America
on acid-free paper

00 99 98 97 96 95   5 4 3 2 1

Library of Congress Cataloging-in-Publication Data
Gilson, Anne Bathurst, 1958–
    Eros breaking free : interpreting sexual theo-
ethics / Anne Bathurst Gilson.
        p.   cm.
    Includes bibliographical references and index.
    ISBN 0-8298-1021-8
    1. Sex—Religious aspects—Christianity.
2. Homosexuality—Religious aspects—Christianity.   3. Feminist theology.   4. Sexual
ethics.   5. Gilson, Anne Bathurst, 1958–   .
6. Episcopal Church—United States—Clergy—
Sexual behavior.   7. Anglican Communion—
Clergy—Sexual behavior.   8. Lesbian clergy—
United States.
I. Title.
BT708.G55   1995
241'.66—dc20
                                    94-39962
                                        CIP

To my mother, Margaret Bathurst Gilson,
and my father, Richard Abbott Gilson,
for standing with and by me

CONTENTS

ACKNOWLEDGMENTS

This book could never have been written without the friendship and encouragement of many people. I am profoundly indebted to Tom F. Driver, adviser, friend, and director of my dissertation at Union Theological Seminary, whose gentle questioning has influenced the shape of this book. For his patience, wise guidance, and sense of humor, I am immensely grateful.

Along with Tom Driver, Beverly Wildung Harrison, Carter Heyward, and Delores Williams served on my dissertation committee. Beverly Harrison's presence throughout the years of my graduate work has been sustaining and her contribution to this book has been invaluable. My years in New York City would not have been the same without her. Carter Heyward has played an essential role in my work since my days as a seminarian at Episcopal Divinity School. The series of conversations we have had on this subject and others over the years, as well as her in-depth reading of various versions of this manuscript, has been critical to my formulation of the final project. Delores Williams's encouragement has spurred me on to make new connections and raise yet more questions. Her support and suggestions for revision of an earlier draft have been enormously helpful.

Ann Kirkus Wetherilt has been a delightful companion during the many months of labor. On days when my eyes were glazed over and I could only babble about whatever section I was working on, Ann was in much the same condition. What an extraordinary gift to have a friend who kept the same weird hours, needed the same walks to the Hungarian Pastry Shop, and had the same propensity for staring into space! For her friendship and her spaghetti sauce, I am forever grateful.

Robin Hawley Gorsline has been a part of this project from early discussions during our years at Episcopal Divinity School to the last-minute redrafting of chapter 6. Margaret Mayman has given crucial suggestions for chapters 3 through 6, and saved me from getting sidetracked. And Marvin Ellison read the entire manuscript and offered numerous suggestions. For these three friends and our innumerable conversations over the years, I am thankful.

Elizabeth Bounds has been present throughout the entire process via telephone consultations and electronic mail. Kathleen Greider's advice to "keep your fingers poised over the keyboard" resulted in the timely completion of this project. Without the ongoing friendship of these two colleagues, my work would have been significantly lonelier.

My editor at The Pilgrim Press, Richard Brown, has been of enormous help in the process of publishing this book. For his belief in the importance of the subject matter of this book and his insightful suggestions, I am truly grateful. Librarians Betty Bolden and Drew Kadel, at Union Seminary's Burke Library, provided crucial assistance and found some of the more obscure references I needed.

My parents, Margaret and Richard, to whom this volume is dedicated, have nourished my commitment to relationships grounded in justice. My sisters, Eileen Williams and Claudia Pontious, and my brother Richard Gilson have likewise informed my work.

Other colleagues in New York City and in Cambridge, Massachusetts, provided companionship, encouragement, and distraction, and I celebrate their presence in my life: Elizabeth Alexander, Angela Bauer, Chris Blackburn, Karin Case, Alison Cheek, Ken Estey, Ann Franklin, Kelly Gallagher, Andrea Sichenze Haldeman, Nan Haxby, Scott Haldeman, Jane Heckles, Jane Hicks, Sandra Jones, Irma Levesque, Sally MacNichol, Diane Moore, James Nally, Michael Orzechowski, Joan Sakalas, Nancy Hamlin Soukup, and Wilma Wake. The children in my life—Anton, Brittany, Tyler, Whitney, Adam, Sydney, Andrew, Emily, Meg, Robin, Beverly, Mónica, Molly, and Brennan—have imbued me with a sense of urgency regarding the adoption of a sexual ethics grounded in justice and love, while reteaching me about the value of play.

Never failing to remind me when it was time to eat, my two feline companions, Ethel and Brattle, have graced my writing hours with the aplomb unique to their species.

I am enormously grateful to all. They have helped eros break free.

INTRODUCTION

Journeying with Eros

I am weary, bone weary, of waiting for the churches to come to their senses about sexuality.

I am weary, bone weary, of hearing about my sisters, my brothers, myself outed and ousted from church positions, careers cut short before they had a chance to be launched. Other sisters and brothers in the clergy live painfully closeted lives, hardly daring to breathe lest the ecclesiastical authorities find out they're lesbian or gay. All this for daring to live lives contrary to a compulsory heterosexuality. This is the price that too many have paid for the church's confusion over sexuality.

I am weary, bone weary, of a church that cannot admit that many heterosexual relationships and marriages involve brutal violence against women and children. So often everyone smiles and maintains the pretense that all is well. "They seem so happy," we hear. "He's such a nice man, the pillar of the church community" (and sometimes even an *ordained* pillar). Yet silence is not golden.

I am weary, bone weary, of the extent to which the message of self-loathing is communicated in christian[1] theology. This message is commonly delivered from the pulpit. The effects are devastating, and too many church people lead alienated, disconnected lives and engage in self-destructive behaviors. Self-loathing is a perversion of christianity.

I am weary, bone weary, of the lack of imagination the churches show in their insistence that *only* female plus male in the context of marriage equals the will of God and is, therefore, representative of the natural order. Such insistence fails to mirror the reality of many people's lives.

I am weary, bone weary, of the subtle and not-so-subtle efforts of traditional theology and the churches to control sexuality in general and female sexuality in particular. The damage that such efforts have wreaked is incalculable. Theological and ecclesiastical investment in the control of sexuality contributes to the propagation of violence as a means of control.

I am weary, bone weary, of the endless stream of committees assigned the task of "studying" sexuality. When one of these committees comes up with sensible recommendations, the powers-that-be dismiss it and call together yet another committee—hoping that this time they'll get it right.

I am weary, bone weary, of waiting to be included. The churches are killing our sexualities, burying eros in the futile hopes of maintaining a grasp on an elusive control. When will they come to their senses?

The churches are in a mess over sexuality. They are preoccupied with questions of what constitutes good christian sexual conduct and have focused these questions on the challenge that lesbian women and gay men pose to church polity.[2] Homosexuality is by no means the only issue of sexuality facing the churches; however, it has become a lightning rod for the sexual confusion and conflict rampant in the churches today. One side insists that justice and eros go together; the other side warns against infidelity to christianity and its doctrines. The debates seem endless as committee after committee is appointed to propose solutions to the "problem."

Because of my experience in the ordination process of the Episcopal Church and the similar experiences of many friends, my investment in what the churches are saying about sexuality is deeply personal.[3] Several years ago when I began to study several denominations' policies on sexuality, I noticed that a pattern began to emerge: lesbian women and gay men were to be received as "children of God" but not as ordained leaders; sexuality was a gift from God and therefore good, but it was a gift to be used only within the confines of heterosexual, lifelong, monogamous marriage. In what were these pronouncements rooted?

I researched the positions on sexuality of mid-twentieth-century ethicists Helmut Thielicke and D. S. Bailey and discovered, to my surprise, that their views were reflected in contemporary mainline denominational policies on sexuality. My curiosity was piqued. At least thirty years had passed since Thielicke and Bailey had written. In the intervening years, pro-feminist theo-ethicists and feminist theo-ethicists had published groundbreaking work on human sexuality.[4] Why was none of it incorporated into denominational statements? Thus began this project.

This book comes from the pen of a feminist liberation theo-ethicist[5] who assumes that traditional theological conceptions of eros and mainline denominational policy statements about sexuality are androcentric in character. Women's voices—indeed the voices of all who are not white, heterosexual, class-privileged males—have not been included in the discourse on eros and sexuality. This has resulted in policies, theology, and ethics that are decidedly limited and oppressive.

I attempt to show the inadequacy of traditional concepts of eros as inherited from such representative theological figures of the twentieth century as Anders Nygren, Helmut Thielicke, D. S. Bailey, and C. S. Lewis and as reflected in the contemporary policy statements of mainline denominations regarding sexuality. I will point to the work done by feminist theorists and feminist liberation theo-ethicists on the subject of eros, and I will engage in the feminist liberation theo-ethical task of moving from an alienated and despised eros toward an erotic mutuality grounded in justice, noting the implications of such movement for contemporary church communities.

In chapter 1, I examine the work of Nygren, Thielicke, Lewis, and Bailey. Nygren saw eros as an unchristian form of love. Thielicke saw value in eros but saw it as an insufficient form of love, in itself, which had to be chastened, shaped, redeemed, and ultimately controlled by agape. For Lewis, eros was acceptable only if combined with other forms of love. Bailey sought to cast eros in a more favorable light than christian history had formerly done, by elaborating upon a theory of gender complementarity as a defense for eros. These four theologians all describe an eros that must be carefully controlled.

Chapter 2, "The Church on Eros," summarizes current debates and policies on sexuality in four mainline denominations. Women's roles; incest and domestic violence; premarital, extra-marital, and postmarital sex; and homosexuality in general and the blessing of same-sex partnerships and the ordination of lesbian women and gay men in particular have all been issues of hot debate in the churches. However, the focus in this chapter is primarily on lesbian and gay issues since they have dominated the headlines and church debates on sexuality. Underlying these issues is the primary subject of this book—the attitude of the churches toward eros. I will also draw out the influence of traditional theologies on these denominational policies.

In chapter 3, "Re-membering Eros," I describe three ongoing movements in feminist liberation theo-ethics: the re-claiming and re-defining of eros, the descriptions of how eros functions in our common lives, and a visioning of the transformative power of eros. The power of eros in women's lives is affirmed via the reclamation and redefinition of eros. The functioning of eros in our common lives is described by three feminist liberation theo-ethicists—Rita Nakashima Brock, Carter Heyward, and Sheila Briggs—all of whom have detailed eros as the source of power in relationships and in justice making. Visioning the transformative power of eros involves elaborating upon the implications of feminist work on eros for the tasks of sexual ethics.

In the final three chapters, I (1) address issues that have arisen in feminist liberation theo-ethical discussions (such as the eroticization of violence), (2) expand the feminist liberation theo-ethical agenda (by talking about movements into an erotic mutuality), and (3) connect the work of feminist liberation theo-ethics on eros to the tasks facing mainline denominations. Chapter 4, "The Problems Begotten of an Eroticized Violence," explores the violence that has its roots in the negative (or, at best, ambivalent) treatment of eros inherited from traditional theology and reinforced by current denominational policies. Chapter 5, "Surviving and Thriving," focuses on the transformation of relational dynamics based on an examination of our relationships with one another and God. Finally, in chapter 6 I address the tasks of our communities of faith in regard to "re-membering" eros.

FEMINIST LIBERATION THEO-ETHICS

In this book I employ a feminist liberation theo-ethical method that is at once historical, analytical, and constructive. There are four pieces to this approach: social location, terminology, the use of social construction theory, and an elaboration upon my own constructive analysis.

Interfacing Privilege and Marginalization[6]

This book was not written in a vacuum. Indeed, many factors have influenced this work—not the least of which are the various aspects of my social location. My particular positions of privilege and marginalization have shaped how I think about eros, sexuality, and sex.

The privilege I am accorded in this society by virtue of race and class comes from several factors. First, I am from the middle economic stratum of U.S. society: economically, my family of origin hangs onto the lower rungs of the middle stratum; culturally and educationally, my family of origin is well toward the upper middle. Second, I am white in the context of a racist society and church. Because of my white skin, I have access to power in ways others do not. Third, I am well educated. My education grants me access to several institutions, including the church and the academy.

My privilege, however, cannot be separated from the ways in which I am marginalized. Because of my economic stratum and education, I have accrued enormous debt. This is both a position of privilege and one of marginalization. On the one hand, if I had not had a family that valued and had access to the benefits of education, I might not have been able to get scholarships and loans and go on to further education. On the other hand, if my family were affluent, I would not have incurred the debt. So, revealing the complexities of contemporary monopolistic capitalist western societies, I have been *privileged* to accrue debt. Our mainline denominations are largely led by persons from the upper-middle class and defined by the socioeconomic interests of those who identify with the maintenance of domination by that class. Class privilege plays an important role in the denominational scramble to maintain control of eros.

I am also female in a society and church that is male-dominated. I have been the target of male violence; between the ages of eighteen and twenty, I was battered by my ex-husband. On a subtler level, my femaleness denies me access to the sorts of power to which males automatically have access. My femaleness has provided firsthand experience of exclusion from the church: before entering the Diocese of Bethlehem, I was rejected in the Diocese of Northwestern Pennsylvania because they did not believe in the ordination of women.[7] In ways similar to class domination, the mainline denominations are led almost exclusively by men and are defined by the interests of those who identify with the maintenance of male domination.

My femaleness, however, cannot be separated from my race. The difference between being a white female and being an African American, Asian American, Hispanic, or American Indian female must be figured into feminist liberation theo-ethical method and praxis. Our mainline denominations are almost exclusively led by white, european-identified North Americans and are defined by the interests of those who identify with the maintenance of the dominant racial or ethnic groups in our society.

As a lesbian woman in a society and church hostile to couplings that are not male/female, lifelong, monogamous commitments, I am, by my very existence, a target of others' fear and rage. I have experienced firsthand the heterosexism and homophobia of traditional theology and the church. Our mainline denominations are almost exclusively led by heterosexual, upper-middle-class white men who time and again have demonstrated their unwillingness to relinquish their domination by accepting and ordaining lesbian women and gay men.

WORKING DEFINITIONS

Because feminist liberation theology takes seriously the different perspectives from which theologians write, a few key terms must be defined from the outset. Others are defined in the contexts in which they arise.

Justice is not about being the power-*full* or the power-*less*, nor is it about power-*over*. Rather, it is about sharing power; it is about power-*with*. Justice is the making of a right relation in which no one person profits at the expense of another and no one group of people uses the particularities of their lives as a determining factor of what should be regarded as universal human truths and values. The praxis of justice entails making certain that all those who are oppressed—by virtue of race, class, gender, sexuality, physical and mental abilities, or religion—are heard, represented in positions of power, and included in the making of policy.

Malestream is a feminist term used to denote how patriarchal viewpoints have constituted the cultural/social mainstream. Patriarchal viewpoints are those that exclude the perspectives of those who are not white, male, heterosexual, and upper middle class.[8]

Sexism is rooted in the negation of that which is female, sexual, eros, and earthy. It is the assumption of female-gender inferiority and the presumption of male-gender superiority. Sexism is the domination of women by men. It is a force that would keep women and men in neatly constrained gender roles. Sexism affects women across generational, racial, cultural, sexual, and economic lines.

Heterosexism is inseparable from sexism. It is the glue that holds sexism in place by cementing male control over female sexuality. Heterosexism assumes that everyone is heterosexual—indeed, that the only possible intimate, sexual relationship is between a man and a woman. It encourages the sexual exploitation of women and is held in place by *heterosexual privilege*. Heterosexual privilege is the security and protection bestowed on women for the price of male control over female bodies.[9]

Compulsory heterosexuality is the institutionalization of heterosexism.[10] It is the foundation upon which the control of sexuality is built, and it assures that heterosexuality is perceived as being normative. Society is structured around the compulsory nature of heterosexuality so that homosexual possibilities—the existence of homosexual images, relationships, and cultures—are kept hidden.

Homophobia literally means fear of the same. It is an attitude reinforced by the structures of sexism and heterosexism and is a social disease that is out of control. It manifests itself in the fear-filled hatred of lesbian women and gay men. Those who would prefer that lesbian women and gay men keep silent and remain invisible fear challenges to the normativity of heterosexuality. Homophobia reveals the extent to which sexuality is controlled.[11]

Sex is a touching of our own and one another's bodies in order to give pleasure to one another. It includes, but is not limited to, genital touching. *Sexuality* encompasses more than sex. By its very nature, it is sensual. Our sexuality can move us toward an erotic mutuality grounded in justice or, when alienated, can move us into eroticized violence. Our sexuality is never ours alone; it necessarily implies relation. As Carter Heyward has noted, it is an embodied, relational response to eros.[12]

The terms *eros* and *sexuality* are often used interchangeably. In chapter 1, Eros[13] is representative of human sexuality in dialogue with the christian love, Agape. In chapter 2, the mainline denominations use the term *sexuality* to represent what Nygren, Thielicke, Lewis, and Bailey would have called *Eros*. In chapter 3, feminist liberation theo-ethicists often refer to both eros and sexuality in identical contexts. Eros is defined constructively in chapter 5.

Feminist Liberation Theo-Ethics and Social Construction Theory

Of the various streams of feminist theory, social construction theory is the most amiable companion to feminist liberation theo-ethics and, as such, needs some elaboration. Social construction theorists believe that sexuality is a construct of society and that the meanings of sexuality are not biologically imputed. Instead, sexuality is shaped by multiple and interconnecting social forces and institutions, including family systems; religious ideologies and practices; economic and social forces; community norms, mores, and regulations; and political agendas and policies.[14] Social construction theorist Jeffrey Weeks notes that the subject of sexuality has not one history but many, and should be understood in a way that takes into account the intricate nature of the subject.

> We must abandon the idea that we can. . . understand the history of sexuality in terms of a dichotomy of pressure and release, repression and liberation. Sexuality is not a head of steam that must be capped lest it destroy us; nor is it a life force we must release to save our civilization. Instead we must learn to see that sexuality. . . . is a result of diverse social practices that give meaning to human activities, of social definitions and self-definitions, of struggles between those who have power to define and regulate, and those who resist.[15]

Weeks stresses that sexuality is not a "given"; rather, it is shaped by "negotiation, struggle and human agency." Put simply, understanding human sexuality involves understanding the *relationships* in which it occurs.[16]

The emphasis of social construction theory on the relational context of sexuality correlates with the centrality of relation to feminist liberation theo-ethics. With its attention to the various overlapping forces that shape sexuality, as well as its insistence that there is no *one* history of sexuality, social construction theory has the potential (though not always fulfilled) to attend to the issue of difference so central to feminist liberation theo-ethics.

Both social construction theory and feminist liberation theo-ethics posit as central to their methodological premises the commitment to seek out, listen to, and act upon the concerns of people from various social locations. Both are open to change; indeed, their continued development is dependent upon change and the inclusion of voices previously unheard. Thus, social construction approaches to sexuality present the most likely theoretical companion to feminist liberation theo-ethics in general and to my own constructive methodology in particular.[17]

Roots, Branches, Trees, and a Feminist Liberation Theo-Ethical Methodology[18]

I have come to believe that a primary theological task is digging for roots.[19] Roots symbolize an intensely powerful *erotic* connecting between human bodies and the earth. They are a

metaphor for life-sustaining and life-enhancing connections between and among ourselves, other earth creatures, and God.[20]

Besides having roots, trees have trunks—which, in this context, can be seen as the main *body* of feminist liberation theo-
ethical work. Without roots, the trunk would cease to exist.
Roots serve to center one in the soil of a wider community and
provide a basis for growth.

Branches are as important to the trunk as roots. They symbolize the importance of reaching out, and they point to the hope of
the future. In a world/church in which white, male, euro-american, and heterosexual perspectives hold sway, branches provide
life-enhancing opportunities to reach out to those who have not
been included. Branches are different from roots in that they require more risk taking. One cannot be "out on a root" in quite
the same way as one can be "out on a limb" (or branch). Branching out into the unknown is as critical to survival as is rooting
down into the familiar soil of community.

Roots, branches, and trunk are part of a whole. From roots
come shoots of roots; roots nourish the trunk, the main body.
From branches come buds, blossoms, leaves, and more branches;
branches derive nourishment from the roots and trunk. Roots,
branches, and trunk dwell in a larger, more complex, ecosystem:
all the parts are interrelated.

Theo-Ethical Roots

Theo-ethical roots push down into the soil of community, preparing a fertile foundation for growth.

The Theo-Ethical Root of Suspicion. Suspicion is an important
tool for critiquing patriarchal tradition. *It entails raising questions
about what has previously appeared to be unquestionable.* In contemplating a feminist liberation theo-ethics of sexuality, the following questions might be among those to arise from a root of suspicion:

> *Who has what to gain by the control of sexuality in general and
> female sexuality in particular?*

> *Why must sexuality be constrained within a heterosexual monogamous model?*
>
> *What if women and men were discovered to be uncomplementary?*
>
> *If compulsory heterosexuality weren't compulsory, would the patriarchal walls come tumbling down?*

The theo-ethical root of suspicion can be used to get at invisible presuppositions, hidden agendas, and historical structures of normativity.

The Theo-Ethical Root of Particularities. Drawing on our particular experiences to engage the questions of theology is part of the power of liberation movements; speaking honestly of our lives and hearing others speak honestly of their lives push open the question of what is "normal" and of what is considered "normative" for human beings as we actually live. Particularities ground us in the everyday realities of our lives and the lives of others. When we share the particularities of our lives with one another, the hold of patriarchal isolation and alienation on our lives is loosened and new possibilities and connections emerge.

The theo-ethical root of particularities means that no one particularity should ever be considered normative. A theo-ethical root of particularities does not aim for "completeness" or "complementarity," "sameness" or that which can be called "normative." Rather, it thrives on *difference,* understood not as "the problem of difference" but as a gift, an opportunity to change. In this root, the differences among us—of race, gender, sexual orientation, age, class, religion, nationality, physical and mental abilities—as well as those things we have in common, matter deeply. They make us who we are. Taking our particularities, our differences, seriously, what is claimed as morally "normative" becomes a question of what enhances or detracts from our well-being and that of others.

The Theo-Ethical Root of Self-Knowing.[21] This root is about *being in touch with oneself,* including, of course, one's body. It does not involve an individualistic navel-gazing but rather an increased understanding of how one's actions affect others. It involves having a sense of who one is and of what one's desires are. If one does not know oneself, one's relations to others and God are unrooted.

The theo-ethical root of self-knowing is particularly important in the context of challenging malestream interpretations of sexuality and eros. Self-knowing enables lesbian women and gay men to "come out," and it enables those who do not buy into prohibitions of sex outside the context of marriage to refuse a patriarchal role. It empowers all who have been relegated to the margins of society to say NO to others' perceptions of who we should be.

Theo-Ethical Branches

Theo-ethical branches enable us to reach out to a wider community.

The Theo-Ethical Branch of Self-Loving. Self-loving has been denounced as an unacceptable form of love for christians. Via its treatment of eros, traditional theology perpetuates self-loathing.[22] It fosters a dis-connection that undergirds violence against women and children, indeed against all who differ from the white, male, heterosexual norm. A theo-ethical branch of self-loving seeks to undo the damage.

For women, this is an especially important branch since we have been socialized into putting everyone else before ourselves.[23] Self-loving means that we must take ourselves seriously. In so doing, we must strategize about how self-loving can be actualized for *all* women, not just for white women. We must eradicate the patriarchal voices that would stifle our creativity, depress us into inaction, and render us null and void.[24] Self- loving requires that a resounding NO be uttered to those self-destructive impulses that in reality do not come from the self but are rooted in a racist, misogynistic, and homophobic church/world order. Self-loving means we need to work together to resist ongoing victimization, finding ways to survive together and perhaps even thrive together. *Self-loving requires that we affirm our right to exist and our capacity to act as moral agents in the world;* it is key to our ability to branch out to others. We must take seriously the critical business of affirming ourselves—of loving ourselves—shamelessly, with passion, and well.

The Theo-Ethical Branch of Loving Our Neighbors as Ourselves.[25] As we engage the process of learning to love ourselves, we find ourselves branching out, reaching out, to our neighbors. Without self-loving, we are unable to love our neighbors. And the reverse is also true: without neighbor-loving, we are unable to love ourselves—much less God.

Combining an explicit self-loving with an explicit neighbor-loving challenges the ideology that would keep the self denied, disciplined, and controlled. Without a love of self, not only is one unable to love one's neighbor very well, but one is also unable to love God.

With a love of neighbor as self, we are more able to embrace our differences and cast out fear—of both our neighbors and ourselves. With a combined love of self and neighbor, the fear that we might see too much of ourselves in our relation with our neighbor—the fear, in short, of eros—can be transformed into desire and energy for relation grounded in authentic engagement with one another. *Love of neighbor as self means that eros is that which enhances the mutual well-being of self and neighbor.* As such, it can be a power of collective transformation.

The Theo-Ethical Branch of Re-connecting.[26] Coming to love our neighbors as ourselves encompasses the theo-ethical branch of re-connecting. Because we are born into a world/church built and maintained on the theory of categorization, pieces of our lives are kept cordoned off and we are deprived of intimate knowledge of one another.

As in loving our neighbors as ourselves, this branch must overcome deeply ingrained fears of re-connecting, of being intimate with one another, of our own bodies. Our fear, if left unchecked, has the capacity to destroy the earth, the human, the sexual, the flesh. Connections between us are destroyed because we have learned to be so afraid. We must begin the process of re-connecting what has been disconnected.

The theo-political work of structural analysis enters into this branch as re-connections are made between sexism, hetero-sexism, racism, classism, and other forms of oppression. The knowledge that oppressions are structurally interconnected has the potential to empower marginalized people to act together. Re-connecting, the friction between us born of our differences creates a life-giving erotic power.

The theo-ethical branch of re-connecting continues the just, mutual, and erotic re-connecting between people begun in the branch of loving our neighbors as ourselves. An explicitly sexual theo-ethical aspect of the branch of re-connecting is one in which the intimate details of our lives can be affirmed within our commonness, within our differences, between and among our bodyselves. Freeing ourselves from fear, we touch and are touched, move and are moved, heal and are healed, earth and are earthed into the loam of one another's and our own bodyselves. Re-connecting, we meet the feelings, the people, and the bodies from which we have been disconnected. Re-connecting, eros is coming—coming unchastened, coming uncontrolled, coming unshaped, coming undenied, coming unbound, coming unruled/unruly.

A Theo-Ethical Branch of Solidarity. Solidarity takes into account the roots and branches (as well as the main theo-ethical body/trunk). In order to be in solidarity, one must have *suspicions* about the status quo. *Particularities,* too, enter in: solidarity requires a working across particularities, across differences. *Self-knowing* is critical if one is to be in touch with oneself enough to demand justice. A grounded *self-loving* is necessary if one is to feel confident enough to engage the risks that solidarity requires. *Loving one's neighbor as oneself* provides a point from which to begin the cooperative work of effecting change. *Re-connecting* loosens the hold on fear and frees the power of eros in our relationships with one another. Yet solidarity is more than the sum of these roots and branches.

In a theo-ethical branch of solidarity, we need to ask: who exactly *is* our neighbor? Our neighbor is not necessarily the one with whom we have the easiest relation or the most in common. We may have to work hard to be in relation—much less a *mutual* relation—with this neighbor.

A theo-ethical branch of solidarity means that we cannot be blinded by either our own privilege or marginalization to seeing the oppression of others. No one oppressed group is elevated at the expense of another, although one form of oppression may be focused on strategically. In a theo-ethical branch of solidarity, we ask, "How do we stand together, you and I? How shall we be accountable to one another? Who are my, your, and our people?" Solidarity entails a willingness to risk, to confront, and to disagree.

A theo-ethical branch of solidarity requires that we walk the boundary together, you and I, and that we "go beyond the isolated self" and risk relation.[27] Solidarity means that you and I come face to face, body to body, into difficult places with one another; come together for sustenance in the struggle; and come together to draw strength from a shared erotic power.

So, come then. Journey with eros.

CHAPTER ONE

Eros—Friend or Foe?

Malestream Interpretations of Eros

Suspicion towards Eros runs deep in the christian tradition. Eros is either completely cast away or re-appropriated, controlled, and tamed. In the pages that follow I sketch the broader protestant theological context in which the control of Eros has flourished. Four mid-twentieth-century theologians—Anders Nygren, Helmut Thielicke, C. S. Lewis, and D. S. Bailey—give voice to the themes echoed in mainline denominational statements decades later.

Anders Nygren and Helmut Thielicke represent a theological suspicion toward Eros. Nygren, a Swedish Lutheran bishop and theologian, and Thielicke, a German Lutheran theologian, are even today considered to be major figures in the ongoing discussion of love and sexuality. Many current assumptions about what "christian" love is and why Eros is perceived as being "unchristian" can be attributed to Nygren's *Agape and Eros* (1932–1938).[1] Many malestream christian theologians consider Helmut Thielicke's *The Ethics of Sex* (1964) to be foundational to the formulation of christian sexual ethics.[2] His work can be cited fairly as representative of a "generic" position on sexual ethics. The agapic redemption of erotic love is the mainstay of his approach.

C. S. Lewis and D. S. Bailey, both British theologians writing in the 1950s and early 1960s, are representative of the Anglican theological tradition's corpus on matters pertaining to human sexuality. Their work, however, has not been limited to that tradition; indeed, it has been used by many struggling to put theology and sexuality together. C. S. Lewis's *The Four Loves* (1960) is his best-known work on the subject of love. In some christian circles, it has very nearly become canon.[3] D. S. Bailey addressed Eros by examining both the institution of marriage and the

16

"problem" of homosexuality. His attention to historical detail contributed in a way paralleled by few others who were engaged in the formulation of christian sexual ethics at the time to the compelling nature of his work.[4]

All four theologians provide a glimpse into the prevailing mindset that has helped shape contemporary church documents on sexuality. The impact of their work should not be underestimated.

ANDERS NYGREN:
EROS AS AN UNCHRISTIAN FORM OF LOVE

Anders Theodor Samuel Nygren (1890–1978) has been characterized as "one of Europe's leading theologians and undoubtedly Scandinavia's best known theologian in the twentieth century."[5] Along with his colleague at the University of Lund, Gustaf Aulén, Nygren has been described as one responsible for bringing Swedish theology to fruition.[6]

Through the historical-critical study of love, Nygren sought to uncover the basic nature of christianity. In tracing his interest in "love" back to childhood, he cited a conversational response of his father's—"But Christian Agape means something quite different"—as that which provided the impetus for him to investigate further "what sort of thing this 'Agape' might be."[7]

The result of Nygren's investigation—*Agape and Eros*—has been called "one of the classics of Christian theology,"[8] and responses to it have varied from praise to criticism. Karl Barth described Nygren as subject to "strangely manichean tendencies," and maintained that Agape would contradict itself if its characteristics were based solely on Nygren's insistence on the antithesis. Barth held that *both* Eros and Agape were experienced by the christian believer.[9]

M. C. D'Arcy charged that Nygren had cut the knot between Eros and Agape, creating not "a peace between the two but only a solitude in which Agape withers."[10] Nygren's antipathy toward self-love was challenged by those who maintained that self-love was biblically rooted and even demanded by "modern psychological thinkers."[11] Daniel Day Williams believed that Nygren's separation of Eros and Agape ultimately failed since it was based on the misinterpretation of "love" in the New Testament as Agape.[12] Other critics described Nygren's assessment of love as being "simply not true" since Nygren had mistakenly associated the perversion of love with "the essence of Eros."[13] Despite the criticisms, Nygren's separation of Eros and Agape, as well as his insistence that Eros is not a christian form of love, widely influenced the shape of contemporary discourse on love.[14]

Assumptions about the Role of Eros

When the religious question, "What is the nature of God?" is raised, the christian responds that God is love. More specifically, God is Agape.[15] In this way, Agape functions as a fundamental motif (*grundmotiv*). In *Agape and Eros,* Nygren insisted that the investigation of the fundamental motif of Agape involved the critique of the motif most directly opposed to Agape, namely that of Eros. In doing so, Nygren took great pains to point out that such motif research, because it was "a type of scientific analysis," guaranteed "that there can be no question of any value-judgement." He further maintained that Agape was not set over and against Eros as right over wrong, but rather the two were to be examined as the christian motif versus a non-christian motif. The difference was to be seen as one of type, not of value, thus, justifying Nygren's so-called value free analysis of Agape and Eros.[16]

As the only form of christian love, Agape had throughout the centuries often been confused with and diluted by the Eros motif.[17] Nygren described Agape as flowing through well-navigated and flood-controlled channels, whereas Eros tended to overflow its banks.

> *The idea of Agape can be compared to a small stream which... flows along an extremely narrow channel and sometimes seems to lose itself entirely in its surroundings; but Eros is a broad river that overflows its banks, carrying everything away*

with it, so that it is not easy even in thought to dam it up and make it flow in an orderly course.[18]

Eros was a chaotic, uncontrolled force that posed a threat to the true christian love, Agape. Noting that all too often the platonic or heavenly Eros was confused with vulgar Eros, which was a sensual, physical love, Nygren was adamant that there was to be no relation between vulgar Eros and christian Agape. He indicated further that if vulgar Eros was the *only* form of Eros at work in the confrontation between Eros and Agape, there would be no problem. No consideration would be given to vulgar Eros simply because it was a physical, sensual, erotic love. By its very nature, physical love was not perceived as a threat to the christian, God-oriented love, Agape. However, that the two forms of Eros were occasionally confused with one another and with the christian Agape lent an urgency to Nygren's mission to disassociate the fundamental motif of christianity from Eros. His task was to make certain that Agape no longer risked being either diluted or compromised by an Eros of any type.

Nygren began the disassociation of Agape from Eros by outlining their basic characteristics. Agape is spontaneous, unmotivated, and indifferent to value; at the same time, it is a value-creating principle. It is a sacrificial love. Agape initiates fellowship with God; it is theocentric. It is primarily God's love. Its movement is downward. When "attributed to" human beings, it is patterned on divine love.[19]

Platonic, or heavenly, Eros, on the other hand, is based on desire; it is an acquisitive, possessive love (in this it is similar to vulgar Eros); it is a yearning, a striving to have the object that it regards as having value. Eros is egocentric. It is primarily humanity's love, and its movement is upward. When attributed to God, Eros is patterned on human love.[20]

Nygren also compared the relation of Agape and Eros to self-love. Sensual, erotic (vulgar) love had been connected to self-love and had been dismissed as unworthy. Platonic Eros, even though distinguished from vulgar Eros, was also characterized as being based on self-love. Even if Eros love was directed toward the neighbor or toward God, it was still based on the self-oriented motive of ascending to the highest good.

In contrast, Agape excluded all self-love.

> *Christian love moves in two directions, towards God and towards its neighbour; and in self-love it finds its chief adversary, which must be fought and conquered. It is self-love that alienates man from God, preventing him from sincerely giving himself up to God, and it is self-love that shuts up man's heart against his neighbour.* [21]

Regarding the commandment of loving God and loving one's neighbor as oneself, Nygren asserted that there were not three commandments: no commandment to love oneself existed. A commandment of self-love would be "alien to the New Testament commandment of love," since self-love had "grown out of a wholly different soil from that of the New Testament."[22]

Nygren associated self-love with a base selfishness which christians must commit themselves to overcoming.[23] Indeed, the very nature of neighborly love excluded and overcame self-love. Any talk of self-love in the context of Agape represented, to Nygren, a compromise between Eros and Agape. The bottom line was that Agape did not and could not admit self-love as being legitimate any more than it could consider incorporating Eros; Agape was the only form of christian love.[24]

Nygren's insistence that Eros is unchristian and that, therefore, any contact whatsoever with christian Agape is unacceptable reverberated throughout the theological world. Whether or not subsequent theologians agreed, Nygren's work had a grave impact on the reflections on Eros which followed. If Eros was *ever* to be considered even marginally acceptable to christians, it would have to be under carefully scrutinized and controlled circumstances.

HELMUT THIELICKE:
THE VALUE BUT INSUFFICIENCY OF EROS

Helmut Thielicke (1908–1986) was a German Lutheran theologian renowned for his preaching and attempts to relate theology to the modern situation.[25] He penned a four-volume work on theological ethics, of which *The Ethics of Sex* (1964) was the second volume. The late 1950s and early 1960s brought a new era of sexual permissiveness and experimentation. Realizing that past theological guidance on sexuality, which stressed the procreational function of married sex, was inadequate for addressing the situation, Thielicke maintained that moral guidelines were needed that did not ostracize Eros completely yet did not leave Eros totally unchecked.[26]

The most serious criticisms of Thielicke's work included the charges that he was not christocentric enough and that he had failed to exegete the "faulty family relationships" that contributed to homosexuality.[27] James Nelson—who later himself wrote several progressive books on sexuality—highly recommended Thielicke's work, although he was quick to point out that he found Thielicke's "judgments at certain points overly conservative."[28] Christian social ethicist Roger Shinn noted that the book had more "substantial theology" than the usual genre of religious books on sexuality. However, he wondered how Thielicke or any male writer could profess to know what sex means to women.[29]

The Differentiation of Eros and Agape

Thielicke's approach differed considerably from that of Nygren. He did not view Eros as having contaminated the river of Agape, nor did he find it necessary to designate one form of love christian (Agape) and the other form of love non-christian (Eros). He claimed that Nygren's description of Agape and Eros characterized them as ideal types which, when placed in a dualistic relationship to each other, were not applicable to the concrete situations of daily life. The problem of the relationship between Agape and Eros was not how to keep Agape untouched by Eros as Nygren had claimed but rather how Agape and Eros were "dialectically interconnected with each other."[30] Thielicke's approach to a theology of sexuality deliberately distanced itself from the abstract and ideal definitions of both Agape and Eros.[31]

Thielicke's preliminary definitions of Agape and Eros were in the shape of two theses about the motives of love: Eros took into consideration the worth of the other person, whereas Agape was concerned with the authentic being, or *Eigentlichkeit,* of the other person. What he termed the "sexual community" (the connection between two human beings) was the place in which the two motives intersected.[32]

Thielicke noted that Agape loves that which is made in the image of God, in spite of its fallen nature. God's love, Agape, was a love that did not look for worth but rather created worth in the object of that love. Eros was the love that measured a person's worth in terms of function and of how one's interests could best be served by the other. Thielicke argued that if the definition of sexuality were to be confined solely to an emphasis on function, then there would be no reason why sexual partners should not be "exchangeable at will" and why "promiscuity should not be legalized."[33] That the majority of people preferred the institution of monogamy proved that most did not interpret their sexuality in terms of mere function. Thielicke asserted that there was more to sexuality than function. That "more" consisted of a deep respect for the other person which was more than Eros alone; it was Agape mixed with Eros. Where there was a regular exchange of partners, there was a "breakdown of personhood."[34] In such circumstances, Agape was not present.

How Agape Transforms Eros

From Thielicke's perspective, it was important that the whole person be involved in the sex community, since only then was fulfillment truly possible. Involving the whole person included seeing that person in his or her relationship to God; only then could one respect the other person and discover personal qualities other than those relating to function. The relation of both oneself and one's partner to God represented the very essence of Agape.[35]

The sex community, as a connection between two people, posited the presence of Agape, which in turn resulted in viewing the other person as a "neighbor." Hastening to point out that not just any "neighbor" could be one's partner in the sex community, Thielicke outlined several conditions that the neighbor had to fulfill.

Among these conditions are that . . . he belongs to the opposite sex, that his age be in a proper relation to mine, that he be my "type," in physique, character, and mind . . . and thus be in a highly specialized complementary relationship to me. Thus the other person must fulfill the requirement of being the bearer of some very definite values. [36]

Eros served as that which lured one to the other; Agape served as that which kept the neighbor, who was the object of the erotic attraction, from being dehumanized, thus acting as the glue holding the sex community together.

In discussing the necessity of Agape transforming Eros, Thielicke relied heavily on the complementarity theory—the assumption that female and male natures "fit together." This theory was illustrated in a variety of ways which both intertwined Eros and Agape and complemented female and male natures. As became evident in the consummation of the marriage relationship, the difference between the two sexes was that the man's sexuality was already wide awake whereas the sexuality of the "untouched woman" was yet to be stirred. In order to avoid a bad start to a marriage, Thielicke recommended that Agape be called forth to shape Eros and to encourage the man to take into account the needs of his partner. He elaborated:

She requires a process of awakening, which takes place in stages over a longer or shorter time. This awakening . . . cannot simply be an unconcerned pursuit of the male sex entelechy, but rather requires self-denial, self-control, and "selfless" compliance. Thus what we have called agape, namely, self-giving, serving love, which therefore also serves to awaken the other person, manifests itself again as an integrating force in the sex community, which breaks down when it is completely absent. [37]

Without an agapic devotion that based itself on seeking the well-being of the other person, without intentional complementing of female and male natures, the sex community could not be fulfilled.

Once female sexuality was awakened, the female yearned to cultivate an ongoing "erotic atmosphere," steeped in an ever-deepening personal intimacy. At this point, Agape was needed to insure balance in the relationship. Thus, marriage provided the Agape-oriented stability required by the often chaotic nature of the erotic atmosphere.[38]

Thielicke further deepened his emphasis on the extent to which female and male natures complemented each other in his assessment of the differing degrees to which the two partners invested themselves in the sex community. A woman's self-image was brought out by the sexual encounter more than the man's because she was vocationally identified with her sexuality.[39] The man invested much less of himself in the sex community, because he was engaged in the work world. He was not defined by his sexuality to the same extent that his female partner was: the woman was "stamped and molded" by her sexual experience.[40] Physiologically, the woman received something from the sexual experience; her male partner relieved himself of something. The man was therefore freer to take a sexual encounter less seriously, whereas the woman had to contend with the "stamping and molding" effect of a sexual encounter, regardless of whether or not she became pregnant. Her nature was traumatized by any relation that was not monogamous.[41]

The so-called natural sexual action for the man was determined by his relationship to his female partner; he was unable to define his sexuality apart from the woman's sexuality. Because Agape portrayed the wife as "neighbor," the husband could only pursue his own sex nature by relating to the sex nature of his wife and honoring "the physical and personal wholeness of the feminine sex nature." To ignore monogamous feminine nature would ultimately deny his own masculine nature.[42]

The presence of Agape in the sexual community underscored the complementary nature of female and male sexuality. Agape did not usurp Eros; rather it shaped one's erotic love of the other person, giving Eros a "meaning and purpose." For Thielicke, Eros shaped by Agape demanded the law of complementarity.[43]

Those liaisons that did not incorporate the law of female/male complementarity were unacceptable to a christian sexual ethics since they were based on an untransformed Eros.[44] Homosexuality was one such relationship.[45] While maintaining that a homosexual relationship was not a "christian" relationship, because it was contrary to the divine plan for women and men, he admitted that it was possible that a homosexual relationship could be a sincere "search for the totality of the other human being."[46] However, Thielicke was clear that homosexuality was part of an "abnormal personality structure" and was contrary to the will of God.[47] Therefore, the homosexual was obliged to refrain from affirming the condition and to seek healing.[48] The homosexual who could not be cured and was constitutionally unable to practice celibacy was to undertake the same sex relationship in a manner that was ethically responsible.[49] Homosexuality, like premarital and extramarital sex, denied the purposes of sexual expression—marriage and parenthood. Ultimately, homosexuality was possessed of an untransformed Eros.

That Thielicke accomplished a great deal in the transformation of the prevailing assumption that Eros was an unfit love is without question. His insistence that Agape and Eros had to be "dialectically interconnected" was a critical paradigm shift in the christian discussion of love and sexuality. No longer were Agape and Eros to be perceived as forms of love that had nothing in common with each other; they had been made accessible to the human sexual community.

C. S. LEWIS:
EROS AS DISTINCT FROM OTHER FORMS OF LOVE

Clive Staples Lewis (1898–1963), unlike other theologians and ethicists of the time, wrote out of a desire not so much to address the sexual revolution (although he was concerned with its societal effects) as to address his relationship to God.[50] The publication of *The Four Loves* was greeted by those grateful that he had taken on the problematic topic of love.[51] Reviewers agreed on Lewis's main point: experiencing human loves helped one learn to love God.

Mixing Loves

Lewis characterized Eros and Agape, respectively, as need-love and gift-love. Need-love was that which cried out to God from our human poverty; gift-love was that which gave of itself and yearned to serve God, often to the point of suffering. Different loves mixed together in the various moments that made up an individual's life; it was extremely rare for a form of love to exist in itself, in isolation, without becoming connected with another form of love.

Distinguishing Features of Eros and Friendship. While Lewis affirmed the intermixing of the forms of love, he went to great lengths to distinguish Eros from Friendship. Although he conceded that it was possible to feel both Friendship and Eros for the same person, he held that love affairs were very different from Friendships. Lovers talked about their love; friends were absorbed in a common interest. Eros was limited by its very nature to two people; Friendship was not. Eros was inquisitive and wanted to know everything about the beloved; Friendship was indifferent.[52]

One of Lewis's purposes in separating Eros and Friendship was to discourage homosexual attraction from arising within friendship.

> *The homosexual theory that good friendships are homosexual . . . seems to me not even plausible. This is not to say that Friendship and abnormal Eros have never been combined. Certain cultures at certain periods seem to have tended to the contamination. . . . Kisses, tears, and embraces are not in themselves evidence of homosexuality. The implications would be, if nothing else, too comic. . . . All those hairy old toughs of centurions in Tacitus, clinging to one another and begging for last kisses when the legion was broken up . . . all pansies? If you can believe that you can believe anything.*[53]

The combination of Eros and Friendship posed a problem. Disturbed by those who saw every Friendship as being homosexual, he felt that the burden of proof was unfairly placed on those friends who were not homosexual. [54]

Lewis assumed that Friendship between members of the opposite sex rarely existed since men and women inhabit such different constellations (e.g., men are educated and women are not; men work and women are idle). [55] In those situations in which Friendship was between a woman and a man, the Friendship very easily passed—perhaps even in the first thirty minutes!—into erotic love. The only exceptions Lewis acknowledged were those physically repulsed by each other or those who loved elsewhere. The occasional coexistence of Friendship and Eros between members of the opposite sex should help skeptical moderns realize "that Friendship is in reality a love, and even as great a love as Eros." [56]

The Not-So-Strange Bedfellows: Eros and Venus

Lewis believed that since God chose to become incarnate in a human body, christian tradition affirmed sex. However, he bewailed the mess that sex had become:

> *They tell you sex has become a mess because it was hushed up. But for the last twenty years it has not been hushed up. It has been chattered about all day long. Yet it is still in a mess. If hushing up had been the cause of the trouble, ventilation would have set it right. But it has not. I think it is the other way round. I think the human race originally hushed it up because it had become such a mess.* [57]

Lewis felt that sex was in a mess because people had totally surrendered to their desires. The situation was made worse by propaganda encouraging lust, which, when combined with the warped nature of humanity, resulted in the view that desires were natural, healthy, and reasonable and that it was perverse to resist them. [58]

Lewis did not condone giving in to temptation. Surrender to one's desires, without discretion, led to "impotence, disease, jealousies, lies, concealment, and everything that is the reverse of health, good humour, and frankness." [59] In order to lead a

christian life and attain happiness, a certain amount of restraint
was needed.

Lewis called the specifically sexual part of Eros, which led one
into temptation, "Venus."[60] Sexuality—Venus—could exist either outside or within Eros. The difference between the two was
that Venus, or sexual desire, outside of Eros wanted the sex or
sensory pleasure alone; Venus within Eros desired the beloved.
Venus outside of Eros focused on pure need; Venus within Eros
encountered pleasure as a by-product. In Venus outside of Eros,
the giving and receiving were distinct; in Venus within Eros, the
distinction between giving and receiving was blurred. Eros functioned as that which transformed Venus.[61] As the sex element
within Eros, Venus had to be taken seriously because it was
part of marriage—the symbolic union between humanity and
divinity.

Sexual Happiness

In an essay published soon after his death, Lewis discussed
whether or not one had a "right to happiness," by which he
meant a right to sexual happiness.[62]

> *When I was a youngster, all the progressive people were saying,
> "Why all this prudery? Let us treat sex just as we treat all our
> other impulses." I was simple-minded enough to believe they
> meant what they said. I have since discovered that they meant
> exactly the opposite. They meant that sex was to be treated as no
> other impulse in our nature has ever been treated by civilized
> people. All the others, we admit, have to be bridled. . . . But ev-
> ery unkindness and breach of faith seems to be condoned pro-
> vided that the object aimed at is "four bare legs in a bed."*[63]

Lewis speculated that the reason for privileging sexual impulses
lay in the very nature of erotic passion. The "being in love" condition of Eros issued an emotional ultimatum: "This is the
chance of a lifetime!" Whether or not the affair lasted was beside
the point; erotic passion demanded obeisance. All talk about a
"right to (sexual) happiness" was based not on one's actual experience of passion but on the feelings one had while in the midst

of it. In actuality, the pursuit of a right to happiness was more likely to result in pain and unhappiness.

Lewis's final point against a right to sexual happiness was that conjugal infidelity was adverse to women, who out of biological necessity were more monogamous than men.[64] Since female physical beauty decreased with each year and it became increasingly harder for women to lure men to their side, promiscuity victimized women.[65] Furthermore, if one allowed a "right to happiness," such a principle would prevail in other arenas as well. It would be the end of civilization if every one followed the prevailing impulse of the moment.

Marriage as Safety Valve. Marriage as the context for Eros provided the chance to know another person thoroughly; one person completed the other in a way that overcame the limits of being only one person.[66] Female and male "were made to be combined together in pairs, not simply on the sexual level, but *totally* combined."[67]

Lewis believed that human love was modeled on divine love and appealed to the authority of scripture to support the headship of the husband.[68] Just as Christ was the head of the church, so too was the husband to be the head of the wife. The man whose marriage was most like a crucifixion, whose wife was least lovable, was considered to be the most Christlike in his headship. Thus, he was "allowed no despair."[69]

Limiting the Natural Loves: Not Eros Alone. Lewis saw the earthly loves as reflecting divine love, although he cautioned that no one was guaranteed salvation through Eros, Affection, or Friendship. The natural loves, including Eros, should be taken seriously in themselves. Through them, something could be learned of divine love.[70]

Eros was a love demanding a total commitment which could serve as an example of the love we ought to exercise toward God and humankind.[71] Eros gave substance to the human understanding of charity—God's love—which otherwise might never be found if one did not take the natural loves seriously.[72] For Lewis, the self-giving nature of Eros served to illustrate the sort of love that ought to enter into every relationship.

While Eros was to be taken seriously, that did not mean that in itself it was sufficient. Alone, Eros could not be itself and could not keep its promises of fidelity. An Eros idolized and isolated from God would be an Eros destroyed: "Eros cannot of himself be what, nevertheless, he must be if he is to remain Eros. He needs help; therefore needs to be ruled. The god dies or becomes a demon unless he obeys God."[73] Access to divine love nourished the natural loves and kept them from becoming perverted. Recognizing that the natural loves were creaturely and therefore in need of transformation opened the door to the love of God—charity. We are urged to press on, claimed Lewis, for there is more to love than the natural loves by themselves can show us.

Lewis called human beings to a risky love, to vulnerability. He admitted that there is no safety; "the only place outside Heaven where you can be perfectly safe from all the dangers and perturbations of love is Hell."[74] But one must take the risk if one is to love fully and lead a christian life—in other words, if life is to be worth living. In this way, the natural loves are redeemed. They become ways to God; it is their only chance to survive.

D. S. BAILEY: EROS CONDITIONALLY AFFIRMED

When Derrick Sherwin Bailey (1910–1984) wrote on the topic of human sexuality, the Quaker Report on Sexuality, affirming homosexual relationships, had just been released and the British Parliament was debating the decriminalization of homosexuality. Believing that the "grave sexual disorder" of his time demanded a "reorientation of the Church's attitude," Bailey called for the development of "a theology of sexual love."[75] Reviewers welcomed his work as an attempt to reflect "Christian spiritual experience" in the man/woman relationship.[76] However, one reviewer claimed that the issue at stake was no other than that of authority and charged Bailey with being an apologist for "a modern Christian view of sex."[77]

The Complementarity Theory as Explanation for Eros

According to Bailey, the creation of humanity in imago Dei, affirmed both sexual duality and human sexuality as being God-given. The interconnectedness of humanity and sexuality meant that in a Christian sexual ethics each person was expected to fulfill two primary duties: (1) to preserve one's sexual integrity (i.e., affirm one's gender and what that implies about one's sexuality) and (2) to accept the duty of sexual partnership.[78] Gender role differentiation—that which was "truly manly" and "truly womanly"—was the key to fulfilling those two duties.

> *To recognize that one is male or female conveys no awareness of sexual polarity and no understanding of manhood or womanhood. But to enter into sincere relation (of whatever kind) with a member of the complementary sex is to move into a new dimension of experience through encounter with another who is human, but in a radically different way from oneself—who is so like one, yet so very unlike. Now, and only now, does sex become meaningful as a personal quality.*[79]

True knowledge of oneself was reflected only in the other—in particular, the other of the complementary gender.[80]

Bailey sought to portray a picture of sexuality in which woman was the equal of man by invoking the theory of complementarity, which served to liberate "the creative dynamic of sex for the furtherance of the common good and . . . the elevation of human life as a whole."[81] Bailey maintained that the theory of complementarity entailed the equal association of men and women in all areas of life but that it did not imply an across-the-board uniformity of sex roles: "Woman finds her true self and destiny, not in rivalling man or assimilating herself to him, but in being accepted willingly and gladly as his partner and complement in all that concerns their common life. The question of her social role, therefore, cannot be settled unilaterally. . . . "[82] Complementarity meant that without women men were incomplete and without men women were incomplete. From the opposite gender came what the other lacked; the two genders provided a balance to one another.

The Nature of Love. For Bailey, love between a woman and a man included equal parts of self-giving (Agape) and desire (Eros). Self-giving involved yielding oneself "completely and unreservedly" to and for the other, desiring the entire person, without seeking to change him or her. Desire was not to be interpreted only in the venereal sense, though it was proper that physical desire should be an element of love.[83] When it was meant in a specifically venereal sense, it was to be held up as that part of a relationship in which verbal communication was insufficient to convey the entirety of what had to be said; it was the climactic event in the nonverbal parlay between lovers.[84] The sexual aspect of Eros, alternating between desire and satiation, recurred "with never-failing novelty" in a "one-flesh relationship." True Eros not only desired physical satisfaction with the beloved; it desired as well a lasting one-flesh union.[85]

Bailey saw Friendship (*Philia*) as the means by which the connection between a woman and a man could be widened so that their relationship did not exist in a vacuum. Without it, an authentic one flesh-union could not take root and flourish. Bailey also insisted that Affection be intertwined with other aspects of love, since desire, self-giving, friendship, and coition were bettered when the "tender loving care" of Affection suffused them.

Within the context of Agape, sexual love was to be interpreted from a perspective portraying the lovers as being "in Christ." Their relationship, transformed by Agape, became one in which the lover was loved for her or his worth to God. Bailey insisted that Agape did not supersede either Eros or Philia. Rather, they were "controlled and enriched" by Agape, which permeated every part of the relationship.[86]

The Meaning and Responsibilities of Sexual Partnership. The goal of love between a woman and a man was "their perfect union as 'one flesh,'" otherwise known as what was termed *henosis*—the denouement of Bailey's complementarity theory.[87] In *henosis*, in the one-flesh union, woman and man each found completion. The woman or man without a sexual partner of the opposite sex therefore remained unintegrated and incomplete.

The love validating the one flesh *henosis* required a mutual vision of perfection on the part of the lovers; it entailed falling in love. To undertake, by means of sexual intercourse, a one-flesh union with a partner through whom one had not seen "the Divine glory" was tantamount to prostitution and indefensible.[88] Only the vision of perfection, a true falling in love, could justify the steps leading to *henosis*.

Bailey viewed the one-flesh union from a holistic perspective. More than a mere pleasuring of the genitals, sexual intercourse was "an attitude of mind in which God, other persons, and the self" were involved.[89] Furthermore, the couple who engaged in the act of sexual intercourse had to be willing to accept the ontological change in themselves, in their relationship, and in their status before their community.

> *In their coming together they either affirm or deny all that sexual intercourse means. In the one case they become knit together in a mysterious and significant* henosis *and fulfil their love as husband and wife; in the other they merely enact a hollow, ephemeral, diabolical parody of marriage which works disintegration in the personality and leaves behind a deeply-seated sense of frustration and dissatisfaction. . . .* [90]

Sexual relation led to a quickening of the one-flesh, henotic relation. Outside of marriage, "in prostitution or casual fornication," the result was a bond forged in irresponsibility and exploitation, eventually impairing one's capacity for relation of any sort.[91] The right act of coition had to be undertaken in a context in which force, deception, or intimidation had no place. The act also had to be within a relationship that was ready for and demanded sexual expression—namely, marriage.[92]

Bailey argued that one should not engage in sexual relations outside of marriage since one could never know how the individuals involved, especially women, would react. What was intended only as a moment's gratification contained unpredictable emotional implications, could well "cause unexpected suffering or unhappiness," and did not contribute constructively to a love relation.[93] The threat of pregnancy and the emotional well-being of unborn children added to his reasons for keeping sexual relation within the context of marriage.[94]

The alternative to building and maintaining one-flesh relationships was to withdraw in fear of "the risk which relation always implied."[95] Isolating oneself offered a certain security; straying from that security demanded a courage rooted in faith: "we can never know what will happen when we commit ourselves to another person. Deep down, we are often apprehensive that in the encounter we may be disturbed or changed—and we may not want change, even when it would be for our good."[96] Nevertheless, Bailey felt that a one-flesh relationship was well worth the risk. Love was "the most remarkable of all encounters in the realm of true relation," offering a different kind of security and a fulfillment that could come only from *henosis*—a one-flesh union.[97] There was no other way of participating and coming to know another's being. And there was no other way of participating and coming to know oneself.

Sex and the Inverts and Perverts

Bailey's research on the subject of homosexuality arose out of his efforts to support the decriminalization of homosexual acts.[98] He was committed to unraveling dangerous attitudes towards human sexuality in general and homosexuality in particular that had been attributed to christianity, and he sought to call the church to account regarding its history.[99]

The term *homosexuality*, as Bailey used it, referred not to actions, but to a condition marked by emotional and sexual leanings toward those of the same gender.[100] The "invert" was a genuine homosexual who could not be held responsible for his or her condition. The invert was not compelled to practice his or her homosexuality and could control physical impulses much as the heterosexual could. Sexual acts committed by the invert were thus open to moral judgment. The "pervert" was not considered to be a "true homosexual." Rather, she or he was heterosexual, engaging only occasionally in homosexual acts "from motives of curiosity or in exceptional circumstances; or habitually, as a prostitute or in pursuit of novel sensual experiences."[101]

According to Bailey, criminal prosecution of homosexuality served to suppress symptoms while ignoring the underlying disease.[102] Understanding "homosexual perversion" as a result of the progressive disintegration of the institutions of marriage and family, he warned that if such disintegration was not thwarted, the entire social order would be at risk. Sexual anarchy would rule the day.

While Bailey believed that the condition of inversion was in itself morally neutral, its expression in homosexual acts required moral judgment. He observed that most male inverts claimed that homosexual acts were natural; for them, heterosexual intercourse would be a perversion.[103] However, Bailey maintained that the sexual organs should never be separated from their "conceptional purpose."[104]

The church's responsibility was to bring the invert to an acceptance of his or her condition via faith and the sacraments, encourage growth of a positive self-image in the invert, and spiritually strengthen him or her to resist homosexual acts.[105] Like heterosexuals outside of marriage, homosexuals were to stress self-control and self-discipline. Close pastoral supervision, not criminal prosecution, was the order of the day.

FROM MALESTREAM THEOLOGY TO DENOMINATIONAL STATEMENTS

Nygren has labeled Eros selfish and unchristian. Thielicke, Lewis, and Bailey have proposed the Agapic redemption and transformation of Eros. It is clear that none of these theologians could bear to let Eros stand alone. Even when combined with Agape, Eros continued to pose a threat to marriage, christianity, and civilization. The solution—argued Thielicke, Lewis, and Bailey—was that physical expression of Eros be confined to the marriage bed.

The theory of gender complementarity, espoused by Thielicke, Lewis, and Bailey, fundamentally shaped their notions of Eros. Based upon humanity's creation in *imago Dei*, the union of female and male was the essence of God-given sexuality

—i.e., *"real* sexuality." Since one was incomplete unless paired with a member of the opposite sex, homosexuality was, by definition, unacceptable. Those willing to say that their homosexuality was a condition and not an active orientation (reflecting the distinction between invert and pervert) stood a chance, however slight, of being accepted in the collective eyes of the christian community.

These four representatives of malestream theology have made clear that Eros must be controlled. As we move to an examination of contemporary denominational positions on sexuality, it becomes increasingly apparent that Eros continues to be perceived as that which must be controlled; christianity, in fact, demands it. What is even more striking is that similar ways of justifying the control of Eros and sexuality continue to be employed.

CHAPTER TWO

The Church on Eros

Contemporary Denominational Policies on Sexuality

T he Presbyterian Church (USA), the United Methodist Church, the Evangelical Lutheran Church in
America, and the Protestant Episcopal Church are
among those mainline denominations that continue to debate a
variety of subjects falling under the rubric of human sexuality. Issues involving the participation of lesbian women and gay men
in the church remain the ones most frequently and vociferously
debated, with the result that discussions of human sexuality become equated solely with lesbian and gay issues.[1] However, the
assumption that lesbian/gay issues are the *only* sexuality issues
facing the contemporary churches is faulty. Lesbian women and
gay men often serve as scapegoats for an eros—a sexuality in
general—which appears to church leaders to be out of control.

Underlying the focus on lesbian and gay issues in this chapter
is the ecclesiastical attitude toward eros. The latter is my main
concern, but the former looms large in contemporary church debates. Issues affecting lesbian women and gay men represent only
the tip of the iceberg in terms of work on sexuality yet to be acknowledged and undertaken by the churches. As the finishing
touches are being put on this manuscript, new challenges are being made to the institutional churches, more people are speaking
frankly of the day-to-day realities of their lives, and increasing
numbers of lesbian women and gay men are demanding justice.
Given the ongoing nature of the denominational sexuality debates, the materials in this chapter cannot help but be dated;
nevertheless, they are endlessly relevant as committee after committee is called to study the matter of sexuality, as report after
report is rejected by denominational legislative bodies, and as

lesbian women and gay men are ousted from leadership positions in church after church.

Despite the continual emergence of new church documents, the ongoing establishment of task forces to study sexuality, and the unceasing attempts to challenge policies, certain basic themes remain intact in both the ensuing debates and the resulting documents. As will become evident, the themes found in the works of Nygren, Thielicke, Lewis, and Bailey continue to influence contemporary discussions.

MAINLINE DENOMINATIONS AND HUMAN SEXUALITY

The Presbyterian Church (USA)

In 1970, the General Assembly of the United Presbyterian Church affirmed the sinful nature of homosexuality.[2] The General Assembly's 1978 decision "welcomed homosexuals" into the church but denied lesbian women and gay men access to ordination. Any person who is a "self-affirming, *practicing* homosexual" could not be considered fit for ordination since the church could not sanction homosexual *practice.*[3] In 1984, at the first General Assembly of the newly merged denomination, the decision was upheld.

Working in the late 1980s and early 1990s, a task force on human sexuality presented a ground-breaking, justice-centered, sex-positive report on sexuality.[4] In June 1991, the denomination rejected the report by a vote of 534 to 31. In its stead, a statement was accepted which affirmed sexuality as a "good gift from God" and the "sanctity of the marital covenant between one man and one woman" as "a God-given relationship to be lived out in Christian fidelity." Furthermore, the General Assembly declared that the church would continue to follow the position on homosexuality of the 1978 and 1979 General Assemblies.[5]

The United Methodist Church

The official statements of the United Methodist Church on human sexuality also recognize it as "God's good gift to all persons," although sexual relations are acceptable only within marriage. Furthermore, even though homosexuals "are individuals of sacred worth," their lifestyle cannot be affirmed by the church.

All persons need the ministry and guidance of the Church in their struggles for human fulfillment, as well as the spiritual and emotional care of a fellowship which enables reconciling relationships with God, with others, and with self. Although we do not condone the practice of homosexuality and consider this practice incompatible with Christian teaching, we affirm that God's grace is available to all. [6]

Since 1984, official policy has barred "self-avowed, practicing homosexuals" from ordination and appointment. Ministers are required "to maintain the highest standards represented by the practice of fidelity in marriage and celibacy in singleness."[7] In 1992, the General Conference upheld the ban on ordination and prohibited church funding for any group promoting homosexuality.[8]

A January 1994 meeting of the executive committee of the Council of Bishops suggested defining the term *homosexual* as follows: "A self-avowed practicing homosexual is a person who engages in sexual acts with a person or persons of the same sex, which are either witnessed or openly acknowledged." The definition was requested by the denomination's Judicial Council, which ruled that the term had to be defined before it could be used to exclude anyone from ministry.[9] Local annual conferences now face voting on the definition.

The Protestant Episcopal Church

In 1976, when the General Convention of the Episcopal Church belatedly approved the ordination of women, a resolution was also passed which, while disapproving of homosexuality per se, stated that lesbian women and gay men were to be treated as "Children of God." A year later, the House of Bishops[10] offered a further clarification of the nature of human sexuality: "Both in the Old Testament and in the New Testament the understanding of sex is rooted in the conviction that the divine image in humanity is incomplete without both man and woman. Hence, the aim of sexuality, as understood in Christian terms, is not merely satisfaction or procreation but completeness."[11] Since homosexuality was by definition "incomplete," the bishops agreed that they would refuse to ordain "an advocating and/or practicing homosexual person."[12]

By the General Convention of 1979, the issue of homosexuality had been studied by the Standing Commission on Human Affairs and Health, which urged the General Convention not to make homosexuality "an absolute barrier to ordination."[13] While the commission supported the possibility of the ordination of lesbian women and gay men, it opposed the ordinations of those who were open and affirming of their sexuality, advocated for "gay rights," and sought "the church's blessing on their 'marriages.'"[14]

The House of Bishops responded to the study by introducing a compromise resolution at the 1979 General Convention. It read:

Whereas, the 65th General Convention recognized "... that homosexual persons are children of God who have a full and equal claim with all other persons upon the love, acceptance, and pastoral concern and care of the Church...";

Therefore be it resolved... that this General Convention recommend... the following... in the selection and approval of persons for ordination:

1. There are many human conditions, some of them in the area of sexuality, which bear upon a person's suitability for ordination.

2. Every ordinand is expected to lead a life which is "a wholesome example to all people." There should be no barrier to the ordination of qualified persons of either heterosexual or homosexual orientation whose behavior the Church considers wholesome.

3. We re-affirm the traditional teaching of the Church on marriage, marital fidelity and sexual chastity as the standard of Christian sexual morality. Candidates for ordination are expected to conform to this standard. Therefore, we believe it is not appropriate for this Church to ordain a practicing ho-

mosexual, or any person who is engaged in heterosexual relations outside of marriage.[15]

While the bishops admitted that the resolution might be perceived to have the impact of legislation, they hastened to point
out that the resolution only *recommended* certain considerations
for screening candidates for ordination.[16] Since 1979, the resolution has been upheld by succeeding General Conventions and
referred to more than once as the reason lesbian women and gay
men should not be ordained.[17]

At the August 1994 General Convention, the bishops passed
a statement re-affirming "lifelong, monogamous union" between
a man and a woman as "the standard for sexual relationships,"
but acknowledging that a minority of people are homosexual in
orientation and that the church must therefore "respond pasto-
rally" to them. Originally intended to carry the weight of a
"pastoral teaching," the statement was downgraded to a "study
document." Statements by more than a hundred conservative
bishops, insisting that the church not sanction homosexuality
and calling for chastity outside of marriage, and a statement by
nearly sixty other bishops, maintaining that they would continue
to ordain lesbian and gay people and bless the relationships of
lesbian couples and gay couples, were circulated.[18]

The Evangelical Lutheran Church in America

The ELCA Task Force on Human Sexuality drafted a report
which—although carefully qualified by calls for further study, reflection, and prayerful consideration—nevertheless made some
advances in affirming sexuality.[19] The draft was released in the
fall of 1993—unfortunately, to the press wire services before the
rest of the church. Headlines such as "Lutheran Church Ap-
proves Gay Marriages and Encourages Masturbation!" generated
thousands of irate calls and several bomb threats. In the aftermath of the publicity, the task force's director, Karen Bloomquist, was forced to resign and the Conference of Bishops quickly
moved to control the damage. With the help of a consulting
panel, the task force has been asked to prepare a second draft
which would be more in keeping with the ELCA's "biblical and

confessional foundations."[20] In the meantime, the first draft has been sent to congregations for further study with the understanding that it is not official ELCA policy.

The ELCA guidelines for clergy stipulate that single ordained ministers must live chastely. Those who are married are expected to be faithful to their partners, expressing sexual intimacy in a relationship that is "mutual, chaste, and faithful." Regarding those who consider themselves to be lesbian or gay, the ELCA policy requires them to "abstain from homosexual relationships."[21]

CHALLENGES TO CHURCH POLICIES

In the ensuing debates over the various denominational sexuality reports, which are almost always more progressive than the denominations would wish, the issue of authority has been central. The debates have focused on those who place unquestioned authority in scripture and church doctrine versus those who bring human experience and a liberation ethos to bear on biblical interpretation. Among the denominational reports, the Presbyterian report stands out as the one that took the biggest strides towards a liberation ethic of human sexuality. Despite its overwhelming rejection by the denomination, it is worth examining in some detail as an example of contemporary challenges to mainstream denominational policies on sexuality.

Reconstructing Ethical Norms

The authors of *The Presbyterian Sexuality Report* maintained that there was room for both scriptural tradition and human experience as sources of authority in the formation of a sexual ethic; they sought to consult with "a diverse, inclusive community of interpreters."[22] Along with experience, the biblical norms of love and justice as well as an accountability to a wider community are meant to act as guideposts to the task of sorting through the challenges facing churchpeople.[23]

The cornerstone of the report consists of a sexual ethic based on the norm of justice-love. Also referred to as right-relatedness, justice-love means that the goodness of sexuality is to be honored; gratitude for the diversity of all people is to be expressed;

special concern for those who are sexually abused, exploited, and violated is to be conveyed; people are to be held accountable for their sexual behavior, considering the well-being of their partners and the entire community; and an openness to learning from the marginalized and preparing for change is to be cultivated.[24]

The concept of justice-love is meant to enhance an ethic of "common decency," and is to replace the norm of heterosexuality. Only those relationships based on abuse, exploitation, and violation of one or both of the parties are to be judged negatively.[25] Among the values flowing from the foundational ethic of justice-love are sexual and spiritual wholeness, mutuality and consent, and a commitment to reclaiming eros and passion.[26] According to the report, the church should not waste time concerning itself with who sleeps with whom and under what circumstances. Instead, it should be concerned over commitment to an ethic of common decency consisting of equality and inclusivity: "We should be asking whether the relation is responsible, the dynamics genuinely mutual, and the loving full of joyful caring. That line of moral inquiry directs people to things that matter."[27]

The authors of the report also claim that celibacy can no longer be presented as the *only* moral choice for those who are single. Justice-love, not marriage, should be the moral norm for determining the appropriateness of sexual activity. The task force also asserted that denying ordination to lesbian and gay persons who affirm their sexuality and engage in "justice-loving sexual relationship" can be seen as nothing but "an affront to the good God who made us all."[28]

In Quest of Eros. "Unless . . . Christians . . . embrace eros," warns the report, "we stand in danger of seriously misunderstanding the full reality of love and . . . of falsely misrepresenting love in our interactions." The report highlights the need to eroticize equality between persons, regardless of the gender combination. Unfortunately, the cultural trend of dominant-submissive relational patterns functions to keep many people from experiencing or knowing what constitutes a truly mutual relationship. Physical, psychological, and/or sexual violence against women and children have no place in justice-love. Since mutuality and consent are denied and bodily integrity and self-determination are systematically destroyed, sexual-spiritual wholeness is impossible for those who suffer abuse.[29] In order to attain the eroticization of equality, it is necessary to equalize power distribution and empower women "to experience the wholeness of their sexuality."[30] With the eroticization of equality, persons can feel more comfortable being both sexually assertive and receptive. Yet, the eroticization of equality extends beyond sexually intimate relationships to engender a "passionate caring for all creation" and influence all relationships.[31] Eros, thus, is integral to the establishment of justice-love.

To say that the sexuality report of the Presbyterian task force was controversial is an understatement. The denomination's news service representative remarked that he had not seen "such furor among Presbyterians since a church agency contributed to the Angela Davis Defense Fund in the 1960s."[32] Stated Clerk of the General Assembly, James Andrews, received inquiries as to how to bring the ordained members of the task force to trial for violating their ordination vows by signing the report. Some churches withheld funds as an attempt to force the discharge of a particular task force member from their area. Another member was denied a job because of her role on the task force. Still other task force members received harassing phone calls and letters and even death threats.[33]

Before the General Assembly met in Baltimore, 89 of 171 presbyteries had voted to register opposition or concern over the report. Some presbytery and synod executives decided that the church could not afford an ongoing debate on the report and sought instead to control the damage it had done. Many of those executives chose to distance themselves from the report and several strategized about how best to defeat it.[34]

The ethic of justice-love would have rejected that which keeps eros negated and in need of being chastened by agape. The fact that the report was so quickly and overwhelmingly rejected speaks volumes about how threatened church leaders were by the specter of an eros affirmed and justice and love combined.

ORDAINING, BLESSING, AND CELEBRATING

Throughout the denominations, lesbian women and gay men continue to seek ordination. A few presbyteries, dioceses, synods, and annual conferences continue quietly to ordain lesbian women and gay men.

On January 20, 1990, two open and affirming lesbian women and one gay man—Ruth Frost, Phyllis Zillhart, and Jeff Johnson—were ordained at St. Paulus Lutheran Church in San Francisco. The ecclesiastical trial of the two churches that sponsored them (St. Francis and First United Churches) took place in June 1990.

In the aftermath of the trial, the two congregations were temporarily suspended from the denomination for a period of five years, after which they will be permanently suspended if they do not change their position. Voice and Vision: Lutheran Lesbian and Gay Ministry was formed following the trial and is now entering its fifth year. Current changes to denominational policy now restrict the ability of congregations to engage in protests on the basis of conscience.

When United Methodist minister Rose Mary Denman came out in the late 1980s and attempted to transfer her ministerial credentials to the Unitarian Universalist denomination, she was told by Bishop George Bashore that her ordination was to be rescinded since her avowed homosexuality meant that she could not be considered to be in good standing. She requested an ecclesiastical court trial, and it was held on August 24, 1987. Her counsel at the trial, The Rev. Dr. John MacDougall, astutely observed at the proceedings that "as far as the church is concerned, Rose Mary has not committed an offense, she *is* an offense."[35] The jury of thirteen United Methodist ministers suspended her from ministry until the next General Conference. In the end, she was denied ministerial standing.[36]

Frank Wulf, an ordained gay man who came out in his church the Sunday after his partner died of AIDS, is facing a second ecclesiastical court trial in the California-Pacific Annual Conference. The first trial, which was on the grounds of disobedience to the order and discipline of the United Methodist Church, failed. The second trial is based on charges of immorality.[37]

One month before the 1991 General Convention of the Episcopal Church, Ronald Haines, bishop of Washington, D.C., ordained Elizabeth Carl—an open, affirming, and practicing lesbian woman—to the priesthood.[38] Presiding Bishop Browning attempted to delay the ordination, citing the upcoming General Convention. Haines went forward with the ordination, reminding critics that the 1979 resolution against ordaining homosexuals was recommendatory, not legally binding.

John Spong, Episcopal bishop of Newark, renowned for ordaining lesbian women and gay men, has pointed out that bishops who oppose the ordination of women have been accorded the privilege of pleading that their "conscience" keeps them from following church decisions. Bishops who ordain lesbian women and gay men to the priesthood on the basis of their conscience are accorded no such consideration. Spong's actions on behalf of lesbian and gay people have been continually denounced by the House of Bishops.[39]

In September 1993, retired bishop and former dean of Episcopal Divinity School in Cambridge, Massachusetts, Otis Charles, wrote a letter to the other Episcopal bishops informing them that he is gay. No longer able to maintain the silence he had kept for decades, he wrote: "I sat silently through the . . . General Convention. I did not join the debate openly and honestly saying, 'Hey, you are talking about me. I am a gay man.' . . . By my silence [I] have given power to the forces that work to maintain the culture of silence within the church and the community."[40] He added that he has been called to speak openly about his experience, especially among his colleagues in the House of Bishops.

Jane Adams Spahr—an open, affirming, practicing, and ordained lesbian woman—was recently called to a Presbyterian church in Rochester, New York. The call was challenged in the Synod of the Northeast's Permanent Judicial Commission, which voted to uphold the call on the basis that the 1978 General Assembly's ruling prohibiting the ordination of practicing homosexuals specified ordination not installation. Furthermore, since Spahr was ordained in 1974, she was covered by a "grandfather" clause protecting those ordained prior to 1978.[41] However, in November 1992, the Permanent Judicial Commission of the General Assembly ruled that no openly homosexual, sexually active person could serve as a minister. The ruling was expected to discourage other lesbian and gay ministers from being open about their sexuality. Spahr responded to the decision, declaring, "This decision says either lie or repent. I will not lie and I will never repent. We are talking about who it is that God made me."[42] She currently travels across the country, working as an evangelist/educator on lesbian/gay issues under the auspices of the Rochester Church.

To the dismay of the denominational hierarchies and conservative critics, clergy have also performed blessings (or affirmations) of lesbian/gay relationships in all four denominations. Resolution after resolution on the subject has been brought before the various legislative bodies. Policy makers continue to stall, and clergy continue to bless and affirm.[43] Episcopal priest Harvey Guthrie stated that he was blessing relationships on the basis of "profound biblical and theological" beliefs and would not permit anybody to say "that they're biblical and traditional and I'm something else."[44]

In November 1993, two thousand women from major Protestant denominations gathered in Minneapolis for a conference on feminist theology called Re-Imagining. An inclusive-language liturgy, invoking the name of Sophia, was used, and women's spirituality and sexuality—including those of lesbian and bisexual women—were celebrated. Although feminists have been having these sorts of conferences for years, this one received a great deal of backlash. The difference with this conference was that it was supported by contributions from mainline denominations and women church executives were involved in its planning. On May 19, 1994, Mary Ann Lundy, a high-ranking Presbyterian Church (USA) executive who assisted in the planning of the conference, was forced to leave her position because "circumstances... made her goal of effective service to the Church unattainable."[45] At the denomination's 1994 General Assembly, a report addressing the controversy of the Re-Imagining Conference was passed by a vote of 516 to 4. The report concludes that "some of the theological content of the conference presentations and worship rituals not only extended beyond the boundaries of the Reformed theological tradition, but also beyond that tradition's understanding of what makes faith Christian."[46] The report was released, in part, to appease conservative groups.

Defending the Status Quo

The challenges to the mainline denominations—including sexuality reports that dare to affirm human sexuality (and eros), ordinations of lesbian women and gay men, blessings of same-sex unions, and feminist conferences that re-imagine theology—have unleashed a firestorm of controversy within the denominations. The defenders of the status quo are desperately seeking to reassert the themes of malestream theology against the rising tide of demands for justice.

Within the Presbyterian sexuality task force, a minority group took issue with the work of the majority. They issued their own report affirming the *complementary nature* of male and female as being that which fulfills the divine plan, and they advocated the church's position of "one woman, one man, lifelong fidelity in marriage," especially given the incidence of sexually transmitted disease and the "instability" experienced by many children.[47] Lifelong fidelity in marriage is seen by the authors of the minority report as being *the* Christian context for sexual relations, fulfilling the well-being of both the woman and the man, as well as God's purposes.[48]

In assessing the problem of homosexuality,[49] the minority report makes a distinction between homosexual *orientation* and homosexual *practice*. It is not homosexual orientation itself with which the church is concerned; rather, it is whether the homosexual chooses to *act* on his or her orientation.[50] While compassionate pastoral care is to be extended to the person of homosexual orientation, a Christian moral position cannot condone homosexual practice. Christians must respect "the single voice with which Scriptures and the church have spoken on these matters" and condemn homosexual acts.[51] The members of the minority group do not see any inconsistency between welcoming homosexual persons into the church and prohibiting the ordination of those unrepentant homosexuals who are "self-affirming" and "practicing."[52]

Referring to the affirmation of eros in *The Presbyterian Sexuality Report*, critic James Edwards complained that the term *agape*, occurring 320 times in the New Testament, was lacking in the report. Eros—mentioned not at all in the New Testament—was elevated instead, connected with "justice" and "spirituality" and associated with "a prophecy of God." Such treatment of eros, charged Edwards, was tantamount to worship in the courts of Baal and Ashtoreth and blatantly disavowed "the love of Jesus, Paul, Saint Francis, and Mother Teresa."[53]

Before the report could be rejected by the General Assembly, a congregation was informed by its pastor that it was "pagan in its doctrine of God . . . wrong in its understanding of justice . . . false in its doctrine of the Incarnation . . . and non-Reformed in its understanding of Scripture."[54] Furthermore, by exonerating "consensual sex under the rubric of 'justice-love,'" the authority of Scripture had been neutralized. Other critics warned that if the Presbyterian Church approved the report, the church would no longer resemble a christian church, but rather would resemble a Canaanite fertility cult.[55]

In Episcopalian circles, the defenders of the status quo stressed "reconciliation" as the remedy to controversy. Presiding Bishop Edmond Browning has emphasized continually the need for reconciliation. Noting "the anguish of gay and lesbian Episcopalians in a church that is torn over how to treat them," he acknowledged the great cost to such persons of integrating their sexuality and their faith. However, Browning was also deeply concerned about church members who were offended and disturbed by the very existence of lesbian women and gay men.

They . . . want . . . to be given clear and unequivocal assurance that their beloved church is not disintegrating into the hedonism that our age seems to have spawned. . . . They view the basic heterosexual relationship as so much a part of the natural order that it is fully normative. . . . They are . . . concerned that full acceptance of homosexual relationships would somehow mean a

breakdown of all forms of sexual morality.... The pain on both
sides is real; neither side has cornered the market on anguish. [56]

When cries for "reconciliation" did not prevent John Spong, bishop of Newark, from ordaining a gay man, pleas for "good order" and "the unity of the church" were invoked: "We decry the action by the Bishop of Newark, which...has polarized our community of faith. What is at stake is the discipline of the church in addressing actions that violate the spirit of our common life....Bishops are called to *safeguard the unity* of the church."[57] Similarly, "We regret the hurt and confusion caused by the ordination and subsequent events...We believe that *good order* is not served when bishops, dioceses or parishes act unilaterally."[58]

Clarence Pope, bishop of Fort Worth and president of the Episcopal Synod of America,[59] warned that if renegade ordinations such as those in Newark were not stopped, "our religion" would be changed. He added that much of the church's teaching would "be altered if we don't take steps." Mark Dyer, bishop of Bethlehem, Pennsylvania, observed that "the Anglican way of discipline is by compassion, not law," and suggested that the bishops do nothing.[60] Ultimately, the bishops released another pastoral statement acknowledging the pain of both sides and asking for "the guidance of the Holy Spirit."[61]

When the first draft of the ELCA sexuality report appeared, twenty-four faculty members at Luther Northwestern Seminary in St. Paul, Minnesota, issued a critique declaring that "love and commitment do not legitimize sexual relations between persons of the same sex."[62] Claiming that the draft would move the ELCA away from the church's traditional understanding of marriage and of homosexual relationships, the authors proposed that the church "receive homosexual persons as we receive all persons who confess Jesus Christ, but not accept the legitimacy of sexual relations between persons of the same sex."[63]

Another critic of the Lutheran report argued that "most men are born with the inclination to more than one wife." If lesbian women and gay men were to gain acceptance because they were "born to it," then men would be able to support their claims to multiple wives.[64]

A representative from the ELCA Division for Ministry maintained that lesbian and gay pastors have brought all the problems on themselves and forced the church to discipline them. Coming out is viewed "as a public confrontation with the church's standards," leaving the church with little choice but to file charges.[65]

ECHOES OF THE PAST

The positions of the Presbyterian Church (USA), the United Methodist Church, the Evangelical Lutheran Church in America, and the Protestant Episcopal Church have not sprung fully formed from the events of the last two or three decades. They have a much longer history and have been influenced by centuries of christian speculation on the nature of human sexuality. The scope of this project, however, has been limited to a few discussions in the twentieth century, and there are common themes to be found between the theologians examined in chapter 1 and the contemporary statements of the denominations highlighted in this chapter.

In the pages that follow, several common themes will be exposed. The ongoing split between eros and agape, the necessity of controlling eros, and the complementarity theory as a means of control are all present in the denominational debates and the works of the four theologians. Furthermore, these themes have fed ecclesiastical panic about "open, affirming, and practicing homosexuals." The extent to which this has occurred and continues to occur will be duly noted.

Splitting Eros and Agape

As we have seen, the degree to which eros and agape have been split varies. Anders Nygren believed passionately that both Vulgar Eros and Platonic Eros contaminated the Christian Agape. Eros promoted a self-involvement, a self-love, indeed, a *selfish* love, incompatible with the selfless and self-giving Christian Agape. There was no room at all in Agape for any piece of Eros.

Helmut Thielicke refrained from positing a separation between Agape and Eros, suggesting instead that Agape serve as that which could transform Eros. More than Eros was involved in the sex community, especially since women were inclined to embody the characteristics of Agape while men were likely to be focused on Eros. Agape acted as the glue that held the sex community together.

Like Thielicke, C. S. Lewis advocated the intermingling of the forms of love. However, Eros and Friendship were rarely combined since most if not all Friendships were between members of the same gender. Defining Eros as the state of "being in love," distinct from the pure sexual activity of Venus, Lewis held that Eros, as the nobler of the two, could transform Venus. Sex (i.e., Venus) within the context of marriage served as the completion of Eros, though Lewis hastened to note that, in order for the natural loves to be made whole, they needed divine love. Without divine love, Eros would be destroyed.

D. S. Bailey also had few qualms about mixing the various forms of love. His concern was that no single love should stand alone. More specifically, Eros was not to stand alone. Eros needed Agape to balance it; only with Agape could the love relationship remain stable. Bailey perceived Agape as that which chastened and shaped, controlled and enriched Eros.

Thielicke, Lewis, and Bailey did not insist, in the tradition of Nygren, that Eros could not be mentioned in the same breath as Agape by good christian people. Nevertheless, they could not accord Eros a status equal to that of Agape. Eros was never permitted to stand on its own as a form of love. Their solution was to bring Agape in to make Eros more respectable.

Within the context of the discussions in the mainline denominations, eros, while not often referred to directly, nevertheless plays a key role. The responses to both the ELCA and Presbyterian sexuality reports were, in part, characterized by a sense of eros as an uncontrollable and chaotic force, which, if left to its own, would result in the destruction of traditional christian moral standards. This attitude was characteristic both of moderate church executives and of conservative organizations.

Church executives, loath to engage in extended considerations of the report, quickly sought to distance themselves from it. The ELCA bishops were not keen to have the denomination perceived as eros- or sex-positive. They hurriedly declared that the first draft was not official policy and sent the task force back to prepare a draft more in keeping with the ELCA's "biblical and confessional foundations." The Presbyterian report's enthusiastic interpretation of sex as a *very* good gift from God, which did not necessarily have to be limited to the context of marriage, posed a threat to conventional ecclesiastical modes of dealing with human sexuality. Conservative groups, more blatant in their reaction to the proposed affirmation of eros, characterized the Presbyterian report as elevating eros at the expense of agape, resulting in a pagan desecration of the love of Jesus.[66]

Episcopalians cloaked their suspicion of eros in a seemingly endless series of debates, studies, and legislative sessions. Eros, as played out in the arena of human sexuality, could not be permitted much, if any, license. The fear of eros as a potentially chaotic and uncontrollable force was particularly evident in the refusal to commit to a pro-active stand on issues of sexuality. Traditional sexual morality was recommended time and again as a guide for christians. Continued attempts to legislate sexuality showed that many potential makers of policy felt that eros—sexuality—was in dire need of being controlled by canon law.

Keeping Control of Eros

Helmut Thielicke, C. S. Lewis, and D. S. Bailey, while affirmative of eros to a certain degree, nevertheless believed that physical expressions of eros had to be limited to the context of marriage. Thielicke, in particular, held that if human sexuality were not provided a specific structure, extramarital sex would flourish and pose a threat to the institution of marriage and to the very nature of christianity. Lewis, maintaining that one could not surrender to *all* of one's desires—since to do so would lead to "impotence, disease, jealousies, and lies"—asserted that a christian life demanded sexual restraint.[67] Erotic passion could not be permitted to privilege one's sexual impulses since such privileging would spread to other arenas and cause the downfall of civilization. Bailey, concurring with the Lewisian prediction, also stressed self-control and self-discipline outside the bonds of marriage.

This attitude is clearly evident in the denominational statements. One of the warnings the Presbyterian minority report issued was that the majority report had accommodated itself to contemporary culture. The prospect of affirming sexual relationships outside the controls of marriage alarmed mainstream Presbyterians. The overwhelming rejection of the report revealed the extent to which the Presbyterian Church was unwilling to grant legitimacy to nonmarital sexual relationships or, more basically, to entertain a less controlling policy on sexuality. Sexual permissiveness was *not* the christian context for marriage. The "marital covenant between one man and one woman" was the only "God-given relationship" and was "to be lived out in Christian fidelity."[68]

In various denominational documents, marriage is uniformly described as the normative "context for moral, intimate sexual expression between Christians."[69] This continual rehashing of the sanctity of marriage has been the response to challenges posed by lesbian women and gay men. The church has stated its willingness to *welcome* lesbian women and gay men as church members, but it will not ordain those lesbian women and gay men who do not *control* their sexuality. In other words, those lesbian women and gay men who are open and affirming of their sexuality and are sexually active cannot be considered appropriate candidates for ordination because they are, by their very existence, "out of control."

This is further evidenced by the plethora of Episcopalian statements in which the term *wholesome* is invoked regarding those fit for ordination. *Wholesome* refers to a particular situation, namely, that of a man and a woman joined in marriage. All others, including single heterosexuals as well as lesbian women and gay men, are to exercise control in order to have any chance of being considered *wholesome*.

The ELCA legislation restricting the ability of congregations to protest on the basis of conscience meant that unruly lesbian women and gay men (representing eros incarnate!) and their

supporters would not be able to mount such a challenge again.
More recently, the ELCA made sure that eros did not break free
in the sexuality report by firing Karen Bloomquist, the director of
the task force, for the controversial first draft and by requesting
that a more acceptable report be submitted.

Other attempts to control sexuality are apparent in the arguments—reminiscent of Bailey and Lewis—likening sex outside of
marriage to a form of social anarchy which results in the destruction of christian family values.[70] The responses of the church hi-
erarchy to Episcopal bishops who have ordained open, affirming,
and sexually active lesbian women and gay men is also indicative
of the threat the offending parties have posed to ecclesiastical
control. Pleas to safeguard the "unity of the church" and to respect "the collegiality among brother bishops" have served as effective tools and excuses for keeping sexuality in good order.

Presiding Bishop Browning's penchant for a so-called reconciliation (read: "compromise") between the lesbian/gay community and their opponents avoids addressing the need for justice.
The focus on being "good christians" and controlling and/or denying one's needs ignores the wrongs committed against an
entire group of people.

And certainly, the protests concerning the Re-Imagining
Conference are indicative of the extent to which church leaders
fear that eros, in the guise of female sexuality, could spiral out of
control. United Methodist Bishop Earl G. Hunt's comment on
the conference—that "no comparable heresy has appeared in
the church in the last fifteen centuries"—reveals the power of
women, the power of eros, to rattle the status quo.[71]

The Complementarity Theory as a Control

The complementarity theory is a particularly effective mode of
controlling eros. It is at work in the thought of Thielicke, Lewis,
and Bailey as well as in the reasoning of the shapers of denominational policies. Thielicke's methodological approach to sexuality
was structured around the complementarity theory. Positing that
female and male natures complemented one another, Thielicke
elaborated upon a schema that portrayed women as monogamous, receptive, and sexually naive, while men were portrayed

as polygamous, active, and sexually knowledgeable. Women were associated with Agape and men with Eros so that not only did female and male nature complement each other, but Agape complemented Eros. Since woman's vocation was to be a "lover, companion, and mother," Agape-oriented marriage provided the stability necessary for the taming of Eros.

Lewis and Bailey agreed that female and male natures were complementary to one another. Humanity was created in *imago Dei,* and thus, the union of female and male was God-given. The two genders balanced one another, and sex role differentiation— far from being something to be overcome—provided the basis for the female/male relationship. In marriage, one person *completed* the other sexually. Thus, by its very nature, sex outside of marriage was incomplete. Bailey's emphasis on *henosis* was the *denouement* of the complementarity theory. One man, one woman, one flesh was all part of the divine plan.

Certainly the negative responses to the ELCA and Presbyterian sexuality reports consist of a major emphasis on the divine intent for a one-man, one-woman, one-flesh relationship. Indeed, that is the entire argument of the Presbyterian minority report as well as some of the more conservative critics and is recorded as being the official church position. According to this view, lifelong fidelity in marriage enhances the well-being of women and men and is the only christian context for sexual relations.

The headlines greeting the release of the ELCA study—that the Lutheran Church affirmed gay marriages and masturbation— flew in the face of traditional theological proscriptions of one man plus one woman. The first statement from Lutheran Northwestern Seminary, declaring that "love and commitment do not legitimize sexual relations between persons of the same sex," also centered around a theory of complementarity as the format for all human relationships.

In the Episcopalian debate, the complementarity theory is evident in many of the discussions and documents. The aim of human sexuality is *completeness,* claims a 1977 document.[72] The complementarity theory in this context, authorized by appeal to scripture, tradition, and divine intent, posits that only woman plus man equals completeness. The frequently invoked 1979 General Convention statement on ordination perpetuates the emphasis on completeness by its insistence on "wholesome examples."[73] This continues to be the theme of debates in both denominations.

The Incomplete Nature of Homosexuality

The complementarity theory is intriguing as it has been one of the most durable arguments in the sexuality debate. It has proved to be an extremely effective way of controlling eros. Homosexuality, though, represents an uncontrolled eros—an uncontrollable sex impulse—and violates the very premise of the complementarity theory.

For Thielicke, a homosexual relationship was not a christian relationship; it was contrary to the will of God and was out of sync with the order of creation. Lewis, too, had an intolerant attitude toward homosexuality. He protested that Friendship and Eros were two entirely different loves and that Friendships should not be presumed to be homosexual. For Lewis, and for Bailey as well, marriage was what completed women and men. All sex outside of that context was incomplete. Indeed, homosexuality, by definition, was incomplete.

While, admittedly, Bailey was a champion for the decriminalization of homosexuality, he did not perceive homosexuality in a positive or even a neutral way. He saw the "problem" of homosexuality as being rooted in a decay of moral standards and a lack of ethical responsibility in heterosexual relationships. Furthermore, Bailey defined *sex* as being the man/woman relationship, which excluded homosexual acts from the panorama of human sexuality. He believed that the purpose of the sexual organs should never be separated from their "conceptional purpose."[74] The only love permitted physical expression was that between a woman and man united in marriage. Ultimately, all three theologians (Nygren did not comment on the subject of homosexuality) felt that homosexuals, if they were not able to switch to heterosexuality, should practice self-control and self-discipline.

As we have seen, lesbian women and gay men fare little better in the recent pronouncements from mainline denominations.

Viewed as contrary to the *imago Dei* and the one-flesh nature of human sexuality, homosexuality is not seen as being a "complete" or "wholesome" expression of sexuality. Like Bailey's distinction between the homosexual invert (i.e., the condition of homosexuality) and the homosexual pervert (i.e., the sexually active homosexual), all four churches continue to make a distinction between homosexual orientation and homosexual practice. Those who agree to refrain from sexual activity *may* stand a chance of being judged worthy for church leadership; those who do not agree to celibacy, but who insist that their sexuality is God-given and "wholesome," are judged unfit for ordination.

The remark of former United Methodist minister Rose Mary Denman's counsel that, in the eyes of the church, she had not committed an offense but rather *was* an offense is an insightful analysis of church attitudes toward lesbian women and gay men. The charges of disobedience and immorality faced by Frank Wulf reveal the extent to which the United Methodist Church—and the mainline denominations in general—view homosexuality and an "uncontrolled" eros as affronts to good christian people.

THE CHURCH'S PRIMARY SEXUAL AGENDA: CONTROL OF SEX AND WOMEN

The issues, both in malestream theology and in the church debates and pronouncements, are complex. But there is one main strand that is woven throughout the material, and that strand is the urgency with which control of sexuality—control of eros—is sought. Eros—sexuality—represents a threat to the status quo of christian polity. Eros represents that which is other—unmale, untameable, and uncontrollable.

The quest to control sexuality is paramount in the denominational discussions, and various tools are employed to keep it controlled. The split between eros and agape, whether it is Nygren's complete split or the use of agape to make eros more acceptable, is one tool. The complementarity theory, positing the unnatural, almost inhuman, nature of non-heterosexual sex is another.

The Splitting of Eros and Agape as Sexual Control

Despite the attempts of Thielicke, Lewis, and Bailey as well as some church policy statements, to change the reputation of eros as an unchristian form of love, the fact remains that their work emphasizes that the way of making eros more acceptable is by supplementing it with agape. As a result, agape has all but eclipsed the presence of eros in intimate relationships. And eros, when it has been untransformed by and resistant to the influence of agape, has continued to be perceived as self-centered and not acceptable to christians.

Why does eros pose such a threat? What characteristics are they assuming agape has that eros does not? Do those assumptions hold up? What does it say about the structuring of divine/human and male/female relationships that compel the transformation of eros by the more respectable agape? How does this contribute to the control of sexuality?

I submit that the effort to make eros more acceptable by combining it with agape is doomed to failure from the very beginning. This is primarily due to the fact that such efforts are dualistic. They presuppose a split *in us* that does not exist between, for example, spirit and body, spirituality and sexuality, male and female, agape and eros. Efforts to redeem a despised eros by bringing agape to the rescue are based on both a faulty anthropology and a faulty theology.

The frantic juxtaposing of eros and agape has underscored and contributed to a false dualism in the christian understanding of love. Eros and agape have been pitted against one another in order to structure and control human sexuality. The widespread concern that without such structure and control premarital and extramarital sex would flourish is based on a belief that any challenge to the institution of marriage is a challenge to the very nature of christianity itself. Loosening the hold of compulsory heterosexuality on people's lives could not be risked, as it surely would mean an unthinkable questioning of traditional christian family values. In short, setting eros and agape in such a distinctively dualistic position, lays the foundation for an ethics of sexuality that has sublimated eros and brought a spiritualized, non-embodied agape, as a necessarily controlling and shaping love, to the foreground.

Several questions can be raised at this point which are important for the chapters that follow. How has the dualistic categorization of love contributed to heterosexism? How has it contributed to misogyny? To what extent does the dualism reflect heterosexism and misogyny? More specifically, have proponents of the agapic transformation of eros been communicating that eros is in need of redemption and that agape is not? Have the intentions of Thielicke, Bailey, and Lewis to affirm eros been undermined by bringing agape to the rescue? If agape did not chasten and shape eros, would God continue to participate in *all* aspects of human relationships (as Thielicke and others have maintained)? If God did continue to participate in human relationships, including an unredeemed and untransformed eros, would God actually participate in eros? Would God participate in the flesh? How? If God participated in the flesh, would God then be involved in femaleness—perhaps held in the female image as well as the patriarchal male image? What would happen to the heretofore structured and controlled nature of sexuality?

A dualistic split between eros and agape has resulted in the characterization of eros as the love that is self-oriented, selfish, and full of self-love. Thielicke, Lewis, and Bailey have all maintained that Eros needs the self-giving nature of Agape in order to supply a corrective to the self-oriented nature of Eros. Nygren, in particular, focused on the inappropriateness of any form of self-love for christian people. "Agape," he noted, "starts with the conviction of one's own lack of worth."[75]

Why is self-love so abhorrent to these (and other) christian theologians? Why are "christian agapic love" and "eros self-love" perceived as being mutually exclusive? The shunning of self-love, indeed the shunning of the *self*, presents immense difficulties to contemporary attempts to formulate a sexual theo-ethics. Stated briefly, the problem is this: the negation of self-love has resulted in severe damage to the souls, psyches, and bodies of women, children, and men.[76]

Excluding self-love from a christian formulation of love results not in *love* of neighbors and God but in a fundamental *disregard* of neighbors and God. The negation of self-love enables policy makers to deny the requests of those who ask that policies on sexuality take into account their multiplex experiences of race, class, gender, and sexual oppression. Their requests are denied or ignored on the basis that they are being selfish when they should be self-less. Ultimately, an abhorrence of self-love encourages a violence against self and neighbor (especially those considered "different" or "other"); this violence is rooted in the dualistic promulgation of a self-denying christian agape.

Despite the assertion of traditional christian theologians to the contrary, agape is "male" in the traditional view. Furthermore, the dualistic nature of agape and eros is thoroughly patriarchal in character. The threat posed by an untransformed eros—an eros allowed to stand on its own, unchastened by agape—to the patriarchal structure of sexuality is real. An untransformed eros would no longer be under the control of that disembodied spiritual principle that patriarchal christianity has named "God." An untransformed eros compromises the control of eros itself, as well as the control of the flesh, the female, and perhaps even God. The affirmation of eros-by-itself would compromise the customary task of christian ethics of bestowing and maintaining order in the realm of sexual relationships.

The Complementarity Theory as Heterosexist Control

As we have seen, the complementarity theory has permeated much of malestream theological and contemporary ecclesiastical literature on sexuality. We have inherited a sexual theological ethos—a sexual ethic that espouses lifelong, monogamous, heterosexual marriage—as the *only* arena in which sex is permissible for faithful christians. The tool of *suspicion* can be used to question what purpose the complementarity theory serves. It has been promoted as being a protector of women, but the effect of the complementarity theory has been to maintain the juxtapositioning of eros and agape and to keep sexuality—and women—controlled. To venture outside the bounds sanctioned by the complementarity theory risks damaging relations with oneself, the community, and probably God Himself (sic). Or so we have been led to believe. Whose interests are really being protected?

The claim that female nature is complementary to male nature functions as the ideological underpinning of compulsory hetero-sexuality by demanding that men be coupled with women and that women be coupled with men. Any aberration is a betrayal of the natural created order. Bailey, Lewis, and Thielicke all por-trayed female nature as needing protection from the stronger male; this protection, of course, was always to be within the con-text of marriage. Thielicke described female sexuality as needing to be awakened by a sensitive male. Promiscuity did not serve women well, according to Lewis, because age eroded the lure of female beauty. Bailey urged against same-sex schooling, fearing the inculcation of "wrong sexual ideas." And church documents claim the one-man, one-woman, one-flesh relationship as the only God-given form of relationship.

The logic of the complementarity theory has served to infan-tilize female sexuality. According to this logic, marriage safe-guards women. Further, the emphasis on the monogamous (agapic) nature of female sexuality, which tames and transforms the polygamous (eros-by-itself) nature of male sexuality, renders marriage necessary since it helps control sexuality, an untamed eros, which might otherwise wreak havoc. The "true man" and the "true woman" come together in this context, deftly redeem-ing and transforming what once threatened to spiral out of control.

And so, once again, we apply a healthy dose of *suspicion*. As-suming for a moment that women are more agape-oriented than men, why should women sacrifice themselves in order to redeem and transform men? And even if eros did need redemption and transformation, why would it have to be undertaken by only fe-male/male couples? Why does being created in *imago Dei* mean that women can only be coupled with men and men can only be coupled with women? How do such assumptions feed violence against women and children? against lesbian, gay, and bisexual people? How have these false assumptions affected our spirituali-ties? our theologies? our psyches? our bodies? our lives?

Creating Alternatives

These questions are merely a beginning. Many more questions can be and need to be asked. The dualistic assumptions that erotic love must be redeemed and transformed by a higher love and that this redemption can happen only between male and female partners in a lifelong, monogamous relationship must be challenged. Indeed, these sexist and heterosexist assumptions have been challenged by increasing numbers of theologians and ethicists. Beverly Wildung Harrison, Sheila Briggs, James Nelson, Mary Hunt, Carter Heyward, Tom Driver, Rita Nakashima Brock, and Marvin Ellison, to name only a few, have attempted to show that the profound devaluing of erotic love and the "romantic" notion of sexual complementarity as redemptive reflect the badly broken spirituality of an oppressive religious tradition.[77] Recent denominational policy statements have ignored this pro-feminist and feminist liberation theo-ethical critique.

In the chapters that follow, pro-feminist and feminist liberation theo-ethical alternatives to the theological and ecclesiastical inheritance of the control, redemption, and transformation of eros will be detailed. The effects of the resultant violence and alienation will be explored, along with a proposal to move beyond the control of sexuality—beyond the control of eros.

CHAPTER THREE

Re-membering Eros
Feminist Liberation Theo-Ethical Voices

I n this chapter, the feminist liberation theo-ethical analysis of eros is examined as a way of developing a response
and alternative to the malestream theological and denominational interpretations of eros. Sheila Briggs, Rita Nakashima Brock, and Carter Heyward have undertaken substantial
work on eros, and so a summary of their work is a primary focus
of the chapter. Other feminist liberation theo-ethicists have
made valuable contributions to the discussion of eros and sexuality, and their work is used supplementarily. This chapter points
to the inadequacies of the earlier treatments of eros and sexuality
and lays out tools for a feminist liberation theo-ethical constructive analysis.

At the same time that secular feminism was being accused of
racism and classism and labeled a "white middle-class women's
movement," feminist theology was also facing those challenges.[1]
In an attempt to broaden the analysis of feminist theology, some
white feminist theologians in the early to mid-1980s began
calling themselves "feminist liberation theologians."[2] Feminist
liberation theology is not intended to be a white, middle-class
movement, but rather is intended to include women from all social locations. Some African American women identify themselves as "womanists" as well as, or instead of, feminist liberation
theologians.[3] And some Hispanic women and Latinas identify
themselves as "mujeristas" as well as, or instead of, feminist
liberation theologians.[4] What these theo-ethicists share is a commitment to the liberation and well-being of all women, with special attention to those who are most marginalized. This concern
cuts across boundaries of class, race, sexuality, nationality, and
culture.

Feminist liberation theo-ethics has been the vehicle for a radical overhaul of malestream understandings of eros and sexuality. This emphasis has everything to do with a privileging of all women's lives, bodies, and experiences. It also has a great deal to do with the feminist liberation theo-ethical commitment to a power analysis in which the personal is political (e.g., sex is political).

In feminist liberation theo-ethics, it is an important part of power analysis to examine the interconnections between oppressions. The attempt is made to do theology across difference, while respecting difference (e.g., race, class, gender, sexuality, culture, age, and physical and mental abilities). Feminist liberation theo-ethics consists of an ongoing effort to open dialogue between all women, keeping in mind that those who identify themselves as feminist liberation theologians and seek to be proactive on issues of race, class, and sexuality are not exempt from needing to work on our own participation in racism, classism, and heterosexism. This commitment to a theo-ethics that takes into account the connections between oppressions is critical to a feminist liberation theo-ethical consideration of eros. Eros cannot be re-membered without taking into account the ways in which its negative treatment has affected *all* women.

In examining feminist and feminist liberation theo-ethical work on eros, three stages emerge. The first is a *definitional* stage, as eros is reclaimed from patriarchal control. The second stage is describing the *functioning* of the newly emergent eros in a feminist context. The third stage of eros is that of feminist *visioning*, in which the transformation of eros, God, and humanity is invoked. In the following pages, we will look at these three stages in the feminist theological and feminist liberation theo-ethical treatments of eros.

RE-DEFINING EROS

From the late 1960s to the early 1980s, feminist theologians—mirroring the efforts of secular feminists—began the process of re-claiming eros from patriarchal control. This process included the basic empowering of women, the affirmation of sexuality in general and female sexuality and bodyselves in particular, and the realization that the control of eros was connected to the control of women's sexuality and reproductive capacities.[5] This realization motivated women to set about the task of re-defining eros and wresting the control of eros from the hands of those who would be threatened by women claiming their own power. Feminist theologians in this stage sought to name the damage that centuries of male-dominated state and ecclesiastical control had wreaked.

The work of feminist theologians and feminist liberation theologians during this period was situated in a concrete socio-historical framework which included the development of secular feminist debate and theory on the topic of sexuality. This secular feminist discourse, taking place almost entirely outside the realm of theology, was foundational for the later feminist liberation theo-ethical response to traditional christian treatments of eros. Indeed, much of the feminist liberation response has been, in large measure, derivative from earlier feminist theoretical developments.

Audre Lorde's "Power of the Erotic"

It is fair to say that no one secular feminist theorist has influenced feminist theology and feminist liberation theo-ethics on the subject of eros more than Audre Lorde. A self-described "Black, lesbian, feminist, mother, warrior, lover, poet, doing my work," Audre Lorde (1934–1992) wrote an essay in the early 1980s re-claiming and re-defining the erotic.[6] This essay has remained a touchstone for feminist and womanist theo-ethicists. As such, it deserves our examination.

Observing that the erotic in our lives is our source of power, Audre Lorde noted that this power has been suppressed and then modeled on male images of power (i.e., that which appears to be rational and controllable). The male-dominant modeling of power has caused women to shy away from claiming our own power. According to Lorde, women have been consistently told that the nonrational, intuitive sources of knowledge within us are not to be trusted, nor are our experiences, and most certainly not the knowledge rooted in our eroticism. The male world, noted Lorde, has warned women against these types of knowledge; but, at the same time, the male-dominant world has valued them enough to have women use them to serve the interests of men. Since men fear these types of knowledge too much to be able to explore their own capacities for them, women's knowledge and eroticism are suppressed, channeled, and controlled via sexism, racism, and heterosexism for the benefit of the male world and the maintenance of patriarchal order.[7]

Lorde also asserted that the erotic has been mislabeled and used against women. "It has been made into the confused, the trivial, the psychotic, the plasticized sensation," wrote Lorde.[8] The erotic has been confused with the pornographic. Eros has been denied. Indeed, eros has been feared. The fear of eros has contributed to the control of women and of sexuality.

Lorde was adamant that eros be re-defined and re-claimed in such a way that its bonds to patriarchal control could be broken. The re-definition of eros would enable women to empower ourselves and one another. To that end, Lorde insisted that the fear of eros be rooted out, since fear only served to prevent us from pursuing our deeper feelings and from unmasking the lies which have hitherto defined the erotic. Asserted Lorde, "we have been raised to fear the YES within ourselves, our deepest cravings."[9] If we fear our desires, then we are less likely to question the reality of these fears or the extent to which our oppression is or is not a given.

In moving beyond paralyzing fear, Lorde sought to re-define and re-claim the erotic as that "resource within each of us that lies in a deeply female and spiritual plane, firmly rooted in the power of our unexpressed or unrecognized feeling."[10] The corruption of this power does not mean that it is irretrievable; rather, it remains there for our tapping. As women move to reclaim the history, language, work, and culture that have been denied, the power of the erotic is unleashed. Lorde understood the erotic as being the life force of women which could begin to bridge the splits between the public and the private, the spiritual and the political. The erotic as bridge taps deep-running passion and

love, for "the erotic is the nurturer or nursemaid of all our deepest knowledge."[11]

Lorde also focused on the erotic as the experience of depth in
our lives. Experiencing our strongest feelings is what the erotic is
about and is also why the erotic has been feared to the extent it
has. She asserted that once we have experienced a certain depth
of feeling and its power, "we can require no less of ourselves."[12]
To turn away from this depth of feeling is a denial of eros and is
destructive both to ourselves and to our relationships with
others.

The Theological Power of Eros Affirmed

It is difficult to imagine feminist theological work on re-
claiming and re-defining eros without Audre Lorde's contribution. Her work has allowed many women in theological circles to
begin to move beyond fear and wholeheartedly re-claim the eros,
"the YES within ourselves." I suspect that this is so because
Audre Lorde spoke from outside the church context and thus had
an understanding of power that was not tied in with a struggle
against dominant male notions of church, God, and sex. In
many ways, Audre Lorde gave feminist liberation theo-ethicists
permission to begin talking about eros.

The re-claiming of eros has gone hand in hand with re-
claiming God/Goddess from patriarchal theology. This process
of reclamation and re-definition has enabled many women to begin to imagine that our bodies, minds, and spirits are part of a
whole. The foremother of feminist theology, Nelle Morton,
writing in the late 1970s, noted the effects of re-claiming and re-
defining eros.

> We can claim our sexuality as pervasive and as ourselves. We
> can claim our bodies as ours and as ourselves and our minds as
> our own and ourselves. This sense of oneness within and with
> one another has brought us into more erotic relationship with one
> another as women. For once a woman comes to see beauty in
> another woman's mind and in her own mind and to love with the
> mind, she discovers another dimension of power that is self-
> fulfilling. [13]

Beverly Wildung Harrison has noted as well the holistic nature of human existence which springs from the erotic: "Our
energy . . . is body-mediated energy. Our sexuality does not detract from, but deepens and shapes our power of personal being.
Our bodies, through our senses, mediate our real, physical connectedness to all things. Our sexuality represents our most
intense interaction with the world."[14] This is key for feminist
theologians: because women have been associated with eros, sexuality, and evil, re-claiming eros from patriarchal control has
resulted in the affirmation of the power of women. Thus, re-
claiming "our bodies as ours and as ourselves and our minds as
our own and ourselves" and re-defining our energy as "body-
mediated energy" open up hitherto unimagined possibilities for
women. And love, which once was constrained in rigid categories, is broken open.[15]

Harrison continues the redefinition of love by maintaining
that the love commandment was never meant to be interpreted
as "an order to feel a certain way," nor was it intended to "create
the power to feel love." Rather, love was meant to deepen human relationships and "build up the power of personhood in one
another." The power of love is thus rooted in a *mutual* love.[16]

In this way, feminist theologians began to deconstruct the patriarchal hold on love in general and eros in particular.[17] A movement toward re-defining eros and incorporating it into a feminist
theo-ethical framework was underway. Having begun the process
of re-claiming and re-defining eros, feminist theologians were
able to imagine what the functioning of eros might look like in
our lives.

THE FUNCTIONING OF EROS

The earlier processes of re-claiming and re-defining eros enabled
feminist theologians to move into a place where they could begin
to consider how this newly re-claimed and re-defined eros might
function. Taking into account the patriarchal resistance to a
freed eros has been important to this task and feeds into how eros
is reconstructed. At the point of describing how eros functions,

the feminist treatment of eros took on a specifically feminist liberation theo-ethical analysis.

The three particular voices of feminist liberation theo-ethics to be considered are Sheila Briggs, an African American feminist Roman Catholic theologian from England;[18] Rita Nakashima Brock, a Japanese/Puerto Rican immigrant American feminist liberation theologian;[19] and Carter Heyward, a white lesbian feminist liberation theologian.[20] Briggs, Brock, and Heyward all have written substantive constructive pieces detailing the functioning of eros, moving from a patriarchal context to a liberative context. Briggs has emphasized self-love and justice as being critical to the functioning of eros. Brock's work has focused on eros as the energy of relationship. And a description of eros as a sensual yearning for mutuality has been Heyward's contribution. The pages that follow detail these three feminist liberation theo-ethical voices.

Self-Love and Justice

> The most well known slogan of the women's movement, "The personal is political," grew out of the painful realization of women, gathering together in groups during the 1960s and 1970s, that their common experiences revealed a socially conditioned shallowness of passion.[21]

Sheila Briggs attributes the negative attitude toward eros and passion to the influence of Hellenism in early christianity. She suggests that a negative attitude was inevitable because the God-human relationship was understood in the socio-historical context of a slaveholding patriarchy.[22] In this situation, eros became associated with passivity, which in turn was equated with the inability to control what was happening to one's own body. The solution arrived at by theologians of the time was to control the body along with those entities associated with it: namely—women, earth, passion, sex, and slaves.

Briggs elaborates on how the connection between the control of eros and the oppression of women and slaves was forged. In doing so, she notes that both the institution of slavery and the sexual exploitation of women within that institution must be taken into account. All women are sexually exploited within a slaveholding patriarchy: "the marriage of the freeborn woman ..." is "on a continuum with the rape of the slave woman."[23] Furthermore, the eradication of slavery did not mean the eradication of sexual exploitation. As long as the mentality and ideology of a slaveholding patriarchy continues, so too does the sexual exploitation and control of women.

This historical perspective is particularly relevant to the earlier theological discussion of eros in chapter 1. Briggs charges that christianity has exhibited a marked lack of willingness to confront the oppression of women. Unwilling to deal with the complex nature of love, theologians have fallen back to insisting on the dualistic nature of love. Citing Anders Nygren as one of the main offenders, she notes that the division of love into eros and agape has encouraged the ongoing exploitation of women in that eros is seen as that which must be chastened, shaped, and controlled.[24] By depositing all that is imperfect about love on the doorstep of eros, theologians have been able to ignore the oppression of women. From Nygren's perspective, the existence of injustice is attributed to the failure of eros and true christians cannot be responsible for the failings of the unchristian love, eros.[25]

The sexist and heterosexist control of women's knowledge and eroticism has played itself out in the assignment of gender roles and the rigid boundaries kept between the public and private arenas. Briggs calls this the "economy of the two loves." Women are charged with the roles of agape (with its emphasis on self-sacrifice), and men are assigned the roles of eros (with its emphasis on self-assertion). These two roles are not placed in opposition to each other (as in the work of Nygren) but rather are portrayed as being *complementary* to each other. The female-associated agape is required in order to make the male-associated eros succeed in the creation and maintenance of the status-quo. Eros must be tamed since it is the human love and therefore given to imperfection and unpredictability. Agape guarantees the reproduction of eros in a way that is both acceptable and controllable. In this way, the two loves work together to insure the health of patriarchal culture.[26]

The functioning of eros, in the context of lesbian sexuality, provides a rich resource for resistance to patriarchal interpretations of love. For lesbian women, the affirmation of eros enables women to say NO to compulsory heterosexuality. Briggs observes the way in which lesbian sexuality disrupts "the symbolism of power" in male-dominant power systems.[27]

> [Lesbian sexuality] subverted sexual intercourse as the representation of male activity and authority and of female passivity and subservience. Passivity was the necessary attribute of those whom nature fitted to be dominated by others. In denying the passivity of women, lesbian sexuality challenged the order of a universe, where it is natural for some to dominate and others to be dominated.[28]

Lesbianism, asserts Briggs, subverts the ideological grounds for the sexual abuse of women within the dual institutions of marriage and slavery.[29]

The oppression of lesbian women results in the suppression of an alternative to the male control of female sexuality. Such oppression reinforces the patriarchal social construction of women's sexuality. It results in the limitation of women's passion to the boundaries set by patriarchal morality. In short, the oppression of lesbian women, according to Briggs, disconnects women from "the erotic affirmation" of ourselves as women and alienates us from a sense of feminist justice.[30] Thus, a feminist justice must commit itself to the opposition of sexual abuse as well as to resistance of the institution of compulsory heterosexuality.

Briggs's affirmation of eros is rooted in the affirmation of self-love. Whether one is lesbian or heterosexual, female or male, the embracing of eros, by definition, involves loving oneself. Malestream theology has been correct in its assumptions that eros and self-love are connected. However, what has not been considered is the extent to which self-love is a central part of our ability to love. Briggs insists that the fusion of self-love with the love of others is a requirement for feminist justice and as such is erotic. She writes:

Erotic love seeks self-fulfillment through relation to the other; it is simultaneously self- and other-directed. As such it shares the structure of compassion, for compassion is not disinterested love nor love without a self-reference. Compassion is an act of empathy in which one is moved to connect the sufferings of another to one's own feelings, to link the material and emotional needs of another to one's own desire for happiness. The inclusion of the self, in the justice which we seek for others, arises out of the realization that eros and compassion together constitute what Carter Heyward has so aptly called 'Our Passion for Justice.'[31]

Briggs highlights an essential point for feminist work on eros. The affirmation of self-love challenges the traditional teachings on eros and transforms love and justice into a both/and instead of the either/or situation it has so often been made out to be.

Not only does eros provide a basis for our struggle for justice, but it reveals to us a God of justice. Briggs suggests further that eros may reveal "the God who sustains the feminist quest for justice" and who pushes us to move beyond the artificial cultural and social boundaries set by a patriarchal order.[32] This God of justice inspires us to become impassioned in the struggle against oppression—for the sake of ourselves, others, and God.

Briggs's emphasis on self-love directly contradicts Nygren's insistence that self-love cannot be a part of christian love. Of course, one of the many differences between Briggs and Nygren is that she considers eros to be a christian love. Her insistence that self-love is an intrinsic part of eros, of christian love, explicitly defies the dualisms of sex and spirit, female and male, eros and agape, self and other present in malestream theology.

Furthermore, Briggs's connection of compassion with erotic love functions as a denial of Nygren's claim that love is disinterested.[33] In her view, love is not something about which one can be "objective;" nor is love something about which "value-free" judgments can be made.[34] A compassionate erotic love, which fuels our desire for justice, arises from particular (subjective) experiences and does not hesitate to make judgments about that which is not compassionate and does not promote justice.

The Energy of Relationship

In the beginning is the divine Eros, embodied in all being. As the incarnate, life-giving power of the universe, divine erotic power is the Heart of the Universe.[35]

In contextualizing her discussion of eros, Rita Nakashima Brock takes stock of the abusive nature of the portrayal of the erotic. She argues that it has been dependent upon a complementary relationship between eros and agape and observes that women's value has been linked directly to our "relational, nurturant abilities" and our "erotic potential."[36] The patriarchal control of eros, maintained through images, laws, and sexual practices, is designed to keep women from seeing other possibilities. Women and eros are treated ambivalently: on the one hand, they are desired and profitable; on the other, they are hated and feared. Thus, Brock associates the repression of eros with the misogyny characteristic of much of christian tradition and rampant in contemporary society. The patriarchal control of eros has created a climate in which the erotic is manifested in violence and abuse toward women, children, and all people of difference. Eros portrayed in this manner contributes to the ease with which compulsory heterosexuality is maintained as compulsory and deviating manifestations of the erotic are deemed "immoral or unnatural."[37] In this context, eros is molded into the confines of a highly specialized role.

In her discussion of eros, Rita Nakashima Brock uses the concept of "heart" as a metaphor for the selves of human beings and human capacities for intimacy. Heart is a holistic concept: it signifies the union, or potential union, "of body, spirit, reason, and passion through heart knowledge," which is also our "deepest and fullest knowing." Heart is the "center . . . and most real, vital meaning and core of our lives,"[38] according to Brock. "Heart is what binds us to others, safeguards our memory, integrates all dimensions of ourselves, and empowers us to act with courage. The union of physical, emotional, and spiritual suggests itself in the very word *heart,* which also is the physical center of our bodies, their vital source."[39]

Brock uses the metaphor of heart not only to signal the inter-relatedness or holistic nature of human existence, but as a way of examining the extent to which patriarchy has a *broken* heart. Heart is a power that allows for a heart-to-heart encounter and leads human beings toward an incarnation of the sacred in daily life.[40] Heart is a fundamental power of life into which we are born. Heart can heal us, make whole what is broken, empower, and liberate. Brock names this the feminist eros or erotic power.[41] She continues her description of the feminist eros, noting that it is "grounded in the relational lives of women and in a critical, self-aware consciousness." Feminist eros dissolves the alienation which has overly compartmentalized our lives and it emerges as "a sensuous, transformative whole-making wisdom" that engages our whole heart in relational contexts.[42]

As "the power of our primal interrelatedness," erotic power both "creates and connects hearts," involving the entire individual "in relationships of self-awareness, vulnerability, openness, and caring."[43] Viewed in this manner, eros is that power from which all other forms of power come. Eros is not about control; it is about connection with our whole selves and the selves of others. It is through our erotic power that we truly experience the depth of our lives as fully integrated selves (mind, body, spirit).

Our personal power comes from our erotic power. Living by heart, we come to experience our responses to the world around us as something unique to us. This experience of heart enables us to affirm ourselves not at the expense of others, but rather in a way that is life-enhancing to us and others. Brock notes: "The paradox of personal power is its relational base. We can only become self-aware and self-accepting through relationships that co-create us, and the maintenance of nonharmful environments requires sustained, nurturing relationships. Self-acceptance, as an ongoing, lifelong process, is possible only through our openness to others and their presence."[44] This personal power, this erotic power, empowers us all to seek intimacy rather than dependency. It entices us toward openness and self-love and away from the altar of self-sacrifice and self-negation.

Ultimately, integration and connectedness come from erotic power. As the grounding force of our experiences, erotic power is the medium through which we can experience the rich textures of our lives. Brock observes that, from this perspective, erotic power is very different from so-called agapic objectivity. Unlike agape, eros is about intimacy. With eros, the entire bodyself is engaged in a relational context.[45]

In detailing the intimate, engaged nature of erotic power, Brock draws on Audre Lorde's description of the erotic and notes that the erotic, by definition, cannot be objectified. It must be felt firsthand "through our own unique presence and the presence of others to us" and is present in "all levels of experience." Echoing Lorde, Brock insists that once having experienced the depth of erotic power, we are enabled "to refuse the convenient, shoddy, conventional, and safe."[46]

Brock also associates erotic power with our deep hunger for justice. When we are in touch with our erotic power, we are able to respond—or to be response-able—to situations of injustice. Unwilling to settle for powerlessness, our embrace of eros gives us life and hope. Eros is the energy of relationship and the basis upon which we attempt to understand one another. Through eros we are able to "see through the faint, fearful, broken heart of patriarchy" and search for connections which empower us to heal brokenness.[47]

By the portrayal of erotic power as the energy of relationship, Brock sketches the theological implications of erotic power as "the incarnation of divine love." Erotic power is the vehicle through which the divine nature of humanity's day-to-day existence is revealed. The connection of erotic power with divine love exists in the midst of human relationships and is co-created by and with one another. This erotic power, insists Brock, is present in our day-to-day concrete lives and is that which provides sustenance throughout our lives.[48]

So how would Brock respond to the descriptions of eros and agape promulgated by malestream theology and the shapers of ecclesiastical policies? Several points can be deduced from her sketch of eros. She lays the blame for the abusive portrayal of eros at the feet of the complementary relationship between eros and agape.[49] Furthermore, she would insist that the so-called complementary nature of eros and agape, of female and male, contributes to the abusive portrayal of eros and women, who in malestream theology represent that which must be controlled. Such control of eros, in Brock's view, perpetuates abuse.

Brock would find Thielicke's description of women's nature as needing to be awakened and protected to be a thinly disguised justification for the deeply misogynistic, male-dominated control of eros.[50] In addition, the judgment of malestream theology and of recent denominational policies that any manifestation of eros which deviates from the proscribed "one-man, one-woman, one-flesh" formula is unwholesome, "immoral or unnatural" further cements what Brock calls the misogynistic repression of eros.[51] Such attempts to control and repress eros contribute to the perpetration of violence against women and children.

Brock's observation that erotic power—or the feminist eros— is very different from "agapic objectivity" serves to highlight further the problems with Nygren's insistence on "value-free" descriptions and "objectivity."[52] Such "objectivity" is founded on dualistic assumptions. Since Brock seeks to introduce eros as a *holistic* rather than dualistic notion, eros cannot be about objectivity. Rather, eros is an intimate, relational engagement between bodyselves. So-called agapic objectivity only serves to distance intimacy, relation, and bodies.

Finally, in contrast to malestream theology and mainline denominational policies, Brock believes that eros is not about control; it is about connection. Eros does not seek dependency (a characteristic often associated with women); it seeks intimacy. Objectivity is not part of eros; rather, eros is concerned with embodied relational engagement. Brock would maintain that the male-dominant understanding of eros as being in need of control lest people be damaged (as Bailey warned) is backward. Instead, she argues that if eros is controlled and repressed "for our own good," it is we who are damaged; indeed, eros as the energy of relationship is damaged.

A Sensual Yearning for Mutuality

With my people—friends, compañeras, sisters and brothers, known and unknown—I realize that our creative power in rela-

> *tion, the power of our godding, is the wellspring of our sexuali-*
> *ties: our yearnings to embody mutually empowering relations,*
> *our desire to live into our YES.* [53]

Carter Heyward, in contextualizing her discussion of eros, ac-
knowledges the virulent opposition that has met any attempt at
combining God-talk and eros-talk. She notes that this opposition, along with the perception of eros as being that love in
which one loses control, has been behind the repression of sexuality. God and eros cannot be talked about in the same breath,
because God is good and eros is not. Heyward maintains that this
maltreatment of the erotic in our common lives denies the message of the incarnation—that our flesh is good. [54]

Furthermore, the dominant theological preference of christian
agape to eros, according to Heyward, results in the predomi-
nance of the message that it is better to "express God's spiritual
love of enemies, strangers, and people we may not enjoy than to
love our friends and sexual partners." [55] The embodied love of
one's close friends and sexual partners is devalued because it is
perceived to be anti-spiritual and full of danger. This dominant
christian perspective on love constitutes an egregious misinterpretation of the love that is of both human and divine origin.
Eros so misinterpreted is eros suppressed.

Agreeing with Audre Lorde, Heyward notes that the patriarchal misinterpretation and suppression of the erotic have made it
inaccessible. When the erotic is not accessible to us, when we
deny our yearnings because of the very fact that we yearn, we are
pulled away from others as well as from ourselves. We remain
unconscious of our feelings and become pornographically objectified by the abusive power dynamics which maintain our subju-
gation and alienation. [56]

Heyward describes the erotic as being "our most fully embodied experience of the love of God." [57] The erotic is that which
moves us to make connections between and among ourselves; it
is that which leads us to the knowledge that in making connections with one another, we are making connections with God.
Our power is a shared power; God is our power and God is erotic
(as well as being agapic and philial). [58]

Heyward makes her understanding of eros more concrete by emphasizing that the erotic is sensual; we know it through our five senses. This sensuality is a source of authority for her.[59] She writes:

I feel passionately my erotic movement in relation to others. I know that, in relation, I am a dynamic, sensual organism. I am bounded by my skin—porous, open, and fluid, with holes larger and smaller through which I take in and put out what I must to live, and through which, with my permission, others may also pass from time to time, sensually or sexually, with me. . . . My eroticism is my participation in the universe.[60]

For Heyward, eros is the sensual embodiment of the divine "between and among us insofar as we are moving more fully into, or toward, mutually empowering relationships."[61] But the erotic is not only characterized by movement *toward* mutuality; it involves a yearning for mutuality. The erotic in mutual relation is "both yet—and not yet, both now—and coming"; it incorporates eschatological movement into mutuality. Eros is shared power, and as shared power it is sacred.[62]

For Heyward, sexuality is an embodied yearning "to express a relational mutuality." Echoing Audre Lorde, she asserts that relational mutuality means that tensions are neither broken nor turned away from, but rather are met face to face. The discomfort of tensions between those in relation are sustained; only by sustaining tension, only by looking it in the face, can tension be resolved.[63]

What exactly is this mutuality of which Heyward speaks? "Mutuality is the process of loving and is a way of speaking of love. It is the experience of being in right relation. *Mutuality is sharing power in such a way that each participant in the relationship is called forth more fully into becoming who she is—a whole person, with integrity.*"[64] Heyward sees mutuality as being a part of relational movement. Mutuality is never static; it changes and grows within particular relationships. Mutuality does not mean that relationships are without conflict, anger, or tension. Indeed, the commitment to struggle through conflict, anger, and tension is a mark of a mutual relationship. As such, mutual relationships require a certain amount of risk.[65]

In engaging the particularly sexual nature of eros, Heyward describes sexual orgasm as "a climax in our capacity to know . . . the coming together of self and other." Orgasm is the coming together of our sexuality and other parts of our lives; it is a tension between the desire to control and the desire to be able to let go. Heyward adds that sexual orgasm brings us to an awareness of the "ongoing movement" or change which is "the basis of our connection."[66] Change is essential to relationship; it is what moves us along in the particular details of our lives and relationships.

Heyward notes that the more mutual and honest a relationship is, the deeper the love is. She is loath to make distinctions between friendship and sexual love when deep feeling, mutual relationship is present, acknowledging that there is an "erotic flow of energy" which binds friends together.[67] Eros should not be confined to the love between lovers. It permeates our life together and draws us into sensual, mutual relationships with one another.

Heyward agrees with Brock that the dualistic nature of malestream theology and mainline denominational policies on eros have resulted in abusive power dynamics.[68] She notes that the designation of God as good and eros as not good—as seen, for instance, in Nygren—has served only to repress sexuality and deny the incarnational message that our flesh is good. Instead, Heyward claims that love is of both human and divine origin.

Heyward's emphasis on mutuality marks a radical departure from the assumptions underlying the malestream interpretation of eros. Far from limiting eros to a specific context between husband and wife, her emphasis on mutuality delimits eros. Eros yearns for relational mutuality, for sharing power. Eros is an embodied connecting movement, not limited to the bedrooms of married heterosexual couples.[69] Another aspect of her emphasis on mutuality that challenges mainline denominational policies is her assertion that conflict, anger, and tension are part of mutual relationships. This is contrary to the stress placed on unity and reconciliation by Episcopal bishops. Unity in the ecclesiastical context means a disdain for and avoidance of disagreement—or for anyone who dares to make a fuss in the name of justice.

Finally, Heyward's move to connect sexual orgasm with other parts of our lives flies in the face of Nygren's adamant refusal to consider that "Vulgar Eros" had anything to do with good christian people.[70] Her unwillingness to make distinctions between friendship and a specifically sexual love violates the careful categories of Friendship and Eros set up by Lewis, as well as the warnings Bailey issued about sexual relations outside of marriage.[71] Heyward's eros refuses dualism, refuses polite dismissals in the name of unity, and refuses to be constrained in carefully constructed categories.

A FEMINIST LIBERATION THEO-ETHICAL VISIONING

More than anything, a feminist liberation theo-ethical treatment of eros points toward the future. It paints a picture of what might be: the "both yet—and not yet," the "both now—and coming" to which Carter Heyward refers.[72] A feminist liberation theo-ethical treatment of eros is part of a process, part of a movement into mutuality. It is about revealing the "broken heart of patriarchy."[73] And it speaks to the importance of self-love for making justice in the world.[74]

This "visioning" of feminist liberation theo-ethicists is important for it keeps us on the edge; it dares us to risk. Visioning provides hope for the transformation of the patriarchal treatment of eros into an eros rooted in mutuality and shared power. As Carter Heyward notes, we have two things in common in this society: "our immersion in nonmutual power relations and our desire for a better way."[75]

The feminist emphasis on mutuality, according to Heyward, provides a vision of a justice which calls people forth to risk and to move into those opportunities that are the most liberative and creative. By its very nature, mutuality entails growth and change in relation. Mutuality is "an invitation into shaping the future together," and together we help create the "not yet."[76]

Along with Sheila Briggs, Jewish feminist liberation theologian Judith Plaskow maintains that the erotic can act as both a personal and a community resource for social change. Tapping the erotic as a resource involves "living dangerously" with the feelings that are no longer suppressed. Being "alive to the pain and anger" caused by oppressive relationships creates energy for change. And on the other side of the struggle for change lies joy. Further, Plaskow insists that being alive entails being sexually alive. To suppress any one type of vitality is to suppress all types of vitality.[77]

Rita Nakashima Brock agrees that the unilateral suppression of eros will not contribute to solving any of the world's problems. Trusting in heart—in erotic power—enables us to challenge those powers that oppress and exploit. Trusting in heart, we face both our own broken-heartedness and our own power to transform the world.[78]

Brock insists that nothing else but our innate need for self-love and intimacy with others can sustain life. The only power that is life-giving is erotic power. Erotic power moves us into the salvific acts of stopping those powers that are life-denying. For Brock, journeying into the depths of erotic power unleashes our power to love; in this journeying we incarnate divine love.[79]

Beverly Wildung Harrison has long insisted on our power as human beings to love one another. She maintains that "we have the power through acts of love or lovelessness literally to create one another."[80] One of the tasks facing a feminist liberation theo-ethics must be to insist that the tradition of christian ethics be held accountable for its role in minimizing the power of human love to transform the world. Christian ethics must face the effects of the denial of love, for it has grossly underestimated and misunderstood "the depth of our power to thwart life and to maim each other." With Plaskow, Harrison notes that we can choose to risk—we can choose to set free our love and God's love—we can choose the transformative, life-enhancing power of love over that which keeps eros repressed, the downtrodden down, and hearts broken.[81]

The vision that feminist liberation theo-ethicists hold for eros is the power to connect, to transform, to liberate. Eros presents the opportunity to connect with ourselves, one another, the wider world, and God. In re-claiming and re-defining erotic power, we reach out to the web of relation of which we are a part.[82] Through erotic power we incarnate God in our everyday communities. Through erotic power we are able to unravel the multi-layers of self-hate. Through erotic power we are able to challenge the life-denying powers of injustice.

SOME QUESTIONS FOR A SEXUAL THEO-ETHICS

The work of feminist theologians, womanist theologians, and feminist liberation theo-ethicists on eros represents a major paradigm shift from that presented in the first two chapters of this book. Eros has been re-claimed and re-defined, and its functioning has been described in some detail. No longer is eros to be shunned by good christian people. No longer is eros to be "saved" by the supposedly more acceptable agape. No longer is self-loving anathema. No longer can love be considered "objective" and "value free." And no longer is eros to be confined only to lifelong monogamous relationships between a woman and a man in the context of marriage.

Eros is breaking free, thus opening up the entire field of sexual ethics. Where once eros was controlled without question, that *carte blanche* control can no longer be assumed. New questions are emerging as to what ethical guidelines are needed in what situations. Should all relationships be monogamous? If not, how do we incorporate non-monogamous relationships into our lives and our communities? How do we understand fidelity?

How do we best protect ourselves and one another from abuse? How can we better educate ourselves about and prevent domestic and sexual violence? How can those who have suffered sexual and physical abuse move beyond surviving to thriving? How can we heal?

Of what does the challenge to the malestream control of eros consist? How do we piece our sexualities and spiritualities back together? Are there any "controls" to be put on sexuality? If so, what are they, and who decides what they are?

What does mutuality actually mean, practically speaking, in our day-to-day lives? How do we struggle to move toward mutuality relationally? What does it mean to hold mutuality as an ethical ideal in the context of a social order that is historically and systemically non-mutual?

What does a feminist liberation theo-ethical perspective on eros mean for our relationships with one another? How are our self-images affected? In a tradition in which self-negation has been the norm, how do we begin to love ourselves? How is our relationship with God influenced and shaped by a feminist eros?

Finally, what are the effects of incorporating eros into "our passion for justice"? What are our strategies for working toward a "feminist justice"? How do we encompass the differences among us—of race, class, sexuality, culture—into our struggles for justice? What do our differences mean in terms of how we experience eros? What do they mean in terms of how we move into relational mutuality? What does solidarity look like when we embrace an erotic passion for justice?

These questions come to mind when considering how a feminist/womanist liberation theo-ethics of sexuality might be shaped. More questions remain to be asked. The process of re-membering eros is an ongoing one. As we move on, the issues change shape and focus. The next two chapters address some of these questions in a constructive movement toward re-membering eros.

CHAPTER FOUR

The Problems Begotten of an
Eroticized Violence

D istorted power relations, fundamental to the control of eros, result in an eroticization of violence. This eroticization of violence is specifically (though not exclusively) manifested in the battering and rape of women and children and hate crimes against lesbian women and gay men. This chapter deals explicitly with the violence that has its roots in the patriarchal attempts to control eros, explores how hetero-sexism and homophobia hold the eroticization of violence in place, and details the subtle but deadly effects that malestream theology and mainline denominational policies on sexuality have on the reinforcement of violence. Attention is also given to the effects of an eroticized violence on intimacy.

SEX DEBATES:
SOME QUESTIONS FOR FEMINIST THEOLOGY

We must push even further the limits of what feminist theology in general and feminist liberation theo-ethics in particular have accomplished. In so doing, there are two issues that deserve elaboration: the lack of attention paid by feminist liberation theo-ethics to the secular feminist sex debates[1] and the lack of concreteness of feminist theological visions.

Debating Sex

The sexuality debates in secular feminism have been primarily about the clashing of radical cultural feminists and libertarian feminists.[2] The debates have continued throughout the 1980s and into the 1990s. The important issue for our purposes is what questions various streams of feminist theory raise that are important for the work of feminist liberation theo-ethics. One of the most overarching issues has to do with pleasure and danger. That radical cultural feminists can be loosely described as being primarily concerned with danger and libertarian feminists concerned with pleasure has polarized the discussion.[3] The important question for our purposes is: Have feminist liberation theo-ethicists adequately addressed the subjects of both sexual pleasure and sexual danger?

There is always more room for theological talk about sexual pleasure. Feminist liberation theology owes a great deal to Carter Heyward for her engagement of the subject. She, more than any other feminist liberation theo-ethicist, has elaborated upon an explicitly sexual theology.[4] However, her work merely marks the beginning of an ongoing conversation feminist liberation theo-ethicists need to have.

Of what does sexual pleasure consist? How do our different experiences of it inform our theologies? our ethics? What is healthy sex, as opposed to unhealthy sex? Some feminist liberation theo-ethicists would suggest that the degree of mutuality present in a particular relationship answers the latter question. We *know* what the authors of church policies and malestream theology would say. This is a critical question for the development of sexual ethics. Feminist liberation theo-ethicists need to engage directly the issue of sexual ethics and not shy away from proposing ethical guidelines.

Libertarian feminists have valorized the concept of consent (i.e., that any sexual activity is acceptable as long as the people involved consent to it), arguing that it is necessary for women to be able to develop their sexualities. Is such a concept adequate for a feminist liberation theo-ethics of sex? Does the concept of consent adequately take into account the different life experiences of women? Radical cultural feminists have maintained that the concept of consent does not take into account the relations of domination that are built into mainstream society.[5] How would a feminist liberation theo-ethics of sex approach this question?

What of sexual danger? Have feminist liberation theo-ethicists adequately addressed eros as "danger"? I believe that there are at least two types of danger connected with eros. The first is that of fear and awe, which requires risk-taking on our parts. This is an inherent part of our eroticism.[6] The second type of danger is that which compromises our physical and psychological safety. This type is the primary focus of this chapter.

There has been a certain reluctance among feminist liberation theologians to engage very deeply the problems of violence and eros. Although Brock speaks of child abuse and broken-heartedness, Briggs speaks of injustice and slavery, and Heyward speaks of the effects of a sadomasochistic society on sexuality, for the most part, the issue of violence has not been sufficiently addressed. Acknowledgement of the dangerous nature—or, more accurately, the distortion—of erotic power is an important first step, but feminist liberation theo-ethicists must move beyond acknowledgement to engagement.

Feminist liberation theo-ethicists need to deal explicitly with the fact that violence is often perpetrated in the name of eros. If eros is the "energy of relationship," as Brock suggests, what do we do about a bad relationship? Feminist liberation theo-ethicists have often explained eros gone bad as a "false" eros, an "alienated" eros, or "anti-eros."[7] But is this not too simple an explanation?

Feminist liberation theo-ethical work on sexuality needs to take seriously the differences in people's experiences of eros. We need to address explicitly the experiences and concerns of survivors of incest and battering; we need to wrestle with the existence of sadomasochism; we need to engage the discussion of the differences between pornography and erotica. In short, feminist liberation theo-ethics needs to do more than acknowledge the so-called danger of eros.

I understand the reluctance of feminist theologians—who are just beginning to reclaim, re-define, and reconstruct eros—to address aspects of eros that are not empowering and, in fact, have damaged women and children. Some feminist liberation theo-ethicists hesitate to engage the issue of a distorted and violent eros, the issue of an abusive sexuality, because of the fear that doing so would evoke "I told you so" responses from those who would keep tighter reigns on eros and sexuality. But by giving into that fear, feminist liberation theo-ethicists risk the power of the unspoken becoming greater than the power of the spoken. Feminist liberation theo-ethics must, for the sake of maintaining the ground that has been broken in the reclamation of eros, face the fact that distorted and violent eros exists and continues to affect adversely the lives of women and children.

There are still other issues raised by non-theological feminists that could broaden the agenda of feminist liberation theo-ethics. As secular feminists must address the fact that any particular ideology does not necessarily address or reflect the actual lived behavior of women, so too must feminist liberation theo-ethicists examine the extent to which their work connects with the everyday lived realities of women. For instance, feminist liberation theo-ethics needs to address the economic realities that interconnect with and oft-times are a determining factor of women's sexual experiences. We cannot continue to talk about eros only from our positions of relative economic security. We also need to listen to women who experience their sexuality as a means of economic survival and not as a means of relational pleasure.[8]

In addition, the concept of "compulsory heterosexuality" needs to be considered both by secular feminists and by feminist liberation theo-ethicists. How does economics affect the structure of compulsory heterosexuality? Is all heterosexuality compulsory? If not all heterosexual behavior is compulsory, we need to examine the nature of our relationships with men. This means that lesbian sexuality cannot be pedestalized as the solution to male domination.

Finally, how exactly do we begin to implement some of the suggestions made by feminist liberation theo-ethicists? Is there a way to make feminist liberation theo-ethical language about eros more concrete? Beverly Harrison urges us to "build up the power of personhood in one another."[9] Well, how? And how, exactly, does Rita Nakashima Brock's feminist eros emerge as "a sensuous, transformative, whole-making wisdom?" What does this mean? Her feminist eros is about connection with our selves and with others.[10] How do we actually connect? Sheila Briggs proposes "a fusion of self-love with the love of others."[11] Well, what are the details of that fusion? And what would that fusion look like in our day-to-day lives? Should we be using the term *fusion*

when women have had to fight so for our own independent identities? Finally, Carter Heyward talks about eros in an eschatological sense, as the "almost, but not yet" in our lives.[12] What do we
do while we're waiting? How do we move toward the "not yet"?
And what of the present situation—the here and now—that is so
terribly fraught with eroticized violence?

INJUSTICE AND EROS: STOPPING THE VIOLENCE

Feminism, in general, has often associated eros with everything
good. This is an idealistic notion and has served to obscure the
injustices committed in the name of eros.[13] The fact of the matter
is that eros, in reality, does not stand for everything good. Feminist liberation theo-ethics finds itself in the position of reclaiming eros from a tradition that has vilified it. The extent of es-
trangement we experience from ourselves, our bodies, our sexualities reveals the extent to which eros has been distorted and
controlled.

As feminist liberation theo-ethics goes about the business of
reclaiming eros, we find that the distortion and control of eros
has wreaked a great deal of violence, especially on those who are
not white, heterosexual, or male.[14] In the name of maintaining
control—in the name of controlling eros, sexuality, and sex—
women end up battered, bruised, broken, and sometimes dead.
In the name of controlling eros, of controlling sexuality, of controlling sex, lesbian women and gay men end up battered,
bruised, broken, and sometimes dead. In the name of controlling
eros, of controlling sexuality, of controlling sex, children are
raped and battered and end up bruised, broken, and sometimes
dead.

The damage wrought by an eroticized violence is not only
physical. There are psychological and spiritual costs as well. This
damage is undergirded by theological interpretations of eros that
posit the necessity to deny, control, and chasten eros. This inherited ethos is reinforced by current mainline denominational
policies on sexuality which mandate a few select forms of eros (if
not *one* select form) as being acceptable for christian people.

This ecclesiastical mandate serves to reinforce the violent character of eros. The churches are complicit in the promulgation of violence because of their insistence that eros be controlled and because of their proclamation that there is one, and only one, true, God-given form for expressing human sexuality.

The Eroticization of Violence

The eroticization of violence is nothing new. In fact, it is a much better established form of relating than is erotic mutuality grounded in justice. It comes from a deep alienation from oneself, one's body, and one's feelings. This alienation is a symptom of the distortion and control of eros. James Nelson, writing explicitly from male experience,[15] described this problem over a decade ago, noting the lack of integration between mind and body.

> *If the mind is alienated from the body, so also is the body from the mind. The depersonalization of one's sexuality . . . inevitably follows. The body becomes a physical object possessed and used by the self. Lacking is the sense of unity with the spontaneous rhythms of the body. Lacking is the sense of full participation in the body's stresses and pains, its joys and delights. More characteristic is the sense of the body as machine.*[16]

Nelson's characterization of alienation is a helpful starting point for understanding the origins of the eroticization of violence. Alienation from one's body, the separation of body and mind, leads to viewing the body as a tool of domination, a tool that, in Nelson's words, "wards off love."[17] Alienation is the climate in which violence is bred.

Gay theorist John Stoltenberg writes of the extent to which violence has been eroticized in the experience of men: "We are *supposed* to respond orgasmically to power and powerlessness, to violence and violation; our sexuality is *supposed* to be inhabited by a reverence for supremacy, for unjust power over and against other human life. We are not supposed to experience any other erotic possibility; we are not supposed to glimpse eroticized justice."[18] Alienation serves effectively to limit the options, to limit imagination, to make one's sexual responses automatic. Any other possibilities are impossible to imagine; eroticized justice is not even a dream.

Nelson compares the alienation experienced in warfare with that associated with sexual violence against women. This violence, he claims, is rooted in historical tradition: "Most societies have insisted that 'manhood' be won by young males through rites of passage involving the willingness to endure and inflict violence. . . . One who fails the ordeal is less than a man."[19] Proving one's manhood has become synonymous with alienation from one's body, feelings, and mind. The more one can cultivate alienation, the more violent one can be. The more violent one is, the more manly one is. This is the context in which many men experience sexuality.

Despite the social construction of male alienation, neither Nelson nor Stoltenberg would excuse male violence. Violence is a systemic problem; our culture is steeped in it. As a result, violence is present in almost every aspect of our daily lives. But, while violence is systemic and is used to maintain the status quo, individuals—most often men, though women too can be violent —*choose* to use it.

Paul Kivel, an activist who works with men who have committed violent acts against women and/or children, maintains that individual men *decide* to commit acts of violence. He insists that violent men be held accountable for their actions; violence cannot be dismissed as "just the way men are," nor can it be excused by virtue of their own abused childhoods. According to Kivel, no matter who commits the violence, no matter whether it is on a societal, institutional, or individual level, violence is the ultimate attempt to control.[20]

It is appropriate when examining the eroticization of violence to bring a well-developed sense of *suspicion* to bear on the discussion. *Suspicion* allows us to be wary of that which keeps violence eroticized and makes a dynamic of control necessary. It allows us to question the assumptions that underlie the proliferation of violence. What makes violence erotic? Why is the need to control so overwhelming? What is it about sexuality that brings forth violent behavior? What are the operating assumptions about sex, violence, and control? Are these assumptions theologically based?

James Nelson, in addressing the issue of sexual violence, describes the false consciousness pervading society.

> The confusion holds that when an act using the sexual organs is performed, sexual pleasure is always the object. It is assumed that a man's sexual response is caused by an external source beyond his control, and hence the responsibility for an act lies with the victim, not the rapist. It is assumed that "romantic love" must involve a dominate-subordinate relationship. It is assumed that men have the right to impose their sexual acts upon others, without regard to the others' feelings or consent. It is assumed that a man's yes prevails over a woman's no. It is assumed that pleasure comes through over-powering another rather than sharing with another. . . . It is assumed that violence is both acceptable and masculine. [21]

It is important to pay attention to the false assumption—namely, that a man's sexual response is "beyond his control." This assumption was also prevalent in some of the assumptions held by Thielicke and Bailey: men were associated with eros and were seen as being in need of domestication; women had an agapic influence and could tame men's base instincts in a context of other-directed love.

"Control" operates, as Kivel also observed, as a goal of violence. This is based on the false assumption that one can maintain control over one's life by acting in violent ways. These assumptions about control operate both as justifications for violent behavior and as that which undergirds the erotic nature of violence.

Many feminists working in rape crisis centers and battered women's shelters maintain that rape and battering are not sexual acts.[22] However, as we have seen, the problem is that rape and battering have been eroticized. They are perceived as being sexual acts by the perpetrators. As Nelson has maintained, this eroticization is based upon false assumptions—in particular, the assumption that overpowering a person is more pleasurable than sharing or mutuality. This assumption is the basis of the eroticization of violence.

Closely connected to the assumption that overpowering a person is more pleasurable than sharing and mutuality is the assumption that romantic love *necessarily* is based upon a dominant/subordinate relationship. This assumption is reinforced by a particular view of female and male natures that associates subordination with female nature and domination with male nature. One of the theological roots of this assumption is Thielicke's and Bailey's promulgation of the complementarity theory, in which the subordinate female nature *complements* the dominant male nature. Thus is domination eroticized and sexual desire associated with the self-oblivion of subordination or the self-assertion of domination.[23]

Intimate Violence and Heterosexism

In examining the eroticization of violence, the tools of *suspicion* and *particularities* can be applied as a way of asking how this violence is held in place. What forms of control are being maintained by the eroticization of violence? What, exactly, is at stake? The first example in looking at this question is that of intimate violence. The term *intimate violence* refers to physical and/or psychological battering and rape within a relationship.[24] It is held in place by heterosexism which seeks to maintain control over women's sexuality (and, thereby, women). This is done by enforcing compulsory heterosexuality.

Theologically, heterosexism is predicated on the belief that male control over women's lives is God's will.[25] Men have the God-given right to decide the whys, whens, hows, and wherefores of women's existence. This "right" is predicated on the sexist assumptions that men are closer to the image of God and, therefore, have dominion over women and that women need male protection. Remember, for instance, Thielicke's musings about female sexuality and how a dormant female sexuality had to be carefully awakened by a male who was willing to put his self-oriented, eros-driven ego aside for the moment.[26] The theological foundation of heterosexism—which emphasizes the need to awaken, shape, and protect female sexuality—feeds into the justification for male violence against women: it is God's will that men be the shapers, protectors, and controllers of female sexuality. And, as a result, violence is too often interpreted as a tool to maintain the dominion over women and sexuality. Because male violence is perceived as being divinely sanctioned, the illusion of control is sustained. And, as long as the illusion of control is sustained, one's manhood passes muster. Violence against women and children thus gains a certain erotic attraction.

When men batter their women partners (and it is almost always men who batter women),[27] when men rape their women partners and their children (and acquaintances and strangers), and when men try to block women's access to abortion, they are exercising what theological tradition has communicated to them as their God-given right to dominion—misinterpreted as domination.[28] Battering and rape are ways of "organizing a relationship so that men continue to feel superior to women."[29] From the perspective of the batterer, "his" woman should be at his beck and call and organize her life around his needs. He feels he has a moral entitlement to make demands upon her, all in the name of divinely sanctioned domination.[30] The better the batterer or rapist feels, the more he feels his manhood is intact and that he truly is the superior one. Violence and eros are thus interlocked, one with another.[31]

Violence against Lesbian Women and Gay Men: The Structures of Compulsory Heterosexuality and Homophobia

If intimate violence is one way of maintaining control over women's sexuality, if heterosexism is the form of that control, and if this control shapes the controller's eroticism, then how does it all play out in violence against lesbian women and gay men? The methodological tools of *suspicion* and the raising up of *particularities* bring questions to the fore concerning how the eroticization of violence and the forms of control it maintains affect the lives of lesbian women and gay men. How do compulsory heterosexuality and homophobia function to feed that violence?

How does the inherited theological ethos of female/male complementarity exacerbate it? What exactly is at stake?

Lesbian women and gay men face the daily possibility of violence.[32] Our children may be taken away from us or discriminated against. We risk losing jobs or not getting them because of our sexuality. Churches, at best, refuse to ordain lesbian women and gay men; and, at worst, they preach that lesbian women and gay men are evil. Our families often disown us or painfully ignore certain aspects of our lives. Ex-husbands track down lesbian ex-wives, seeking vengeance. Some family members have been known to batter or kill their lesbian or gay family members. On the street, lesbian women and gay men face being verbally harassed, beaten, or killed. Charlie Howard was thrown off a bridge in Bangor, Maine, and drowned by male teenagers seeking to defend their manhood. In the spring of 1992, a gay man was attacked and raped near Columbia University by a group of fraternity brothers. What is at the root of this violence?

Lesbian women have stepped out of line by refusing to have their sexuality dictated by and dependent upon men. A lesbian woman's independence from men is often perceived as hatred of men. Lesbian theorist Suzanne Pharr describes lesbian women as stepping outside "the acceptable, routinized order of things."

> *[A lesbian woman] is seen as someone who has no societal institutions to protect her and who is not privileged to the protection of individual males. Many heterosexual women see her as someone who stands in contradiction to the sacrifices they have made to conform to compulsory heterosexuality. A lesbian is perceived as a threat to the nuclear family, to male dominance and control, to the very heart of sexism.*[33]

A lesbian woman, by her very existence, flies in the face of male domination. From the depths of her *self-knowing* and *self-loving,* she utters a resounding "No!" to the interpretation of male domination as God-given and God-demanded. Such no-saying can trigger the wrath of men who believe that their sense of manhood is dependent upon any woman's availability to them.

Unlike lesbian women, gay men, *because they are men,* have a certain degree of male privilege, even while battling hetero-sexism and homophobia. While lesbian women represent a threat to male domination, gay men are perceived as traitors. The very presence of open gay men is a presence that breaks rank with established patterns of male control of female sexuality. As traitors, gay men face extreme hatred. Traitors often are killed for their crimes. Gay men stand outside the prescribed gender roles and are seen as not being "real men."

> [Gay men are] *identified with women, the weaker sex that must be dominated and that over the centuries has been the object of male hatred and abuse. Misogyny gets transferred to gay men with a vengeance and is increased by the fear that their sexual identity and behavior will bring down the entire system of male dominance and compulsory heterosexuality.* [34]

Open gay men face the hatred that goes along with having once been part of the dominant group. To have broken rank risks male-dominant rage, as those who are threatened by the exis-tence of gay men seek to regain control of the sexual order. That is why heterosexual men sometimes bash, rape, and/or kill gay men. The bashing, rape, and murder of gay men represent an eroticized violence in which the perpetrators desperately seek to dominate the out-of-line other.

What is at stake here? Why the attempt to control violently those who do not measure up to the status quo? The claim that female nature is complementary to male nature functions as the ideological underpinning of that which flows from heterosexism —namely, compulsory heterosexuality. Theologically, compul-sory heterosexuality is based on the belief that the one-man, one-woman, one-flesh relationship in the context of lifelong marriage is not only God-given but God-*demanded.* This belief fuels resistance to anything that deviates from the norm. After all, any deviation from the norm is contrary to the will of God, violates the natural order, and is therefore sinful.

In the works of Thielicke, Bailey, and Lewis surveyed earlier, these assumptions are firmly in place. All three believed strongly in a God-given, even God-demanded, heterosexual order for human sexuality. Compulsory heterosexuality, the complementarity of female and male, reflected the divine order; indeed, it reflected the very "Be-ing of God."[35] Thielicke maintained that homosexuality was not part of the "normal created order of the sexes" and was contrary to the will of God.[36] Lewis believed that women and men "were made to be combined together in pairs."[37] Bailey understood the "problem of homosexuality" as arising from a "decay of moral standards" in heterosexual relationships.[38] That this kind of theology is used to justify violence against lesbian women and gay men and that, furthermore, the violence is based on a desire to maintain *sexual dominance,* reveals its inadequacy.

Like the structure of compulsory heterosexuality, the feeling of homophobia fuels the fires of violence. *Suspicion* might lead one to ponder, of what are people so afraid? What is the power behind fear? Beverly Wildung Harrison, in detailing the connections between misogyny and homophobia, discusses the break with the safe and familiar that homosexuality represents: "The fear of the power of, and revulsion from sexuality itself is an important element in homophobia. . . . [Homosexuality] is a break with that strong social patterning which, because it is familiar, makes sexuality seem safe and conventionally channeled."[39] Homophobia is about more than fearing lesbian women and gay men. It is a fear of losing the institution of compulsory heterosexuality (i.e., loss of male control of women).

If one fears sexuality per se and if one's response to that fear is to constrain one's sex life in a rigid, narrow, predictable, and— most importantly—controllable fashion, then lesbian women and gay men represent that which has spiralled out of control. Homophobia is fear, writ large, of losing control; it is, ultimately, a fear of not being in control.

As Harrison has noted, homophobia is really fear about sexuality and fear of cultural and institutional change. Lesbian women and gay men exist beyond the realm of the safe and familiar and represent, in the minds of homophobes everywhere, an uncontrolled, and perhaps even uncontrollable, expression of sexuality. Violence against lesbian women and gay men is fueled by a desire to stay in control, by a desire to maintain a position of sexual dominance. In homophobic acts of violence—whether those acts be beatings, rapes, or even murders—the goal is to maintain sexual dominance, assert one's own masculinity (for, like intimate violence, the majority of the perpetrators are male), and literally "straighten out" the victim. Like the structures of heterosexism and compulsory heterosexuality, the feeling of homophobia is justified by appeal to divine will. The AIDS epidemic has exacerbated homophobic violence because the perpetrators see AIDS as a manifestation of God's punishment of "gays."[40] Homophobia added to eroticized violence is a volatile combination.

VIOLENCE AND MAINLINE DENOMINATIONS ON SEXUALITY

Suspicion and the raising up of *particularities* are once again drawn upon to pose several key questions: How have the churches encouraged the eroticization of violence? How have the churches been complicit? What impact have the mainline denominational policies on sexuality had on the perpetuation of violence?

Invisible Violence

It is my contention that sexual violence—and certainly the eroticization of violence—have been virtually invisible in the eyes of the churches.[41] While some strides have been made by establishing task forces to examine violence against women and children,[42] the violence perpetrated against lesbian women and gay men goes virtually unacknowledged.[43] Why is this?

There has always been a reluctance in the mainline churches to acknowledge the scandals of violence which exist right under their very noses. One reason for this is that the perpetrators of violence against women and children are often among the most upstanding members, if not among the leadership, of church communities. There is a reluctance to believe that good christian people could act in such a way. One result of this reluctance to believe that violence exists is a tendency to disbelieve the victim of violence and/or make excuses for the perpetrator.

Certain theological assumptions reinforce and feed the violence. In the denominational statements themselves, the emphasis on "one man, one woman, lifelong fidelity in marriage"
provides the theological justification, whatever the authors' intent may be, for enforcing both male dominance over female
sexuality (heterosexism) and for punishing those who refuse to
conform to the dictates of compulsory heterosexuality. As the
emphasis on the one-woman, one-man, one-flesh theory helps
shore up intimate violence, sexual or not, so too does it sustain
violence against lesbian women and gay men. Invocation of the
complementarity theory, along with the constant reiteration
that scripture condemns homosexual practices, feeds the fires of
homophobic violence.

In the debate over issues affecting lesbian women and gay
men, the Presbyterians declared that lesbian and gay people were
members in good standing; the Episcopalians likewise insisted
that lesbian and gay people were to be treated as "Children of
God;" the Methodists maintained that God's grace is available to
all.[44] These gracious sentiments were followed by refusals of both
denominations to ordain those lesbian women and gay men who
insisted on being open and affirming about their sexualities.
Both churches have drawn clear distinctions between those lesbian women and gay men who are homosexual in *orientation* and
those who are homosexual in *practice*.[45] The message is that sexual acts between members of the same gender are wrong.

The distinction between orientation and practice (as in
Bailey's distinction between invert and pervert), is, I believe,
one of the biggest contributions to the ecclesiastical sanctioning
of violence against lesbian and gay people. It does a great deal to
further the general message that sex should be controlled, that
sexual abstinence is to be privileged over sexual activity, and
that those who do not conform to such demands are less than human, sinful, and therefore deserving of punishment. Those
lesbian women and gay men who dare to come out, affirm themselves, and admit to being sexually active risk ecclesiastical
censure (a revoking of the "Child of God" status) as well as the
perpetration of violence against them for being sexual human be-

ings. Open lesbian women and gay men are often perceived as deserving this censure and violence.

The churches' calls for unity in the midst of the sexuality debates are also contributing factors to both violence against women and children and violence against lesbian and gay people. It is fascinating to note that when lesbian women and gay men become too demanding, Episcopal bishops resort to calls for unity. The tradition of unity in this instance (as opposed to "unity" in the feminist liberation theo-ethical concept of solidarity) means that all must toe the party line in order to defend the status quo—in order to protect God, Christianity, and the tradition of male dominance.

The same is true of calls for reconciliation. All four churches have issued calls for reconciliation in the heat of conflict over issues affecting lesbian and gay people. Church leaders characteristically insist that the pain of both sides—the oppressor and oppressed—must be attended. Reconciliation is urged even in the face of continued injustice in order to ease the discomfort of staid, upstanding christian people. This is an instance where the theological weight of the concept of reconciliation is brought tumbling down on top of those seeking sexual justice. Those who resist reconciliation without justice are open to charges of not being good christians. Furthermore, the resistance to premature reconciliation provides additional grounds for the perpetuation of violence against the resisters.

Finally, aspects of the churches' complicity in violence against lesbian women and gay men are apparent in the political strategies of church hierarchies to distance themselves from controversy. Two examples of this are the eagerness of Presbyterian officials to control the "damage" wrought by the progressive sexuality report and the speed with which the Lutheran bishops directed the Sexuality Task Force to draft a second, more acceptable, report. Another instance is the propensity of the four denominations over the last twenty years for proposing that the issue of sexuality needs further study. These political strategies delay the concrete and serious engagement of human sexuality that is so desperately needed. The calls for further study reveal a refusal to take seriously the ways in which sexuality issues are life-and-death issues for many people and need to be acted upon constructively, justly, and in a timely fashion.

Until church policymakers realize that sexuality is a justice issue, the lives of all women, children, and lesbian and gay people will continue to be at risk. The churches must be prepared to take responsibility for the outcomes of that risk since eroticized violence is so closely connected to the theological discourse regarding sexuality. In addition, the churches must acknowledge that not only are people's lives and physical well-being at stake, but so too is people's *spiritual* well-being.

The spiritual damage wrought by ecclesiastical complicity in violence is incalculable. Incest survivors who have been taught to associate the father with God, the father as all-controlling and all-knowing, are faced with the task of putting their spiritualities back together. Battered women who have internalized the christian message of the value of being humble, forgiving, and obedient to men—if they are lucky enough to survive—face searching for a spirituality that will affirm their very existence. Lesbian women and gay men who have suffered theologically sanctioned violence face finding a spiritual home that will not only affirm their "child of God-ness," but that will affirm their humanity, their needs for sexual fulfillment, and their capacities for leadership.[46] All women and men face finding theologies that are sex-positive instead of sex-controlling.

INTIMATE FEAR, INTIMATE VIOLENCE

Eroticized violence is not just something that happens to someone else. Rather, all of our relationships are grounded in a context of eroticized violence. That is not to say that the extent of the violence does not vary; from the preceding discussion, it is clear that there are tragic, as well as subtle, manifestations of eroticized violence. What *is* true, however, is that our abilities to be intimate with one another—our experiences of eros—are expressed in an atmosphere permeated by fear and violence.

Carter Heyward has noted the effects of this violent atmosphere. She observes that all of us reside "in a praxis of alienation" from which there is no escape.

> *All of us are, to some significant degree, in bondage to wrong relation, alienated power relations, which frequently we do not recognize as problematic. Those who are justice-minded tend to perceive the alienation in racism, sexism, and other transparently oppressive structures of alienated power. But we have . . . trouble realizing ways in which these structures have shaped our own psyches and spiritualities, our capacities for friendship and sexual pleasure.* [47]

Alienated power—an eroticized violence—blocks our ability to be intimate; indeed, it blocks our abilities to know what true intimacy—or what mutuality—actually is. Given the context in which we reside, we have known but a very few glimpses of it, and those glimpses have come our way all too rarely. For many of us, our relationships have been marked by what Dorothee Sölle calls an "impoverishment of feeling, pleasure without imagination, and an absence of spirit." She remarks further that from the ruins of this relational impoverishment arises a heresy that implies "that wholeness is impossible." [48]

Once again, the methodological tools of *suspicion* and the raising up of *particularities* can be used to get at some of the components of eroticized violence. What, specifically, are some of the blocks to intimacy? Whom do they affect and how? How might intimacy be possible?

Fear Writ Large

One of the primary blocks to intimacy is fear. The violence in which our lives are grounded breeds fear. Fear functions in such a way as to keep us separated from one another. At times, the fear is intense. Experiences of being female in a male-dominated world; poor in an economy of global capitalism; African American, Hispanic, Asian American, or American Indian in a racist, white-dominated, euro-american culture; lesbian, gay, or bisexual in a heterosexist world all contribute to the propagation of fear as a coping mechanism. This coping mechanism has often been necessary—particularly in dealing with recovery from experiences of eroticized violence, including incest, rape, sexual harassment, forms of intimate violence, and hate crimes. Such experiences cannot help but impact our relationships with those closest to us as well as our capacities for intimacy.

It is important to differentiate fear arising from life experiences of oppression and violation from that fear which is rooted in maintaining privilege. From a position of privilege, fear functions as a way of closing oneself off from challenges; it represents change and possible losses of power. Sometimes, both the dynamics of protecting privilege and struggling to survive are at work in fear. However, in attempting to move beyond fear, the issues are markedly different for those operating from marginalized positions and those operating out of positions of privilege. One requires empowerment for resistance of violence;[49] the other requires the courage to give up privilege and power, to stop causing violence, and to find deeper, more meaningful, ways of relating.

What are some of the *particularities* of this fear in relation to intimacy? Of what are we so afraid that we choose dis-connection and isolation over connection and intimacy? Granted, connection and intimacy often take more conscious work to achieve and maintain; but dis-connection and isolation also take a great deal of energy—whether conscious or not—to defend. The latter, of course, is an effect of the prevailing climate of eroticized violence.

I suggest that a great deal of fear is based upon a romanticization of intimacy.[50] We all carry images around with us about what intimacy should be. Often the word *intimacy* conjures up images of perfect people in a perfect relationship, together forever, perfectly. Those are the images that popular culture gives us. They are also the images given to us by malestream theology and current denominational policies. The inheritance of the "one-man, one-woman, one-flesh" complementarity theory serves to communicate a romanticized, unrealistic, and overly idealistic expectation of intimacy. When reality fails to measure up to those images, people suffer in silence, convinced that the failure is

theirs, and all too often, especially in the case of women, convinced that they are not good enough and therefore not deserving of intimacy. Fear of rejection, fear of loneliness, fear of being
alone hold sway.

Fear is also based upon a "bank-deposit" mentality in which
one is afraid one will never have enough intimacy, enough love,
and therefore feels the need to hoard what little one has. This
feeds the need to possess the other person. It also makes one hes-
itant to "spend" or "invest" oneself, one's time, or one's life in
anyone or anything else. One banks on the ideal residing in the
future rather than the realities of the present. In this context, relationships are commodities and are marked by distinct and unmoving boundaries.

Fear and Boundaries: Protective and Defining or Controlling and Abusive?

A "boundary," according to the *Oxford English Dictionary*, is
"that which serves to indicate the bounds or limits of anything. . . . " It is also "the limit itself."[51] Boundaries have traditionally been used as protection against intruders. Originally,
boundaries were used to mark and protect one's land; they were
stone walls, offering protection to a farmer's sheep. Today, they
are still invoked as a form of protection, as well as definition of
who we are in relation to each other. But *suspicion* and the *particularities* of our lives lead us to ask—what exactly is being protected? Who needs protection, and under what circumstances?
Does the one being protected have anything to say about it?
Who is doing the defining? How do boundaries function in different situations?

The invocation of boundaries in order to protect and define
has its helpful and necessary aspects.[52] Boundaries may serve to
protect survivors of abuse from their former abusers. All people
have physical boundaries. My body, bounded by my skin, is distinct from yours, bounded by your skin. We are only to cross over
those boundaries when we have been invited to do so. Boundaries, as Margaret Craddock Huff has observed, can be our source
of connection.[53] But when we have not invited a crossing over of

those boundaries—when, for instance, sexual abuse occurs—those boundaries are violated. This is one sense of boundaries.

For many people, especially women and children, it is important to learn to set boundaries, to say "no," and to nourish oneself.[54] Doing so is important for learning to love oneself. Defining limits can enable one to move from being victimized to being a survivor.

However, boundaries invoked as protection can also serve as a force that limits and controls. Too often we take refuge behind boundaries. Boundaries can become an excuse not to risk relation and intimacy, not to branch out into *self-loving* and *neighbor-loving*.[55] Boundaries sometimes provide an excuse to refrain from connecting, much less re-connecting. When misused, they become walls promising safety at the price of intimacy and provide a false sense of security, a false sense of control. Boundaries, when employed in this manner, do nothing to ease fear; rather they are based upon it.

A friend of mine, who is a survivor of incest, has been served well by boundaries invoked as protection and definition. Such boundaries have aided her recovery process. The problem has been, however, that she has moved from boundaries invoked as protection and definition to boundaries invoked as control. She shies away from what she cannot control. She fears taking relational risks. She hides in the name of boundaries. Boundaries invoked as control have paralyzed my friend. She is afraid of life. Not only has she been unable to contemplate the move from surviving to thriving; in many ways she has moved from being a survivor to being a victim.

Boundaries invoked as control also serve to keep those in power from facing the consequences and responsibilities of their power. Boundaries are invoked in this way when people are attempting to maintain the status quo. They do not want to be touched or moved, changed or challenged. Boundaries invoked in this way often become abusive.

When boundaries are used by those in power to maintain control—often in the guise of protecting—the very individuals they were meant to protect are hurt. Boundaries invoked in this manner are abusive. Structured and reinforced by the so-called authority figures in our lives, this sense of boundaries carries over into our friendships and lover-ships with one another. If I am insisting on rigid boundaries in relating to you—my lover, my friend—e.g., if I am keeping the pieces of my life in carefully controlled categories, boundaries can become my excuse for not relating, not taking risks, not being willing or able to move beyond fear into a love of self and neighbor. Boundaries also can become my way of controlling you and can invoke isolation, alienation, violence, and crazy-making secrecy. Boundaries can save lives and permit healing. Meant to offer necessary protection and definition, boundaries—if there is never any chance of their changing—stunt growth and kill intimacy and sometimes even people. Rigid boundaries—closed forever to the possibility of change—can block healing and engender abuse.

FROM SURVIVING THE VIOLENCE, TO TRANSFORMING IT, TO A VISION OF THRIVING

We have hardly begun to understand the problem, and there is much to be done. From a justice-oriented perspective, there are many possible paths to take. In the discussions that follow, the intent is to begin a journey exploring some constructive ways of moving away from eroticized violence. Given where we have been—from the malestream theology of Nygren, Thielicke, Lewis, and Bailey and current sex-negative denominational polices to feminist liberation theo-ethical reflections on eros— how do we proceed? Many of us have moved from being victims to being survivors. Dare we think of moving from surviving to thriving?

CHAPTER FIVE

Surviving and Thriving

Movement Toward an Erotic Mutuality Grounded in Justice

I n the previous chapter, the effects of eroticized violence on intimacy were discussed at some length. In this chapter, movement into erotic mutuality is explored by focusing on particular relational dynamics. The subjects of incarnational sexuality, sexual incarnation, God's sexuality, erotic mutuality, and the challenges facing the churches are discussed in terms of their contributions to the transformation of alienated relational dynamics and to a movement from surviving to thriving, grounded in an erotic mutuality.

Before proceeding further, however, it is important to detail what exactly is meant by *eros* in this constructive context of transformation and movement. Throughout the preceding pages, eros has been examined from several different perspectives. Eros has been portrayed as unchristian and as that which needed to be controlled and chastened. Eros has also been represented as something that was acceptable as long as it functioned within prescribed situations (i.e., lifelong, monogamous marriage between a woman and a man). In chapter 3, feminist liberation theo-ethicists re-membered eros from the ruins of patriarchal discourse. The potential of eros for alienation and violence was portrayed in the preceding chapter. With the sole exception of the feminist re-membering of eros, the difficulty that these interpretations present is that they are sex-negative and thwart movement into an erotic mutuality.

More appropriate to the feminist liberation theo-ethical construction of a sexual theo-ethics are the descriptions of eros from progressive pro-feminist theologians and feminist liberation theo-ethicists. James Nelson writes that eros is the form of love "born of our hungers and our need for one another." He adds that this eros is connected with God. The divine eros is a "fundamental energy of the universe."[1] He suggests that "We need to recapture a vision of the divine eros as intrinsic to God's energy, God's own passion for connection, and hence also our own yearning for life-giving communion and our hunger for relationships of justice which make such fulfillment possible."[2] For Nelson, eros, by its very nature, is interconnected with our yearnings, God's yearnings, and our struggles for justice. Sheila Briggs connects eros with a strong self-love and a movement toward justice. Eros involves resistance to violation.

Carter Heyward argues that our experiences of eros are connected with our experiences of God. The erotic serves as that which interconnects and involves us with one another; it "moves transpersonally among us" and "draws us more fully into ourselves."[3] Along with Beverly Harrison, Heyward understands eros as a "body-centered energy channeled through longing and desire." Echoing Audre Lorde, both Heyward and Harrison believe that eroticism is not only essential to our well-being but that it is also the source of our creativity.[4]

Rita Nakashima Brock's concept of "the feminist eros" is that eros is the "power of our primal interrelatedness." It has the power to heal us, make us whole, empower us, and liberate us. Eros is located in the "matrices of our connectedness to self, to the body, to others, and to the world." It connotes a certain intimacy via the engagement "of the whole self in a relationship."[5] Judith Plaskow also sees eros as being "our fundamental life energy."[6] *The Presbyterian Sexuality Report* defines eros as being our "passionate desire for intimate connection." Erotic power is that which centers us and encourages us to create justice "with love for ourselves and all others."[7]

Overall, these theologians and ethicists see eros as a life-giving force, permeating all aspects of our lives and intimately connected with the pursuit of justice. Eros is the source of our creative energy; it is that which connects us with God. But, there is yet another aspect attributed to eros that must be considered— and that is the specter of abusive power relations.

Heyward maintains that abusive power relations are rooted in alienation. To some extent, no one is exempt from experiencing abusive power dynamics since they are part of the social fabric.

She adds that these dynamics are the result of an alienated and distorted eros which moves us away from just and mutual relations.[8] Brock also sees that dominance and control are a result of the denial of erotic power.[9]

Critics have charged, however, that this description of eros is inadequate. Kathleen Sands accuses feminist theologians of being idealistic about eros and refusing to take into account the demonic or tragic aspects of eros.[10] Her point is that the feminist liberation theo-ethical treatment of eros is too closely associated with an ethical ideal of the good.[11] Arguing that linking eros with the divine only serves to distance eros from the human realm, she notes that feminist liberation theo-ethicists' response to the question of how to reconcile violence with eros—namely, that violence is the opposite of eros—sounds like "proclamations of erotic faith." Sands further charges that theologies such as Heyward's and Brock's fundamentally require "sex to carry too much moral and ontological weight."[12]

With Sheila Briggs, Rita Nakashima Brock, Marvin Ellison, Carter Heyward, Beverly Harrison, Mary Hunt, and James Nelson, I claim that eros is a yearning for embodied connection with one another, a movement toward embodied justice. As a *christian* feminist liberation theo-ethicist, I not only believe that justice and eros are inherently interconnected; I believe as well that justice within sexual relationships is what must be morally normative.[13] Sands is correct: this *is* a proclamation of erotic faith. Experiencing what I have experienced in terms of domestic and sexual violence and believing what I believe about justice and eros, I must insist that eroticized violence is part of an alienated eros; it is an eros disconnected from an embodied justice and an erotic mutuality.

Because love—specifically, eros—and justice are fundamentally interconnected, an eroticized violence cannot be any part of an eros that is connected with erotic mutuality and embodied justice making. Eroticized violence is, indeed, part of an alienated and disconnected eros and part of the fabric of a sadomasochistic culture and society.[14] Finding ways to de-alienate and reconnect an alienated and dis-connected eros is precisely the agenda for feminist liberation theo-ethics.

One way to re-connect a dis-connected eros is to insist that it be linked with the divine. Historically, eros has been negated, cast out, perceived as anathema, and labeled as contrary to God's love, agape. It has been perceived as something to be controlled, lest it contaminate good christian people and christianity as a whole. Linking eros with the divine serves to bring an earthiness, a humanness, a sensuousness, a "sexualness" to God. Far from removing eros from the common, human realm, linking eros with God immerses God in the common, human realm. Sands's assumption that such a link would make eros more distant reveals her conception of God as a being predicated on distance from humanity. Linking God and eros connects us all more closely one with another and moves us closer to incarnations of justice in this world and, more particularly, to incarnations of justice in our most intimate relations.

And so, I define eros as a body-centered love marked by a yearning, a pushing and pulling toward erotic mutuality, a movement toward embodied justice. It can be specifically sexual, but it is not limited to that form of expression. It celebrates the sexual, the bodily, the earthy; it is rooted in body-experience and seeks the integration of body and spirit, human and divine. Eros connects a strong self-love, an opening to love of neighbors, and a love of God. It requires a commitment to the well-being of all people and, in that sense, is liberative. Eros works toward the eradication of violence; it is rooted in a process of overcoming alienation and dis-connection. Finally, eros is the action of human beings and God together, seeking incarnations of God, of justice, of mutuality in this world. But who or what is this God of whom I speak? What kind of God is this who is so intimately connected with us?

NEARER TO GOD ARE WE

I believe that God is She who is with us. God is She who is moved and changed and touched by and with us. God is embodied in female presence and in male presence. God is most often "She" for me because of the damage wrought by centuries of exclusive male God language. I believe that God is reflected in you and in me. And we are reflected in God.

God is very much part of nature for me. Earth, sea, water, and air creatures . . . soil, wind, and ocean . . . trees, roots, and branches. . . . All reflect and are reflected in God.

To be more specific, God is not the God of Nygren, Thielicke, Lewis, or Bailey. God is not the God of restrictive denominational policies. Most definitely, God is not a God who has the male-defined, misogynistic characteristics of the Christian God.[15] Nor is God an ideal, far removed from our lives.

I have come to be *suspicious* of any God who is described as "objective." God combined with objectivity usually means a God who is distant from humanity. I have come to be *suspicious* of any God predicated on distance. God combined with distance usually means a radically dualistic theology—one in which divine is over human, spirit is over body, male is over female, and agape is over eros. I have come to be suspicious of any statements about sexuality that are deemed God's will, part of God's plan. Such statements are usually aimed at the control of sexuality and women's bodies by a male-dominant order.

If God is not to be held at an objective, controlling distance from us, that means that God is involved in the nitty-gritty, day-to-day, *particularities* of our lives. I believe that God is a radically immanent God.[16] This means that God is present with us, here and now. God is as present in my life as in yours, and vice versa. My experience of God may not be the same as yours. Our life experiences are not the same. Our experiences do not need to be the same. There is room for all.

Self-knowing is intricately connected with God-knowing. As I was leaving an abusive marriage on my twentieth birthday, I had my first glimpse of God-knowing. In the act of leaving, I knew I would somehow survive. I knew for the first time that God existed; I knew God's presence. I knew as well that God was not a God who tolerated abuse. God is on the side of those most marginalized.

My own *self-knowing* and coming out as a lesbian woman was marked as well with God-knowing. Coming to know myself was part of coming to know God. Once I was able to affirm my sexuality, I knew that it was not contrary to God's will. I knew that as I looked into the mirror at my lesbian self I reflected God's image. And God was reflected in my image. And it was good.

Self-loathing keeps God at a distance because of the sense of being unworthy to have God near. God is wrapped up in our *self-loving*. Self-loving is not selfish; it is self-full—of both knowing and loving. Through self-loving, God comes nearer. Self-loving enables us to claim our moral agency, together with one another and God, to seek justice in this world, to stop the eroticized violence, the evil, that is predicated on self-hate, other-hate, God-hate.

As God is wrapped up in our self-loving, so is God immersed in our *loving our neighbors as ourselves.* Self- and neighbor-loving heal the dualistic split between self-loving on the one hand, and neighbor- and God-loving on the other. Bringing together self-loving with neighbor-loving is marked by a sharing of power, a sharing of eros, a sharing of God. Loving our neighbors as ourselves helps us see God embodied in our neighbors as in ourselves.

God is also a God who thrives on connecting, on *re-connecting* between you and me and between us and God. Through the casting out of fear, human-divine connectedness is affirmed—and, once again, as in the beginning, God is radically immanent. Re-connecting is that which serves to bring God down to earth; it is that which brings us and God together in a divine-human home-coming. God is not an unmoved mover. God is not an unchanged changer. God is not an untouched toucher. God moves and is moved, changes and is changed, touches and is touched.

I believe that God is a God who is moved, changed, and touched into an *ongoing solidarity* in which we move, change, and touch while standing *with* one another. Being with God in solidarity means that God does not walk away from relation nor from conflict. We are all in it together, always.

God is the power of eros,[17] affirming bodyselves, yearning with us away from eroticized violence and into embodied justice and erotic mutuality. Connecting eros and God, justice and God, brings God more fully into the human arena. God as the power of eros is not over and against us but with us. God as the power of eros is not distant but nearer than we know.

God as the power of eros is She who is with us, who is moved and changed and touched by and with us.

BODYING FORTH

In the explicit linking of eros and God, we open up a variety of possibilities for incarnating God among us. My conception of a specifically incarnational eros is rooted in my belief that God's incarnation in Jesus was not a one-time event but rather represents God's continuing acts of incarnation in our world.[18] If God's incarnation is ongoing, and if eros is connected with God, then God is fully present to us in every way. Made in God's image, we not only bear a responsibility to incarnate God; we bear a responsibility to see ourselves reflected in God.

Self-knowing and self-loving are important in a consideration of incarnating God in eros. Because self-loving is seen as a primary component of eros, it has been denounced as an unacceptable form of love for christians.[19] To this day, self-loving continues to be devalued. Linking God and eros is a constructive step which begins to undo the theological inheritance of self-loathing. It makes possible as well the re-connecting of that which has been dis-connected.

Being made in the image of God and incarnating God in all aspects of our lives invokes a divine imperative to take ourselves seriously. *Self-loving* helps reveal that we are made in the image of God. This has a variety of implications, depending upon one's social location. As a white woman and a lesbian, self-loving affirms my femaleness and lesbianism, both of which are not affirmed in the wider society and church. However, self-loving could have different implications for an African American woman or a Hispanic woman whose femaleness, skin color, culture, and sexuality are negated in the wider social and ecclesiastical order.

Seeing ourselves as made in the image of God can be a powerful source of creative energy for transforming oppression. Combined with *suspicion,* attention to the *particularities* of our lives, *self-knowing,* and *self-loving,* the fact that we are made in the image of God allows us to discern the impact different positions of privilege have on our lives. For instance, if I were a white, heterosexual man, the moral imperative of seeing myself as being made in the image of God would be different than if I were a

Hispanic lesbian woman. The former would bear a responsibility for finding ways to give up some of his power and privilege; the latter would bear a responsibility for taking herself seriously and mounting resistance, together with others, to that which devalues her.

In terms of being made in the image of God, *self-knowing* and *self-loving* mean that we have the creative power—from joining individual selves together—to incarnate God among us. This ongoing incarnation of God among us means that through *self-knowing* and *self-loving* we are better able to work toward a justice-centered eros and move into an erotic mutuality.[20] Together, we can proceed to de-alienate and re-connect an alienated and disconnected eros. Without *self-knowing* and *self-loving*, without an affirmation of ourselves as being made in the image of God and being capable of incarnating God between and among us, we have a difficult time surviving, much less thriving. And we will find it difficult to begin to imagine that eros is good—and more specifically, that our sexuality and sexual passions are good.

TOWARD AN INCARNATIONAL SEXUALITY: JOINING THE SEXUAL AND THE DIVINE

Marvin Ellison has declared that "an incarnational faith skittish about the goodness of the body and about sensuous pleasure may well bore itself to death."[21] Tom Driver has revealed the presence of the breath of God in our most body-centered undertakings.[22] And Carter Heyward writes about the erotic as "the divine Spirit's yearning, through our bodyselves, toward mutually empowering relation."[23] If we believe that eros, God, justice, and mutuality are interdependent and interconnected, then we cannot exclude God's connection with and incarnation in the specifically sexual aspects of our lives.

I am talking here about a specifically incarnational sexuality. This means that we cannot disconnect sexuality from the presence of God, no matter how much we may want to do so. An incarnational sexuality has very little to do, however, with a theo-ethics that is based on limiting sexual contact only to a woman and a man in the context of lifelong monogamous marriage. This is not meant to disparage the choice of such a life-style; the operative word here is *choice*. To the contrary, where there is pleasure and a movement toward embodied justice and erotic mutuality, God is being incarnated.

Love of neighbor as self is helpful when considering the joining of the sexual and God. A well-grounded love of neighbor as self lets us move into a detailed discussion of the differences among us without fearing a loss of, or threat to, our self-identity. With *self-loving* intact, we know that our identities are strong and deep where they need to be and that the possibility of being changed by and with the other does not spell disaster to our own selves. This ability to engage our differences is critical to the consideration of an incarnational sexuality because we do not leave our differences behind when God and sexuality are joined together. Indeed, entering into such intimate spaces with one another and God can magnify differences and require intense and costly work to move ourselves through places of change toward a more embodied justice and erotic mutuality.

An incarnational sexuality involves working toward justice relationally in all aspects of our lives, especially those with whom we are most intimate. The combination of justice and sexuality means that justice concerns continue behind the bedroom door. This means that we need to find ways, together, to communicate —to both speak and listen. Together, we need to search out concrete ways of moving, as best we can, toward an erotic mutuality.

An incarnational sexuality also involves pushing against unjust social policies that control our bodies and/or those of others. The inadequacy of AIDS prevention, treatment, and research programs; sterilization abuse; restricted access to abortion; policies restricting the civil rights of lesbian women and gay men; and the movement toward limiting comprehensive sex education for children all need to be taken on as issues affecting our bodyselves, our sexualities. This is part of what loving our neighbors as ourselves entails for an incarnational sexuality.

Sexual Incarnation: God's Participation in Human Sexuality

At first glance, "sexual incarnation" may seem identical to an "incarnational sexuality." However, there are important differences. Incarnational sexuality describes the joining of the sexual and the divine; it denotes God's blessing of human sexuality. Sexual incarnation, on the other hand, moves an incarnational sexuality further by calling forth God's presence and participation in human sexual experiences.

The idea of God's participation in human sexuality is a bit startling at first. It is one thing to describe sex as a spiritual experience and quite another to assert that God participates in sex. But if we are to insist that God, justice, eros, mutuality, and sexuality are all interconnected and that we have the shared power together to incarnate God and justice between and among us, then we cannot just leave God outside the closed bedroom door.

Let me provide an example here. It is common when in the midst of sexual ecstasy to utter a divine name (among other things). "Oh God!" "Jesus!" or "Oh Lord!" are among the choice utterances. A friend once related to me the occasion when on the brink of an orgasm, he invoked the name of God. He was so startled at the prospect of God's presence in that intimate moment that "it almost ruined everything."[24] What many would regard as blasphemy and scandal can alternatively be interpreted as a form of prayer or an experience of God's presence. There is an ecstatic character to eros which can be closely connected with an ecstatic experience of God.[25] Such utterances and invocations are representative of our collective power to incarnate God, to call forth God's presence.

It could be argued, of course, that experiences such as the above only point to a passive presence by God. However, the divine presence is not passive, but rather, active. God participates. Insofar as we attempt to move toward justice, toward mutuality, in our intimate relations, we are incarnating God—calling forth divine presence and participation. God is as present and participating in our love-making as in other aspects of our lives. As Carter Heyward has noted, the erotic God yearns "through our bodyselves, toward mutually empowering relation."[26] The movement towards mutuality that we are participating in is sacred, even—or especially—the movement under the sheets! God is being incarnated, called forth, and is participating in our movement together.

If this is so, is God also present and participating in manifestations of eroticized violence such as rape, incest, and bashing? This is a crucial question. With Elie Wiesel, I maintain that God is present when evil is being perpetrated.[27] However, while God is present in evil situations, we fail to call forth God's active participation to the extent that we are not moving toward erotic mutuality, toward embodied justice. God is not all-powerful. God cannot stop the violence we perpetrate against one another. Otherwise, we would not be embroiled in struggles against injustice. The fact that God is present but does not participate in manifestations of eroticized violence means that we have moral agency in our lives. From this viewpoint, the case for God's participation in human sexuality is even more compelling: we have the power to choose embodied justice, to choose erotic mutuality, and to incarnate God in our most intimate interactions.[28]

As *neighbor-loving* is central in the development of incarnational sexuality, so too is it in sexual incarnation. In sexual incarnation, the love of neighbor as self helps us branch out toward the neighbor and toward God. It helps us *re-connect*. Sex, intimacy, and God are scary subjects standing alone, much less together. As we call forth God's presence and participation in our sexual intimacy and assert our moral agency, we discover that our fear can be tapped and transformed into desire for authentic engagement. Our fear is, in part, based on the unknown, and the resolution of fear rests in actual acts of coming to know.

When we are able to acknowledge that our bodies are holy and that God is indeed present in the sexual energy that flows between us, then we are better able to value the bodies of our neighbors. In loving our neighbors as ourselves, we move toward overcoming the alienation and dis-connection that have kept us apart. We move more freely into letting go of the fear of those who are like us as well as those who are not like us.

Neighbor-loving as self also means that we commit ourselves to doing as much as we can to end eroticized violence. Those who suffer the ravages of rape, incest, bashing, and battering need our embodied presence and participation in their processes of recovery. And if we ourselves have suffered eroticized violence, then we need to know that we are not alone. We need to come into one another's presence and search together for ways to heal, re-connect, and resist any ongoing violence. In so doing, in moving toward the possibilities of sexual incarnation, we incarnate God. Together, we and our neighbors invoke God's active participation in the sexual aspects of our lives.

God's Sexuality

Viewing our sexual encounters as holy, not to mention bringing God into the act, is scandalous. Imagining God's sexuality crosses the border into heresy.[29] Or so some would say. Nevertheless, as scandalous and heretical as it may be, unless we view God as an unmoved mover or an unchanged changer, we must consider the issue of God's sexuality. Such consideration is important to a movement into an erotic mutuality in which eros and God are interconnected.

One of the primary points of incarnational sexuality and of sexual incarnation is that God is interconnected with the details of our lives in profoundly intimate ways; we see that our bodies and passions are holy. Indeed, we have found that God is with our bodies and passions as we move together, under the sheets and elsewhere, toward justice-centered, erotic mutual relating and into physical acts of incarnating God in our midst.

If this is so, then we cannot avoid the consideration of God's sexuality. If God participates in our sexuality, do we participate in God's? Is God sexual?[30] To the extent that we call forth God's presence in our sexual pleasuring, we are participating in God's sexuality. We are participating in making God incarnate; we are participating in the coming of God. As God is present in the midst of our sexuality, our sexual encounters, so too are we present in God's. Our relation with God is not a one-way street. It would be very odd then to consider that our actions to incarnate God in our midst—explicitly, but not exclusively, in sexual interconnections—are not also participation in the sexuality of God. God is moved by our moving. God is changed by our changing. God is touched by our touching. As we love our neighbors as ourselves, we incarnate God and love Her. And She loves us back.

TOWARD EROTIC MUTUALITY AS
INCARNATING THE DIVINE

Consideration of incarnational sexuality, sexual incarnation, and the sexuality of God is titillating to say the least. It sounds great, but how do we get there from here? The fact of the matter is that we have some serious problems to address.

The eroticization of violence has permeated all of our lives. This violence places serious blocks in our paths as we try to incarnate an intimacy between and among us that is connected with embodied justice and erotic mutuality. We need to work together to find ways to end the violence; we need to recover mutuality. And we need to be as concrete as possible, knowing that our "concreteness" is not writ in stone but open to being changed and re-shaped as people begin speaking of their different needs and experiences.

Mutuality and Eros

In the movement toward an erotic mutuality, we are seeking to *re-connect* that which has been dis-connected by the eroticization of violence. The intent of moving toward erotic mutuality is not to make eros like agape or to make eros more acceptable. Eros, unlike traditional conceptions of agape, is not a mechanism for control of others or ourselves. And, unlike traditional conceptions of agape, it is both sex-positive and justice-centered. In this movement toward erotic mutuality, we must confront the fears that have had such a crippling impact on our lives and begin to undo the myriad ways in which violence and the need to be in control have been eroticized.

The movement toward an erotic mutuality can be aided by a movement toward *re-connecting.* We need to build into the movement toward an erotic mutuality a web of analysis that takes into account the devastating effects that racism, classism, heterosexism, and sexism have had on our abilities to be connected, to feel, and to enter into relations of erotic mutuality. Re-connecting contributes an awareness of the differences among us in terms of power and privilege. As the movement expands, it must seek ever-increasing circles of input. All who are marginalized in terms of race, sexuality, class, gender, and physical/mental capacity must be heard from and be instrumental in undertaking this movement. If, from the start, it is not owned and supported by a chorus of diverse voices, movement toward an erotic mutuality will stall.

This movement requires all of us, as many of us as can be mustered. It will fail if it is limited to just the perspectives of white feminist women. Voices of difference are key to shaping the movement into erotic mutuality.[31] As a white woman, I cannot conjecture in isolation how eroticized violence and erotic mutuality might be manifested in the lives of women who are marginalized.[32] This fact, however, cannot exempt those of us who are white feminists from engaging the questions that factors of difference raise and asking how those factors of difference might shape our work.

Quite simply, I do not know where else to begin besides talking with one another. Once we begin to hear one other, I expect that other ideas will soon be generated. But first and foremost, I believe we need to *create* particular ways of being in dialogue with one another concerning the differences in our lives.[33] We need to be intentional and concrete about this. Many of us have been talking for years about how we need to talk. Enough already! In twos or threes or larger groups; around kitchen tables, around the churches, in our bedrooms, around the seminaries, in our living rooms: we need to organize specific opportunities to have these conversations. Given the conflict people feel around the topic of sexuality, such conversations do not just happen on their own.

Some beginning points for conversation might include the following. The *root of suspicion* leads us to begin by asking: what has kept us apart? what has kept us from talking to one another? what continues to get in the way? We need to share our experiences of sexuality and then ask one another "So what?" What do our *particularities*—our commonalities and differences—mean for a sexual theo-ethics?

In *loving our neighbors as ourselves,* we encounter the relationships that make up our lives, and are called into "being real" with one another in a context in which we come face to face with the fears that have kept us apart, the differences that have been made divisive. *Re-connecting*, we come together to ask how racism and classism compound the effects of violence. How do those of us with varying degrees of privilege in our patriarchal society participate in the oppression of other women? How do differences of sexual orientation, race, class, age, church experience, and physical and mental capacity shape our sexualities?[34] influence our movements into an erotic mutuality? what works for particular women in the movement into erotic mutuality? what doesn't? *Solidarity* brings us to ask of each other how we move and, indeed, who is *able* to move from surviving into thriving.

In the midst of these questions and the others that are bound to arise, we may find ourselves uncomfortable over the differences, the conflict, and the anger that may erupt. That is the risk, without which real conversation among us will not take place. Out of discomfort, out of chaos, out of pain, often comes connection. But until we can be real with each other—until we can stop feeling threatened by our differences and until white women especially stop ducking conflict and start paying attention to what women of color are already saying—our movements into erotic mutuality will be stifled and compromised.

From our conversations, new ideas will be raised up. Our work will take on different shapes. We will learn how to empower one another. And strategies for change in our various communities will develop. But none of this will happen unless we open our hearts, open our ears, and open our mouths.

Sharing Our Power

Before going any further in the casting of movement toward an erotic mutuality, it is important to define the term *mutuality*. Mutuality is not synonymous with equality. It is not about equal power relations but rather about sharing power. Nor is mutuality a reciprocal give and take.[35] Rather, mutuality is a process, an ongoing movement.

Carter Heyward has written extensively about mutuality.

[Mutuality] is a process of relational movement that most often is charged with tension. . . . Mutuality is a process of getting unstuck, of moving through impasses, of coming into our power to-

gether. It is the way of liberation, of calling forth the best in one another, and, in so doing, of empowering one another to be who we are at our best. Mutuality is the process by which we create and liberate one another. . . . Mutuality is a way of redirecting wrong relational power. [36]

Mutuality is not an easy process; it is often messy and full of fear and anger. The important point is that one try to work through the difficult points, seeking the help of others when necessary.

Because mutuality is not a concrete, fixed entity, but a *process,* definition is difficult. Mutuality as process takes different shapes for different people in different contexts. It is a slippery concept because of the very room for process, movement, and difference built into it. It is also difficult to describe because of both the "here-ness" and the "not yet here-ness" inherent in it. Nevertheless, several concrete things can be said about mutuality. First, the process of moving toward mutuality requires a commitment to an embodied justice across boundaries of race, class, sexuality, gender, and culture. Second, it requires a deeply rooted commitment to being as honest as possible with one another. Mutuality requires a commitment to listening and actually hearing what is said. It also requires a willingness to speak. Third, mutuality requires a commitment, insofar as that is possible, to stay with the process and our companions in the process—whatever the ultimate outcome of the process may be. It requires patience, too, for taking each day as it comes. Fourth, the process of moving toward mutuality requires a commitment to feel, to re-member how to feel, to learn how to feel, and to communicate the feelings. Although none of these aspects of mutuality can be construed as the final word, they do provide some concrete ways to re-connect the particularities of our lives with a movement toward mutuality.

Mutuality and the Erotic

What is erotic about mutuality? Mutuality is erotic in that it is about a meeting, an engagement—in the context of our sexuality—that is face-to-face, flesh-on-flesh. Erotic mutuality is about sharing power, sharing difference, sharing space, sharing our-selves. It is about connecting in embodied, justice-centered ways. Erotic mutuality is about moving and being moved, changing and being changed, touching and being touched. As such, it involves vulnerability, risk, and affirmation of sensuality/sexuality. Mutu-ality is erotic in the very sharing that goes on between us; it is erotic in that it is about embodying justice, incarnating God. Mu-tuality is also erotic in that movement toward it is never complete; there is always some tension, some "not-yet" character to it.

The movement into erotic mutuality is neither easy nor turbulence-free. It is a scary movement, one calling up age-old voices of recrimination which have been reinforced by the in-herited theological ethos and held in place by an eroticized violence. It is scary if only because many of us are so used to the illusion of "safety"—the illusion of being in control. Erotic mu-tuality is not about control. It is about letting go, risking, and sharing.

How exactly do we move into erotic mutuality? Because of our differences, because we face different blocks to intimacy and mu-tuality, there is a limit to what can be laid out concretely here. Yet, one thing is clear and actually very concrete in our lives: moving through fear and moving beyond survival are both essen-tial in the movement toward an erotic mutuality. Moving through fear is important because fear has either the power to stop movement toward erotic mutuality or to inspire movement. Moving beyond survival is essential because erotic mutuality calls forth our visions of what can be and someday will be. It pushes us to dream; it pushes us to embody justice and incarnate God under even the most trying of circumstances. It gives us hope, which keeps the movement going. Both moving through fear and beyond survival are rooted in the day-to-day realities of our lives and influence the shapes of our futures.

Moving through Fear

Fear means very different things to different people. To some, it is the fear of change, the fear of being vulnerable. To others, it is the fear of giving up old, familiar, though damaging habits in favor of the unknown. To others, it is the fear of loving oneself, the fear of intimacy, the fear of the power of re-connecting. And, to still others, it is the fear for one's life and the lives of loved ones.

When we are afraid, we need to express it. It is as simple—and as complicated—as that. We need to find someone to tell. If it cannot be the one with whom we are the most intimately related, we need to find someone else. We need to sit down, face-to-face, body-to-body, and figure out ways of engaging the fear. Fear is not to be ignored. Like anger, it only festers when kept under wraps.[37]

If the fear is of change, of being vulnerable, we need to do our best to assure one another of our respect. It is paramount that one another's bodily integrity be respected and that we continue to find ways of becoming more comfortable and in touch with our bodies.

If it is fear of breaking out of self-damaging habits, we need to affirm one another's right to exist, to be healthy and happy, and to be able to find less self-destructive ways of responding to life's stresses. We need to sit down, together, and find other, self-full, self-respecting ways of responding to stress.

If the fear is of *loving oneself,* we need to examine together, with *suspicion* and by raising up *particularities,* what it is in our lives that keeps self-loathing in place. The particular messages that undergird self-loathing need to be called forth, one by one, and revealed for what they are: lies—namely, patriarchally rooted efforts to control. If the fear is of intimacy, of *re-connecting,* then, having made a situation as safe as possible, fear needs to be examined in terms of what actually could happen. Somehow the disadvantages of continuing to live in fear and the advantages of risking relation, risking re-connection, need to be brought into focus. We need to encourage one another to leave fear behind insofar as it does not serve as warning of bad relation and physical danger. We need to re-connect with one another, branching out into relations that increasingly move toward mutuality.

If the fear is for one's life and the lives of loved ones, particularly if that fear is grounded in threats from perpetrators of eroticized violence, we need to connect with community-wide resources to ensure the safety of those involved. Together, we need to find ways to put a stop to violence and to hold the perpetrators accountable for their actions.

The important point to remember in our journeys through fear is that fear is real, regardless of the situation. My friend, whose life has been paralyzed by fear, has had good reason for being afraid; her past experiences have confirmed it. The point of moving through fear is not to dismiss it out of hand. The point is not to "get a grip" and just stop being afraid. Rather, the point is to take fear seriously, examine it in detail, and, together, find ways to begin to move through it—perhaps, even carrying it with us if need be—as we move into new ways of relating to ourselves, to one another, to the world around us, and to God.

Sex as Resource. In a process of *re-connecting*, in the movement through fear, we might consider sex as a resource (one among several). To some, that might seem odd since the sort of self-love, intimacy, and vulnerability that sex can represent is often what many people actually fear. However, since fear is so often embodied and since eros is most definitely embodied, it would be odd not to consider sex as a way of moving through fear.

In considering sex as a resource for moving through fear, it is important to be clear that sexual intimacy is not synonymous with losing ourselves, nor with losing control. That is an illusion fostered by the deeply entrenched alienation and the eroticized violence characteristic of our social order. It is an illusion which would keep us unmoved and unmoving, untouched and untouching, and unchanged and unchanging.

Sex and our sexual desire can be ways of moving through and with fear into a homecoming into ourselves and into one another. It can be a way of searching for a physical/spiritual home, of painstakingly searching out the interconnections between us. Because fear, eros, and sex are embodied, the touching of our bodies, the embracing of our desire, the coming to know and trust our bodyselves can sometimes move us from a place of "stuckness" into a place of intimacy, of re-connection, where we

can truly come back into our own. Embracing our desires can engender a sense of deep self-knowing that we are moving in a way
which physically and spiritually moves us more and more out of
alienation and into mutuality—into coming home.[38]

Sex as a way of moving through fear is never without its mix of
fear and hope, certainty and trembling. In this context, sex is
about learning to be present—with oneself and one's lover. Sex
is about choice—to have sex or not. Sex is about an embodied
movement into incarnations of justice between us. Sex as a resource is a way of acting our selves into relation, into a more
deeply embodied connection with the erotic. It is about finding
justice and mutuality titillating, both in and out of bed.

There is, of course, much debate about good sex versus bad
sex, healthy sex versus unhealthy sex. The important point to re-
member in a movement through fear is that sex can be a movement away from the eroticization of violence and a movement
into *re-connecting,* into erotic mutuality. Unhealthy sex fails to
respect bodily integrity. It impedes one's ongoing movement into
an embodied mutuality. It prevents healing.

The question on so many minds these days—what about
sadomasochism?—is important to consider in this context. To
the extent that it represents the sadomasochistic dynamics present in society, it furthers the eroticization of violence and hin-
ders the movement into an erotic mutuality.[39] Feminist theorist
Ann Ferguson helpfully distinguishes between those sexual practices that are basic, risky, or forbidden, in what she names as a
"transitional feminist sexual morality." The key is whether or
not specific sexual practices reinforce relations of dominance
and submission. For instance, forbidden sexual practices would
include incest, rape, and domestic violence. Risky practices
include those "suspected of leading to dominant/subordinate relationships" and would include sadomasochism, capitalist produced pornography, and "nuclear family relations between male
breadwinners and female housewives." Basic feminist sexual
practices would include "casual and committed sexual love, co-
parenting, and communal relationships," marked by "self-
conscious negotiation" of differences in power relations (economic, social, age, and gender).[40] The designation of S/M as a

risky practice is, I believe, appropriate for a conscious movement toward sex as a movement through fear and into an embodied mutuality.

It is clear that sex as a resource for moving through fear should not be romanticized. It entails hard work to reclaim sexuality, sometimes even to be able to re-connect the words "sex" and pleasure," and to come to the knowledge that we deserve to feel good. It is often a painful movement into embodied mutuality, into re-connecting sexuality and spirituality, especially for those who have withstood the ravages of eroticized violence.[41] But, it is also important to value fun, pleasure, and play as part of sex, as part of a movement into embodied mutuality. Sex is a way of increasing self-knowing, self-loving, neighbor-loving. Sex is a way of re-connecting, embodying justice, incarnating God. As such, it deserves body-positive, sex-affirmative celebration.

Moving beyond Survival

Many of us have been able to move from being victims to being survivors. Dare we think about the possibilities of moving beyond mere survival? Is it possible to move from bare bones surviving to fully embodied thriving? If so, for whom? What would thriving be like? And how would such movement be affected by dynamics of race, class, gender, and sexuality?[42]

In any discussion of surviving and thriving, it is critical to take into account the dynamics of oppression which determine who is victimized, who survives, and who is able to thrive. The fact that I am a white, educated, lesbian woman pondering the movement from surviving to thriving is important because it communicates that the factors of my white skin and my access to higher education have something to do with thriving. But, of course, it is also important to note that I am a lesbian woman thinking about thriving in a culture which values neither lesbianism nor femaleness.

Delores Williams writes of the ethical principle of "survival and a positive quality of life for black women and their families in the presence and care of God."[43] This ethical principle is used to evaluate whether certain realities enhance or detract from the survival and quality of life of African American women. There is a lot to be said for surviving. Without surviving, we die. Without surviving, we cannot begin to dream of thriving.

The impact of difference is important when talking about the movement from surviving to thriving. For many, sex is a mode of economic survival. Whether a woman is a sex-worker or a woman who stays in an unhappy or abusive relationship for economic reasons, the result is the same: few women in those situations have the luxury of imagining sex as anything but an economic fact of life.[44] The same is true when contemplating the move from the eroticization of violence to an erotic mutuality. Too few have glimpsed mutuality. Those who face violence every day of their lives, who have nowhere to live, and who do not know from where the next meal is coming have little time or energy to contemplate surviving, much less thriving. Women who must survive in a racist social order also face obstacles in the movement from surviving to thriving. The struggle to survive often takes all of one's emotional, physical, and sexual resources. It is important to factor this into any discussion of thriving.

Nevertheless, I believe that thriving is a possibility that deserves attention. Perhaps, though, *thriving* can best be understood in a sense similar to Williams's emphasis on a "positive quality of life for family and community."[45] Thriving is sometimes only a glimpse of what could be. It is a hope for the future—if not ours, then our children's futures. But, thriving is not entirely based in the future. It is based on the belief that we are all creatures of value, deserving of relatively safe environments in which to flourish—now. It sometimes involves a sense of fun, pleasure, and excitement about life, which can be erotic. Thriving involves a zest for living, for creating, for incarnating. Visions of thriving help spur us on to resist that which detracts from the quality of life for our neighbors and ourselves. These visions spur us on to claim that which enhances movements into erotic mutuality.

The movement from victim to survivor to one who thrives does not happen overnight, nor does it happen once and for all. Indeed, I believe that many of us move back and forth between the positions at various times. The movement between the positions, however, is imperative: it is best not to get stuck in a victim or, ultimately, even, a survivor position.[46] Too often, there is little movement from the focus on being a "survivor" to a focus on anything else. In this sense, being a survivor becomes a badge of membership: it sometimes serves as a justification of keeping non-members out; it functions as a control over the extent to which one may be urged to risk relationship.[47]

So, the term *survivor* has at least two primary connotations. It connotes the day-to-day struggle to survive, to stay alive, to put food on the table, have a roof over one's head, and/or resist violence. The other consists of a misuse of the survivor position as it is used to keep others out and to defend oneself against the challenge—or the need to grow—into erotic mutuality; it is often based on fear. In both senses, then, the possibilities of thriving could add to the quality of life of survivors.

In imagining how this might be so, it is helpful to remember that movement into thriving is rooted in a particular community and moves outward. A healthy sense of *suspicion* must, of course, be employed to examine what keeps people from thriving, from surviving, and what undergirds ongoing victimization. At the same time, the raising up of *particularities* brings in the differences that privilege and marginalization make in determining who is victimized, who is able or unable to survive, and who is able to imagine movement into thriving. *Self-knowing* functions as that which helps us determine what our needs and desires are and how our quality of life might be enhanced. And *self-loving* is absolutely essential to continue surviving and even to be able to consider thriving. Without it, one's energy for the long-term struggle to survive, much less thrive, is severely diminished. If we do not believe we deserve to survive, or we cannot imagine thriving, we will be caught in a seemingly endless mentality of victimization.

Loving our neighbors as ourselves is also critical to surviving, for it is much easier to survive if we are not undertaking it alone. And love of neighbor as self is essential to the movement into thriving, because those who thrive with no regard for their neighbors are oppressors, victimizers, and perpetrators of violence. *Re-connecting* helps us in the movement through fear into an erotic mutuality; it enables us to find our ways together, working with conflict and with our differences, into a movement from victim to survivor to one who can—even if only vaguely— imagine what it might be like to thrive. Re-connecting actively takes into account the dynamics of racism, sexism, classism, heterosexism, ageism, speciesism, and able-bodyism and their impact on how we move toward surviving and thriving together; it will not do to leave anyone behind. [48]

Moving beyond survival, then, is essential to a movement into erotic mutuality. The possibilities of thriving, both now and in the future, add to the momentum of erotic mutuality. It brings to the movement into erotic mutuality a rigorous analysis of differences in power. If the movement into erotic mutuality is to be a lasting one, we need to enhance the quality of life for all. We need to be nudged beyond our daily struggles. We need the impetus of hope and vision that the possibility of thriving contributes to a movement into erotic mutuality.

SOLIDARITY AND THE WORK
OF THE CHURCHES RECONSIDERED

Solidarity requires that we re-member that while one of us is victimized, while one of us struggles daily to survive, our work is not done. It means that we cannot stop struggling against forces which keep eroticized violence in place; it means that we must keep the momentum going and the dream of thriving alive for the sake of our ongoing relations with our selves, one another, and God. Solidarity requires a relentless and rigorous commitment to constructing a theo-ethics that affirms human bodies, sexualities, and sex and takes seriously the damage inflicted by that inherited theo-ethical ethos which posits the need to control, chasten, and shape eros.

We have been on a long journey with eros. We have seen the ways in which it has been despised, negated, and chastened. We have seen the panic that eros instills in some church people and the resulting attempts to keep it on a straight and narrow path. We have also seen the attempts by progressive church people and feminist liberation theo-ethicists to unravel some of the damage done by the inherited anti-eros ethos, as well as a constructive positing of a movement out of the eroticization of violence and toward erotic mutuality. We need to ask so what do we do now? Where do we go from here? More specifically, what is the work of the churches?

BUILDING SOLIDARITY:
THE CHURCH BECOMING EROS COMMUNITY

At the expense of eros, our churches have been known as "agape communities." These agape communities have all but eclipsed the existence of eros. In this context, eros—human sexuality—is blatantly ignored as something that good christian people do not think about. We have seen the results of this self-imposed ignorance: the various manifestations of eroticized violence speak to this as does the alienation of vast numbers of people from both their sexualities and spiritualities. Agape communities have imposed a great deal of pain on their members.

It is time to consider the church as eros community. The phrase, *church as eros community*, undoubtedly calls forth to some people images of worshipers in the courts of Baal, dancing naked around a steaming cauldron, and committing all sorts of "non-christian" acts together.[49] That the phrase *church as eros community* could call forth these images indicates the extent to which eros has been deemed an unchristian and wildly uncontrollable love.

But if we remember that eros is love that is marked by a yearning, a pushing and pulling toward erotic mutuality, a movement toward embodied justice; that it celebrates the sexual, the bodily, the earthy; and that it is rooted in body-experience and seeks the integration of body and spirit, human and divine; then the phrase *church as eros community* takes on a different meaning. The church as eros community could be a place where sex—in a relational context that embodies a commitment to an erotic mutuality—is seen as a life-enhancing way to express *self-loving*, *neighbor-loving*, and *God-loving*. It could be a place where the well-being of all people is important and where justice is more than an intriguing biblical concept applicable only to safe, un-threatening charitable causes. The church as eros community could be the sort of place where, in the pursuit of an eros-centered embodied justice, all would work against the ravages of eroticized violence.

I suspect that the church as eros community would be a crowded place. Those people who have left the churches because of the irrelevance of church to their lives would return, for they would feel that the church is a place that would offer acceptance and affirmation of their lives. The church would be a place of creative celebration of the various aspects of our lives, of our differences and commonalities. It would be a place where, together, we would incarnate God and embody justice. The church as an eros community would be a true home. It would welcome and or-dain (though perhaps the church as eros community would have little need of a distinction between clergy and lay people) open, affirming, and sexually active lesbian women and gay men. It would talk about sexuality openly; seeking out a wealth of experi-ences; addressing topics of interest to teenagers, single people of all ages and sexualities, people living together, elderly people. In short, the church as eros community would be an alive and lively place, unlike so many of the churches we know today.

But what do we do in the meantime? How long do we wait? How can we inaugurate some of these visions? For the reality is that this is what these are—visions of something yet to come. What is the work of the churches to be?

CHAPTER SIX

Re-membering Eros in Church
Tasks for a Sexual Theo-Ethics

The churches, as I noted at the outset of this book, are in a mess over sexuality. The fault does not lie with lesbian women and gay men, as some would maintain. Nor does it lie with uppity women. The debates over lesbian and gay sexuality and the role of women are a symptom of a much wider disarray and disorientation on the subject of human sexuality. As Marvin Ellison has forcefully noted, the church has inculcated and maintained a deep fear of sex and passion.

> [The church] is coming perilously close to killing off our love of life in the flesh and our passion for justice in the church and in the world. . . . The church must also overcome its preoccupation with questions of sexual orientation and cease its endless harangues about the dangers and illegitimacy of sexual diversity. It is high time for the church to "come of age" about sex and sexual pluralism in the church and in the society.[1]

Indeed, it is past time for the church to come of age. There are no longer any acceptable excuses. Time has run out. And the situation is dire. As the authors of *The Presbyterian Sexuality Report* assert, because of the church's inheritance of patriarchal structures, there are "many things to unlearn, as well as to learn."[2]

Solidarity is central to the construction of a sexual theo-ethics for the church. Solidarity means that good christian people may well be a bit uncomfortable, ill at ease. Ada María Isasi-Díaz writes that if solidarity were truly understood, more people would be threatened by it and it would be less "fashionable" than it is, because it is about truly radical change.

*Solidarity is not a matter of agreeing with, of being supportive of,
of liking, or of being inspired by, the cause of a group of people.
Though all these might be part of solidarity, solidarity goes beyond all of them. Solidarity has to do with understanding the interconnections among issues and the cohesiveness that needs to
exist among the communities of struggle.* [3]

Discomfort notwithstanding, solidarity requires a commitment
to an ongoing process of sitting down face-to-face, body-to-body,
with those who are different from us.

Solidarity calls us to examine the consequences of our own
privilege on others' lives and to connect the particularities of our
own oppression(s) to the oppression of others. It calls us to open
our eyes and see the concrete effects our lives have on others. In
the church context, solidarity means that policies on sexuality
cannot continue to be formulated without undertaking a liberation analysis of power and privilege, i.e., an analysis that begins
with an epistemological privilege of the oppressed.

The results of a liberation analysis re-shape the channels of ecclesiastical accountability. Solidarity holds the shapers of policy
accountable to those beyond the immediate circle of power holders, to those who are marginalized. In the formulation of policies, it means that the "invocation of unity" with regard to those
in power cannot be heeded. In this context, *unity* has meant the
control of sexuality and eros in the hands of a few by imposing
across-the-board agreement in order to maintain institutional
power and privilege by the leaders of the church. *Unity*, in a
church context that takes justice and solidarity seriously, must
come to mean a commitment to keep struggling together, in all
of our differences, for the sake of incarnating God, embodying
justice, and moving into erotic mutuality.

Solidarity means that the church must seek out, listen to, and
learn about the lived realities of people's lives. The church needs
to hear from, listen to, and learn from African American,
Hispanic, American Indian, and Asian American women and
men. It needs to hear from, listen to, and learn from single parents, lesbian women, bisexual women and men, gay men, heterosexual couples living together, and single people of all persua-

sions. The church needs to hear from, listen to, and learn from a range of age groups and those with differing levels of physical ability. Knowledge so obtained must figure decisively in what results. Not only must all these people be heard from, listened to, and learned from, they must be well represented on policy-shaping committees (e.g., lesbian women and gay men must be active leaders, not the objectified "other," on committees debating ordination issues). The authors of *The Presbyterian Sexuality Report* did well in undertaking this process of hearing, listening, and learning. That the report was so overwhelmingly rejected betrays the extent to which these voices continue to be ignored by those invested in maintaining control of sexuality.

As the old invocation of "unity" has ceased to be useful, so too has "reconciliation." Reconciliation cannot be prescribed; it cannot happen without justice, for such a reconciliation is false. Movement toward reconciliation must come from those who have been hurt, *if and when* they are ready and have seen change on the part of those who have perpetrated violence. Reconciliation requires that shapers of ecclesiastical policies repent of their contribution to injustice and the maintenance of eroticized violence.[4]

Solidarity means that the life-denying split between orientation and practice, insisted upon by the churches in reference to lesbian women and gay men, must be overcome. The orientation/practice split sends a sex-negative message, and—as has been noted above—reinforces eroticized violence against lesbian women and gay men. It also has served to divorce sexuality from identity, thus forcing upon lesbian and gay people a "non-wholesome" (non-integrated) lifestyle. Only those lesbian women and gay men who reject such posturing and are "open, affirming, and practicing" can, by any stretch of the imagination, be considered wholesome. And we are rewarded for such wholesomeness by being rejected by the churches.

The old order must pass away. The former task of christian sexual ethics—of bestowing and maintaining order—is no longer tenable. The ethic of one woman, one man, one flesh, based on the complementarity theory, no longer maintains the control over eros that was intended. It has ceased to be relevant to people's lives (if it ever was) and, indeed, causes damage. The only "order" it maintains is that of eroticized violence.

RE-IMAGINING: SOME CHALLENGES FROM EROS FOR CHURCH LEADERS

Church conservatives are right when they charge that the various denominational reports on sexuality and the challenges posed by feminist liberation theo-ethics in general and lesbian women and gay men in particular are heretical and contrary to Christianity. If church leaders were to heed the challenges posed in these pages, the churches would never again be the same.

What I have suggested consists of a direct challenge to the structure of the mainline churches as we know them. Indeed, they cannot be "Christian" in the same way. I have proposed a radicalized theo-ethics moving beyond dualism. In this theo-ethics, the doctrines of God, incarnation, creation, and sin would be radically re-imagined. With the re-imagining of doctrine would come a re-structuring of malestream Christianity.

The limits of current church policy on ordaining self-affirming, sexually active lesbian women and gay men must be challenged. The churches cannot be permitted to get away with a "love the sinner, hate the sin" mentality. If, as the churches assert, lesbian women and gay men really are created in the image of God and are members in good standing, we must be eligible for ordination on the same basis as heterosexual women and men. Of course, heterosexual people have access to marriage; lesbian women and gay men do not. Therefore, it would be essential to do away with the marriage or celibacy requirement—especially since most church authorities turn a blind eye to the nonmarital sexual relationships of many heterosexual clergy. Until open, affirming, and "practicing" lesbian women and gay men can be ordained on the same basis as people who are not lesbian- or gay-identified, lesbian women and gay men will continue to be on the periphery of the church and will continue to leave it . . . and be left by it. The church has much more to gain from the contributions of self-affirming and practicing lesbian women and gay men than lesbian women and gay men have to gain from the churches in their current condition.[5]

In addition to changes in doctrine and discipline, the implications of moving beyond dualism require liturgical changes: inclusive language must be the order of the day, not the exception. Our understandings of who we are in relation to God and who God is in relation to us have shifted so that much religious imagery needs to be evaluated in terms of how it reflects our theologies.

A re-imagined eros must be incorporated then, as soon as humanly possible, into the doctrine, discipline, and worship of our churches, as well as into our daily lives.

Eros must be able to stand alone, meeting the gaze of christianity, and be respected, cherished, and affirmed as a love that need not be feared, controlled, denied, or rescued by agape. Until then, church policies will continue to find sexuality to be something less than respectable.

Re-imagining eros requires that the churches cease operating out of, and educating its members into, a sense of fear about sexuality. Rather, a sense of joy and excitement about bodies, sex, and God needs to be affirmed and reflected in church teachings and proclamations. The churches need to go beyond their statements that "sex is a good gift from God." It is more than that! It is life-enhancing, indeed, faith-enhancing. Without such enthusiastic affirmation, little change is likely.

Erotic mutuality—between and among us and God—requires an end to attempts to control sexuality by fitting it into a narrow, prescribed model. Such control creates damaged persons, a damaged church, and a damaged society. Accepting the challenge of being erotically open and affirming instead of closed and controlling will help the churches begin to stop the damage.

The churches need to realize that the complementarity theory—until now justified by a theory of God's will/God's demand—is outdated; fails to take the plurality of people's experiences into account; and helps maintain heterosexism, compulsory heterosexuality, and the eroticization of violence.

The effects of eroticized violence must not be underestimated. To do so is dangerous and costs lives. The existence of the varying degrees of violence—from alienation, isolation, and self-negation to battering, incest, rape, and hate crimes—must be acknowledged. But acknowledgement is not enough. The churches need to take responsibility for their participation in eroticized violence and send out the theo-ethical message that violence is unacceptable. The theological inheritance of an ethos that is used to justify violence must be rejected. A constructive effort must reflect an affirmation of self-love, different ways of loving, and sex itself.

The churches must support educational efforts that are grounded in a concentrated listening. There is no time for listening only to the least discomforting voices. A panoply of different voices must be sought, and these voices must reflect a diversity (and, mostly, a non-dominant perspective) in terms of experiences, race, class, sexual orientation, and gender. These voices must not only be listened to, they must participate from the very beginning in the construction of a sexual theo-ethics.

Education must include basic sex education, at all levels (including clergy), which is sex-positive. Information on sexual violence, as well as community resources for those who have need of them, should be made available. So too, should explicit information about AIDS and safer sex practices. There is no need to start from scratch. Many already existing resources, such as *The Presbyterian Sexuality Report* as well as many secular resources, can be used.

Church policies must reflect an understanding of eros as a movement away from alienation and violence and a movement toward an erotic mutuality, an embodied justice. Sexuality needs to be understood as something that God created. Eros as movement toward an embodied mutuality, an embodied justice, should be affirmed as a way of incarnating God, embodying justice, in our midst.[6]

Finally, *solidarity* means that the churches must cease being an arena that creates victims. They must become a place where *all* survive, where *all* can come to be affirmed and held accountable to a theo-ethics of embodied justice and erotic mutuality. They must become a place not only where all survive, but where all can begin to find ways of thriving.

DARING TO CLAIM AUTHORITY: SOME IMPLICATIONS OF EROS FOR CHURCH PEOPLE

The work facing all of us is vast. Often the push for change in the church is stalled by church leaders who say "the people aren't ready." Nothing insults church people more. The fact of the matter is church people are ready—indeed, more than ready. Movement into an erotic mutuality grounded in justice is not entirely dependent on ecclesiastical power holders with an investment in maintaining the status quo. Challenging eroticized violence and disembodied teachings about sexuality is also the work of everyone in the pews. In many ways, daring to claim erotic power in mutual relation frees us all for new life. This power for new life can be brought into being when all of us dare, with God, to create it. I suggest all justice-loving people dare to dig deep to recover the roots of suspicion, particularities, and self-knowing and branch out into self-loving, neighbor-loving as self, re-connecting, and solidarity.

1. *Let us dare to be suspicious.* Ask heretical questions. Claim our authority to question that which has always been. Let us question the relevance of christian doctrine to our lives. Question unjust church policies. Let us dare to be brash about it. Ask how our sexualities have been influenced and controlled by malestream theology and church policies. Let us ask why those policies define "wholeness" as existing only within life-long, monogamous, heterosexual marriage. How does that influence our lives and the lives of our friends and lovers?

2. *Let us dare to speak honestly of the particularities of our lives and loves.* Let us bring those particularities into church with us. Take the time to ask people about their lives and loves. Let us dare to value the differences between us and embrace those differences. Let us dare to experience conflict as opening possibilities.

3. *Let us dare to know ourselves.* Let us dare to take the time to make our own acquaintance. Let us come to

know our own bodies, learn from them, and listen to them. Let us dare to search out ways to integrate our bodies, minds, and spirits. Let us dare to come out as who we really are.

4. *Let us dare to love ourselves.* This is not an indulgence; it is a necessity. We are made in God's image and are therefore good. Let us dare to put away patterns of self-loathing. Let us come to know that we deserve love. Let us dare to take ourselves seriously. Let us dare to love ourselves shamelessly, with passion, and well.

5. *Let us dare to combine love of ourselves with love of our neighbors.* Let us dare to reach out to our neighbor and to love her or him. Reach beyond the pew, out to the streets, across to the other side of the tracks, and beyond. Let us be open to our neighbors. Be open to confrontation, challenge, and change from loving our neighbors. Let us dare to share the news that eros enhances the mutual well-being of ourselves and our neighbors. Let us dare to think about the collective power of transformation fueled by eros.

6. *Let us dare to re-connect, to be intimate, to transform fear.* Let us dare to find the connections between our oppression(s) and others' oppression(s). Let us dare to touch and be touched. Let us dare to move and be moved. Let us dare to change and be changed. Let us dare to desire and be desired.

7. *Let us dare to stop being good, to stop being nice.* Good and nice do not suffice when confronting the limits of church policies. Let us move, together, into true *solidarity.* Let us dare to be sex-positive in sex-negative environments. Let us dare to take seriously our own moral agency, demanding inclusion and change, directly challenging the limits of church policy. Let us dare to risk relation. Dare to risk eros and bring our friends.

Let us dare to break free.
I dare you. I dare myself. I dare us.
For we, the people in the pew and out of the pew, are ready.

NOTES

INTRODUCTION

1. I have lowercased *christian* and *christianity* in order to acknowledge the ways in which christianity has been employed as a tool of colonialism and imperialism.
2. Throughout this book, the terms *lesbian women* and *gay men* are used in place of *lesbians* and *gays*. The words *lesbian* and *gay* are used as adjectives rather than nouns to avoid contributing to the objectification of the sexuality of lesbian women and gay men. Use of the adjectival form also denotes a social constructionist, rather than essentialist, approach. Kevin Gordon also used this designation in "From the Task Force to the Consultation: Revisit, Revise, and Revision: Introductory Essay," in *Homosexuality and Social Justice*, ed. Kevin Gordon (San Francisco: The Consultation on Homosexuality, Social Justice, and Roman Catholic Theology, 1986), 1–64.
3. In the spring of 1985, while a seminarian at Episcopal Divinity School and a postulant for ordination in the Episcopal Diocese of Bethlehem, Pennsylvania, I told my bishop that I was a lesbian woman. My bishop invoked the 1979 General Convention statement, which declared: "We believe it is not appropriate for this Church to ordain a practicing homosexual, or any person who is engaged in heterosexual relations outside of marriage." When I refused to take a vow of celibacy, the bishop promised to present my situation to the Diocesan Commission on Ministry. Predictably, the Commission voted unanimously to oust me from the ordination process.

   These events were chronicled in the pages of *The Witness*. See Anne E. Gilson, "Therefore Choose Life," *The Witness* 68, no. 9 (September 1985): 22; Mary Lou Suhor, "In the Matter of Sherwood and Gilson," *The Witness* 69, no. 1 (January 1986): 4; and The Witness Editorial Board, "Open Letter to the Presiding Bishop," *The Witness* 69, no. 9 (September 1986): 13–14.
4. *Pro-feminist* refers to men who are supportive of feminist issues and incorporate that perspective into their work. The term *theo-ethicist* is an attempt to hold the interrelated fields of theology and ethics together.

5. Feminist liberation theo-ethicists share a commitment to the liber-ation and well-being of *all* women, with special attention to those most marginalized. For a further exposition of feminist liberation theo-ethics, see chapter 3.

6. By the term *privilege*, I mean the power one is automatically ac-corded (or not) in this racist, classist, sexist, and heterosexist soci-ety by virtue of one's skin color, class stratum, gender, or sexual ori-entation. This so-called privilege is to be critiqued in terms of how those who hold it seek either to maintain it or deconstruct it by em-powering those who are not white, male, economically comfort-able, or heterosexual. For a womanist perspective on privilege, see Delores S. Williams, "Womanist/Feminist Dialogue: Problems and Possibilities," in *Journal of Feminist Studies in Religion* 9, nos. 1–2 (spring/fall 1993): 70–71.

7. This took place in the late 1970s and early 1980s. The Diocese of Northwestern Pennsylvania now accepts women priests.

8. Conversations with Elizabeth M. Bounds, Kathleen J. Greider, and Margaret Mayman. "Malestream" was originally coined by Mary O'Brien in *The Politics of Reproduction* (London: Routledge and Kegan Paul, 1981), 5ff.

9. See Carter Heyward, *Touching Our Strength: The Erotic as Power and the Love of God* (San Francisco: Harper and Row, 1989); Andrea Dworkin, *Woman Hating* (New York: Dutton, 1974); Zillah R. Eisenstein, "Developing a Theory of Capitalist Patriarchy and So-cialist Feminism" and "Some Notes on the Relations of Capitalist Patriarchy," in *Capitalist Patriarchy and the Case for Socialist Feminism*, ed. Z. Eisenstein (New York: Monthly Review Press, 1979), 5–55.

10. bell hooks, *Feminist Theory: From Margin to Center* (Boston: South End Press, 1984), 155. See also Adrienne Rich, "Compulsory Het-erosexuality and Lesbian Existence," in *Powers of Desire: The Poli-tics of Sexuality*, ed. Ann Snitow, Christine Stansell, and Sharon Thompson (New York: Monthly Review Press, 1983), 177–205; Carter Heyward, *Touching Our Strength*; Carter Heyward and Mary Hunt, "Lesbianism and Feminist Theology," in *Journal of Feminist Studies in Religion* 2, no. 2 (fall 1986): 95–106.

11. For more on homophobia, see Beverly W. Harrison, "Misogyny and Homophobia," in *Making the Connections: Essays in Feminist Social Ethics*, ed. Carol Robb (Boston: Beacon Press, 1985), 135–51.

12. Heyward, *Touching Our Strength*, 193–94.

13. "Eros" is capitalized only in the context of the traditional theological treatment of it in chapter 1.

14. For other resources on social construction theory, see Ann Ferguson, *Blood at the Root: Motherhood, Sexuality, and Male Dominance* (Boston: Unwin Hyman/Pandora Press, 1989); Ellen Ross and Rayna Rapp, "Sex and Society: A Research Note from Social History and Anthropology," in *Powers of Desire: The Politics of Sexuality*, ed. Ann Snitow, Christine Stansell, and Sharon Thompson (New York: Monthly Review Press, 1983), 51–73; Maryviolet Burns, ed., *The Speaking That Profits Us: Violence in the Lives of Women of Color* (Seattle: Center for the Prevention of Sexual and Domestic Violence, 1986); and Rennie Simson, "The Afro-American Female: The Historical Construction of Sexual Identity," in *Powers of Desire*, 229–35.

15. Jeffrey Weeks, *Sexuality* (London: Tavistock Publications, 1986), 25. Weeks's other works on sexuality include *Sex, Politics, and Society: The Regulation of Sexuality Since 1800* (London: Longman, 1981) and *Sexuality and Its Discontents: Meanings, Myths, and Modern Sexuality* (London: Routledge and Kegan Paul, 1985).

16. Weeks, *Sexuality*, 25, 28.

17. It is important to note here that both radical cultural and libertarian feminist theorists have made important contributions to the discussion. The distinction lies in the more congenial political and intellectual relation between social construction theory and feminist liberation theo-ethics. For a critique of social construction theory, see Carole S. Vance and Ann Barr Snitow, "Toward a Conversation About Sex in Feminism: A Modest Proposal," *Signs: Journal of Women in Culture and Society* 10, no. 1 (autumn 1984): 126–35.

18. I am indebted to those who have offered constructive suggestions throughout the last decade: Katie Geneva Cannon, Alison Cheek, Robin Gorsline, Beverly Wildung Harrison, Carter Heyward, Joy Mills, Larry Rasmussen, Nancy Richardson, Elisabeth Schüssler Fiorenza, Owen Thomas, and Wilma Wake. Tom F. Driver has most recently influenced the shape of this method.

19. I have drawn the image of roots from Frederic Denison Maurice's use of *digging* as a metaphor for theologizing. See Frederic Maurice, ed., *The Life of Frederic Denison Maurice*, vol. 11 (New York: 1884), 137.

20. For more on the development of this method, see my treatment of it in "Keeping Sex in Order: Heterosexism and Episcopal Church

Policy," *No Easy Peace: Liberating Anglicanism,* ed. Carter Heyward and Sue Phillips (Lanham, Md.: University Press of America, 1992), 161–86.

This root originated in conversation with Tom F. Driver, New York City, April 1993.

22. The extent to which this is so is elaborated upon in the exposition of the works by Nygren, Thielicke, Bailey, and Lewis cited in chapter 1.

23. Feminist resources on self-love include Susan Dunfee Nelson, "The Sin of Hiding: A Feminist Critique of Reinhold Niebuhr's Account of the Sin of Pride," *Soundings* 65, no. 3 (February 1982); Valerie Saiving, "The Human Situation: A Feminine View," in *WomanSpirit Rising,* ed. Carol Christ and Judith Plaskow (San Francisco: Harper and Row, 1979; originally published, 1960), 25–42; Judith Plaskow, *Sex, Sin, and Grace: Women's Experience and the Theologies of Reinhold Niebuhr and Paul Tillich* (Lanham, Md.: Univ. Press of America, 1980); Sheila Briggs, "Sexual Justice and the 'Righteousness of God,'" in *Sex and God: Some Varieties of Women's Religious Experience,* ed. Linda Hurcombe (New York: Routledge and Kegan Paul, 1987), 251–77; and Carter Heyward, *The Redemption of God: A Theology of Mutual Relation* (Lanham, Md.: Univ. Press of America, 1982).

24. For an elaboration of the effect of self-hate and loss of self on women, see Dana Crowley Jack, *Silencing the Self: Women and Depression* (New York: HarperCollins, 1991).

25. I am greatly indebted to the work of Carter Heyward on this topic. See especially *The Redemption of God.*

26. Here I am indebted to the work of Beverly Wildung Harrison, especially her book *Making the Connections.*

27. Ada María Isasi-Díaz, "Solidarity: Love of Neighbor in the 1980s," *Lift Every Voice: Constructing Christian Theologies from the Underside,* ed. Susan Brooks Thistlethwaite and Mary Potter Engels (San Francisco: Harper and Row, 1990), 36.

CHAPTER ONE

1. Anders Nygren, *Agape and Eros: A Study of the Christian Idea of Love* (London: SPCK, 1953).

2. Helmut Thielicke, *The Ethics of Sex,* trans. John W. Doberstein (New York: Harper and Row, 1964).

3. C. S. Lewis, *The Four Loves* (San Diego: Harcourt, Brace, Jovanovich, 1960). His earlier work, *Mere Christianity* (New York: Macmillan, 1943), provided a foundation for his later reflections on love; and selected essays of his, which were posthumously published, illuminate his thoughts on the nature of sexual happiness. See also *God in the Dock: Essays in Theology and Ethics*, ed. Walter Hooper (Grand Rapids, Mich.: William B. Eerdmans, 1970) and *The Allegory of Love: A Study in Medieval Tradition* (1936; repr. New York: Oxford Univ. Press, 1958). The latter is primarily a history of allegorical love literature spanning from the early Middle Ages to the latter part of the sixteenth century.

4. D. S. Bailey, *The Mystery of Love and Marriage: A Study in the Theology of Sexual Relation* (New York: Harper and Row, 1952); *Homosexuality and the Western Christian Tradition* (London: Longmans, Green, and Company, 1955); and *Common Sense About Sexual Ethics* (New York: Macmillan, 1962).

5. Thor Hall, "The Nygren Corpus: Annotations to the Major Works of Anders Nygren of Lund," *Journal of the American Academy of Religion* 47, no. 2 (June 1979): 269–89.

6. Nels F. S. Ferré, *Swedish Contributions to Modern Theology: With Special Reference to Lundensian Thought* (New York: Harper and Row, 1967), 30; and Gustaf Wingren, "Swedish Theology Since 1900," *Scottish Journal of Theology* 9 (June 1956): 123–24.

7. Anders Nygren, "Intellectual Autobiography," in *The Philosophy and Theology of Anders Nygren*, ed. Charles W. Kegley (Carbondale: Southern Illinois Univ. Press, 1970), 6.

8. Hall, *Anders Nygren*, 37. See also Ferré, *Swedish Contributions*, 219.

9. Karl Barth, *Church Dogmatics* IV/2, trans. G. W. Bromiley (Edinburgh: T. and T. Clark, 1961), 741, 746–47.

10. Martin D'Arcy, *The Mind and Heart of Love, Lion, and Unicorn: A Study in Eros and Agape* (Cleveland: World, 1962), 96.

11. John M. Rist, "Some Interpretations of Agape and Eros," *The Philosophy and Theology of Anders Nygren*, ed. Charles W. Kegley (Carbondale: Southern Illinois Univ. Press, 1970), 172–73.

12. Daniel Day Williams, *The Spirit and the Forms of Love* (New York: Harper and Row, 1968), 8–9, 79.

13. William Lillie, "The Christian Conception of Love," *Scottish Journal of Theology* 12 (1959): 235–36.

14. David K. Clark, "Philosophical Reflections on Self-Worth and Self-Love," *Journal of Psychology and Theology* 13, no. 1 (spring 1985): 7.

15. It does not matter that the noun *Agape* is mentioned only twice in the synoptic gospels (the term is developed further by Paul). According to Nygren, this is not because the concept did not exist, for the term did occur in rare instances in pre-Christian sources (although he quickly qualifies this by adding that the meaning was not the same as the Christian use of the term). Rather, the important point was that the reality for which the term *Agape* stood was unmistakably present in the synoptic gospels. See Nygren, *Agape and Eros,* 113–15.

16. Nygren, *Agape and Eros,* 38–39. Nygren's characterization of motif research as "a type of scientific analysis" was intended to guarantee the objectivity of his work.

17. Augustine's synthesis of Eros and Agape was precisely what Nygren saw as being the error that occurred throughout christian history, and his self-appointed task was to undo the damage that the combination of the two motifs had caused. According to Nygren, Augustine was unaware that Eros and Agape were "diametrically opposed to each other and that the relation between them must be an Either/Or; instead, he tried to make it a Both/And." Augustine's mistake was attempting to hang on to both Eros and Agape, when the fact that platonic Eros and New Testament Agape came from two entirely different religious contexts meant that any connection between them was not only undesirable but simply impossible. See Nygren, *Agape and Eros,* 470.

18. Nygren, *Agape and Eros,* 49.

19. Ibid.; see discussion, 75–80, 210.

20. Ibid.; see discussion, 175–78, 210.

21. Ibid., 217.

22. Ibid., 100–101.

23. Self-love is so abhorrent to Nygren that, in quoting Luther he remarked, "On the basis of Christ's words in John 12:25, it is a fundamental principle for [Luther] that: "To love is the same as to hate oneself." Ibid.; see 711ff.

24. Ibid.; see 216–17.

25. In 1944, the leaders of a plot against Hitler asked Thielicke to write part of a revolutionary statement on the nature of church-state relations. He narrowly escaped death when the Hitler regime discovered the plot. "Obituary of Helmut Thielicke," *The Christian Century* 103, no. 10 (19–26 March 1986): 290.

26. In an essay written in 1990, I examined Thielicke's position on many of the subjects addressed in the remainder of this chapter.

Since that essay was written, I have nuanced differently my interpretation of Thielicke's work. See Anne E. Gilson, "Keeping Sex in Order: Heterosexism in Episcopal Church Policy."

27. See Paul G. Schrotenboer, "Review of *The Ethics of Sex*, by Helmut Thielicke," *Westminster Theological Journal* 29 (November 1966): 107–10; and William E. Hulme, "Review of *The Ethics of Sex*, by Helmut Thielicke," *Pastoral Psychology* 15, no. 141 (February 1964): 63–65.

28. James B. Nelson, "Review of *The Ethics of Sex*, by Helmut Thielicke," *Theology and Life* 8 (winter 1965): 308–9.

29. Roger Shinn, "Review of *The Ethics of Sex*, by Helmut Thielicke," *Union Seminary Quarterly Review* 20 (January 1965): 203–5.

30. Thielicke, 27.

31. Ibid., 28.

32. Ibid.

33. Ibid., 23.

34. Ibid., 23–24.

35. Ibid., 26.

36. Ibid., 33–34.

37. Ibid., 51.

38. Ibid., 58.

39. Ibid., 80–81.

40. Ibid., 81.

41. Ibid., 83, 85–86.

42. Ibid., 89 and 93.

43. Ibid., 94 and 97.

44. Ibid., 200–201.

45. In his discussion of homosexuality, Thielicke referred exclusively to male relationships. However, he raised the question as to why female homosexuality was not punished as much as male homosexuality. He suggested that perhaps female homosexuality was punished less because it was less socially harmful. The female homosexual was not forced into the same "shady circumstances" as her male counterpart. This difference aside, Thielicke failed to see why the two forms of homosexuality should be "differentiated in value." Ibid., 269, 289.

46. Ibid., 271–72.

47. Ibid., 282–83.

48. Ibid., 283.

49. Celibacy was understood to be a vocation and thus not an option for most people. Ibid., 284.

50. A. N. Wilson, *C. S. Lewis: A Biography* (New York: W. W. Norton, 1990), 274. For others' comments on his work, see Lee W. Gibbs, "C. S. Lewis and the Anglican via Media," *Restoration Quarterly* 32, no. 2: 105; Norman Pittenger, "Apologist Versus Apologist: A Critique of C. S. Lewis as 'Defender of the Faith,'" *Christian Century* 75 (1958): 1104–7; C. S. Kilby, "C. S. Lewis: Everyman's Theologian," *Christianity Today* 8 (3 January 1964): 11–13; Edwin D. Cuffe, "Insight and Common Sense," *America* (3 September 1960): 602; and Michael Novak, "The Way Men Love," *Commonweal* 72 (19 August 1960): 430.

51. The primary source considered in these pages is Lewis's *The Four Loves*. His *Mere Christianity*, written years earlier, and an essay on the right to sexual happiness, published posthumously, provide supplemental material.

52. Lewis, *The Four Loves*, 91f, 102–3.

53. Ibid., 93.

54. Ibid., 90–91. It is interesting to note that one of Lewis's most intimate friends, Arthur Greeves, was homosexual. See Walter Hooper, ed., *They Stand Together: The Letters of C. S. Lewis and Arthur Greeves (1914–1963)* (New York: Macmillan, 1979).

55. Lewis, *The Four Loves*, 105.

56. Ibid., 98–99.

57. Lewis, *Mere Christianity*, 91.

58. Ibid., 92.

59. Ibid.

60. Lewis, *The Four Loves*, 132.

61. Ibid., 136–37, 139–40. Compare the Lewisian concept of "Venus" to Nygren's "Vulgar Eros."

62. C. S. Lewis, "We Have No 'Right to Happiness,'" in *God in the Dock*, 317–24. The same essay was published in *The Saturday Evening Post* a month after his death.

63. Ibid., 320.

64. Helmut Thielicke also argued this point. See *The Ethics of Sex*, 87–98.

65. Lewis, *God in the Dock*, 321–22.

66. Lewis himself did not marry until he was in his late fifties, although he lived with his "friend," Mrs. Moore, for several decades.

67. Lewis, *Mere Christianity*, 95–96.

68. Ibid., 102–3. The argument that the permanence of marriage is at some point dependent upon the headship of the husband was also made by Helmut Thielicke in *The Ethics of Sex*, 154–62.

69. Lewis, *The Four Loves*, 148–49.
70. Ibid., 20.
71. Ibid., 153.
72. Ibid., 158.
73. Ibid., 160.
74. Ibid., 169.
75. Bailey, *The Mystery of Love and Marriage*, ix.
76. See Franklin D. Elmer, "Review of *The Mystery of Love and Marriage*, by D. S. Bailey," *The Journal of Religion* 33 (July 1953): 231–32; and Henlee H. Barnette, "Review of *The Mystery of Love and Marriage*, by D. S. Bailey," *The Review and Expositor: A Baptist Theological Journal* 50 (April 1953): 252–53.
77. Robert M. Grant, "Review of *Sexual Relation in Christian Thought*, by D. S. Bailey," *The Journal of Religion* 40 (July 1960): 212–13. See also, Charles R. Stinnette, "Review of *Sexual Relation in Christian Thought*, by D. S. Bailey," *Anglican Theological Review* 42 (October 1960): 366–68.
78. Bailey, *Common Sense about Sexual Ethics*, 82.
79. Ibid., 87.
80. According to Bailey, same-sex association could not supply the same self-knowledge. Bailey even urged against single-sex schools for children as they could encourage "false sexual ideas." See D. S. Bailey, *Sexual Relation in Christian Thought* (New York: Harper and Row, 1959), 286.
81. Bailey reported that the twentieth century had seen "the latest, the most successful, and probably the last of several emancipation movements in the West." *Common Sense About Sexual Ethics*, 89–91.
82. Ibid., 92–93.
83. Ibid., 109–10.
84. Ibid., 113.
85. Bailey, *The Mystery of Love and Marriage*, 25.
86. Ibid., 27.
87. Ibid., 18.
88. Ibid., 19–20, 22.
89. Ibid., 53.
90. Ibid.
91. Bailey, *Common Sense About Sexual Ethics*, 97.
92. Ibid.
93. Ibid., 127.
94. Ibid., 134.

95. Ibid., 108.
96. Ibid.
97. Ibid.
98. Bailey chaired the Church of England Committee—the Moral Welfare Council—responsible for addressing concerns about homosexuality. The Moral Welfare Council provided three major documents to the Wolfenden Committee, including "The Problem of Homosexuality" (1954); "The Homosexual, the Law and Society" (1955); and "The Homosexual and Christian Morals" (1955). The three documents were published in D. S. Bailey (comp. and ed.), *Sexual Offenders and Social Punishment* (Being the Evidence Submitted on Behalf of the Church of England Moral Welfare Council to the Departmental Committee on Homosexual Offences and Prostitutions, with Other Materials Relating Thereto), (London: Church Information Office, 1956).

    For more information on the Wolfenden Report and its context, see chapter 12 in Jeffrey Weeks's commentary in *Sex, Politics, and Society,* and Jonathan Sinclair Carey, "D. S. Bailey and 'The Name Forbidden Among Christians,'" *Anglican Theological Review* 70 (April 1988): 152–73. See also Charles E. Raven, "Towards a Wholesome Sex Ethic" (review of Bailey's *Homosexuality and the Western Christian Tradition), The Expository Times* 66 (August 1955): 331.

99. Bailey also sought to reveal that "the legend of the 'persecution' of the homosexual by the Church" was an exaggeration, just as the idea of "warped and narrow-minded clerics, obsessed with a horror of sodomy, delivering hordes of innocuous inverts to the *vindices flammae*" was an "invention of modern rationalism." See Bailey, *Homosexuality and the Western Christian Tradition,* x.

100. Ibid., xi.
101. Ibid.
102. Sexual acts between women were mostly ignored by church and state. However, Bailey was convinced that, most often, it was the lesbian who interfered with heterosexual marriages by seducing married women and causing marriages to fail. Ibid., 162, 166.
103. Ibid., 169.
104. Bailey, *Sexual Offenders and Social Punishment,* 76.
105. Ibid., 94.

CHAPTER TWO

1. There are other issues under discussion, although they do not receive anywhere near the attention as do issues affecting lesbian women and gay men. These issues include sex beyond the perimeters of marriage and violence against women and children.

2. The northern (United Presbyterian Church, USA) and southern (Presbyterian Church in the U.S.) branches of the Presbyterian Church, which had originally split during the Civil War, merged in 1983. The merger of the more progressive northern churches with the more conservative southern churches preceded a time of institutional retrenchment. The national headquarters moved from New York City to Louisville, Ky., in 1988.

3. See Calvin Gay (pseud.), "To the Presbyterians on Homosexuality: You Spoke from Ignorance," *Christianity and Crisis* 38 (30 October 1978): 254–59; Chris Glaser, *Uncommon Calling: A Gay Man's Struggle to Serve the Church* (San Francisco: Harper and Row, 1988); and C. Dwight Smith, Jr., "Presbyterians on Homosexuality: Studying 'Others,' Finding Self," *Christianity and Crisis* (20 February 1978): 22–27.

4. *Presbyterians and Human Sexuality* (Louisville: The Office of the General Assembly, Presbyterian Church (USA), 1991). See also John J. Carey, "The Presbyterian Church and Sexuality: Why This? Why Now?" *Church and Society* 80 (November–December 1989): 1–5. The report is discussed further in the pages which follow.

5. Recorded in the *General Assembly Minutes*, 1991.

6. Adopted by the General Conference as part of the social principles, as printed in *The Book of Discipline of The United Methodist Church* (Nashville: United Methodist Publishing House, 1992), 91–92.

7. As quoted by Gail Hovey, "In the Matter of Rose Mary Denman: Life and Times of a Minister," *Christianity and Crisis* 47, no. 16 (9 November 1987): 379.

8. Reported in *Open Hands*, summer 1992.

9. *The United Methodist Newscope* (28 January 1994). In June 1990, the Western Pennsylvania Annual Conference passed a resolution further defining a "practicing" homosexual as a person who is "emotionally, mentally, spiritually, or physically practicing." *Open Hands* (spring 1992).

10. The House of Bishops is one of two legislative houses in the Episcopal Church. The other legislative house is the House of Deputies, which consists of a clerical order and a lay order.

11. The House of Bishops, "The Port St. Lucie Pastoral Letter," October 1977.

12. Ibid. Psychiatrist and theologian Ruth Tiffany Barnhouse also argued against the acceptability of homosexuality, insisting that the *imago Dei* was "not complete without both man and woman." "Homosexuality," *Anglican Theological Review*, Supplementary Series 6 (June 1976): 107–34 (especially 127 and 130).

13. "Commission: Statement on Homosexual Priests," *The Living Church*, 1 July 1979, 6. That same year, the first open and affirming lesbian woman, Ellen Barrett, was ordained to the priesthood by the Rt. Rev. Paul Moore, bishop of the Diocese of New York.

14. Ibid.

15. Emphasis mine. Recorded in "Summary of General Convention Actions," *The Daily of the General Convention of the Episcopal Church*, 20 September 1979.

16. The recommendatory nature of the resolution was also stressed by the bishops in a pastoral letter to the national church. The resolution was to be interpreted as offering guidance on the question, not legislation. See "Toward Tomorrow: A Pastoral Letter from the House of Bishops," *The Living Church*, 21 October 1979, 13–14.

17. A dissenting statement, signed by 23 bishops and 136 deputies, focused on the recommendatory nature of the resolution. Expressing appreciation for the ordained ministries of known homosexual persons "formerly and presently engaged in the service of this church," the resolution asserted that many homosexual relationships contained "a redeeming quality" . . . which was "no less a sign to the world of God's love than . . . Christian marriage." They added:

> We have no intention of ordaining irresponsible persons, or persons whose manner of life is such as to cause grave scandal or hurt to other Christians; but we do not believe that either homosexual orientation as such, nor the responsible and self-giving use of such a mode of sexuality, constitutes a scandal in and of itself.

> [Recorded in *The Daily of the General Convention of The Episcopal Church* (18 September 1979).]

18. Gustav Niebuhr, "Episcopalians Soften Stance on Sexuality,"

New York Times, 25 August 1994, A13; conversation with Carter Heyward, 2 September 1994.

19. "Lutheran 'Sex Wars'" in *Open Hands* (winter 1994): 28 and *The Lutheran* (April 1994): 33.

20. *The Lutheran* (January 1994): 37.

21. Evangelican Lutheran Church in America, *Visions and Expectations: Ordained Ministers in the Evangelical Lutheran Church in America* (1990), 13.

22. *Report of the Special Committee on Human Sexuality: Majority Report* (Louisville, Ky.: Office of the General Assembly, Presbyterian Church, USA): 11. [Hereafter referred to as *The Presbyterian Sexuality Report.*]

23. By way of comparison, the United Methodist report refers to Scripture as "the primary source and criterion for Christian doctrine." See *The Church Studies Homosexuality: A Study for United Methodist Groups Using the Report of the Commission to Study Homosexuality* (Nashville: Cokesbury, 1994), 16. The ELCA report views Scripture as "our interpretive center." *The Church and Human Sexuality: A Lutheran Perspective, First Draft of a Social Statement* (Chicago: Division for Church and Society of the Evangelical Lutheran Church in America, October 1993), 2.

24. *Presbyterians and Human Sexuality,* 9–10.

25. Ibid.

26. Ibid., 21–22.

27. Ibid., 28.

28. Ibid., 54.

29. All the denominational reports denounce violence against women and children, as well as against lesbian women and gay men.

30. The report also notes that, in the context of a patriarchal culture, women have denied themselves by turning over their lives to men when such self-denial has not been expected of men. The continual expectation of self-denial is sinful. See Susan Dunfee Nelson, "The Sin of Hiding: A Feminist Critique of Reinhold Niebuhr's Account of the Sin of Pride" in *Soundings* 65, no. 3 (February 1982): 321–22. Quoted in *The Sexuality Report,* 35.

31. *The Presbyterian Sexuality Report,* 33.

32. Jerry Van Marter, quoted by Randall L. Frame, "Sexuality Report Draws Fire," *Christianity Today* 35 (29 April 1991): 37.

33. Jim Gittings, "A Bonfire in Baltimore: Presbyterian Task Force

Reports on Sexuality." *Christianity and Crisis* 27 (May 1991): 177.

34. Ibid., 172–73.

35. Rose Mary Denman, "Looking Forward, Looking Back," *Christianity and Crisis* 48, no. 1 (1 February 1988): 7.

36. See Hovey, "In the Matter of Rose Mary Denman," 379–80.

37. Conversation with Frank Wulf, 25 May 1994.

38. Elizabeth Carl received the dubious distinction of having George Bush comment on the unacceptability of her ordination. Dorothy Mills Parker, "Avowed Lesbian Ordained Priest in Washington," *The Living Church*, 30 June 1991, 6; Bishop Ronald Haines, "Statement Before Ordination of Elizabeth Carl," *Episcopal Life* (July 1991): 19; and "Lesbian Ordained," *The Christian Century* 108 (26 June–3 July 1991): 647.

39. "Bishops 'Disassociate' from Newark Ordination," *The Living Church* (14 October 1990): 8; John S. Spong, "A Call to Confront Homophobia," *The Witness* 73, no. 11 (November 1990): 22–25; and Richard Walker, "Bishops Narrowly Reject Homosexual Ordination," *Christianity Today* 34 (22 October 1990): 55.

40. "Retired Bishop Reveals He's Gay," *Episcopal Life* (October 1993): 6.

41. "Lesbian's Call to New York Approved: Synod Says Grandfather Clause Protects Jane Spahr," *The Presbyterian Layman* 25, no. 5 (September–October 1992): 1, 4.

42. Ari L. Goldman, "Highest Presbyterian Panel Bars Homosexual Minister," *New York Times*, 5 November 1992, B21. A documentary of the Spahr case is an invaluable educational tool. See "Maybe We're Talking About a Different God—Homosexuality and the Church," directed by John Ankele, produced by Mary Byrne Hoffman, distributed by Current Production Group, 423 West 55th St., New York, N.Y. 10018.

43. At the 1994 General Assembly of the Presbyterian Church, a resolution prohibiting the blessing of same-sex unions was passed. It has yet to be approved by the Presbyteries. See "Ministers 'Not Permitted' to Bless Same-Sex Unions," *The Presbyterian Layman* 27, no. 4 (July/August 1994): 1, 8.

44. Doug LeBlanc, "Conservatives Feel Betrayed by 'Affirmation Service,'" *United Voice* (November 1992): 1–2. The Rev. Dr. Harvey Guthrie was dean of Episcopal Divinity School until 1985.

45. Memo from James D. Brown, executive director of the Presbyterian Church (USA) General Assembly Council, 19 May 1994. See also Peter Steinfels, "Cries of Heresy after Feminists Meet," *New York Times*, 14 May 1994, 28.

46. As quoted in Robert P. Mills, "GA's ReImagining Report Affirms Boundaries," *The Presbyterian Layman* 27, no. 4 (July/August 1994): 1.

47. See chapter 1 for a detailing of the complementarity theory.

48. *The Presbyterian Sexuality Report*, 110.

49. The minority report consistently used the term *homosexual* rather than *lesbian* and *gay*.

50. *The Presbyterian Sexuality Report*, 112–13.

51. Ibid. The minority report cites Gen. 39, 2 Sam. 11, Matt. 5:28, and Heb. 13:4 as supporting this emphasis. Regarding the passages cited for the condemnation of homosexuality, see Lev. 18:22, Lev. 20:13, Gen. 19, Judges 19:22, 1 Cor. 6:9–10, Rom. 1:26–27, 1 Tim. 1:10, 2 Pet. 2:6–7, and Jude 7.

    The minority report also noted that the arguments of scholars such as Robin Scroggs, George Edwards, and John Boswell which attempt to "neutralize" the bible's message about homosexuality are simply without substance because they "overpress the evidence" and lack accuracy in "linguistic matters." See the minority report, 112. For further reference, see Robin Scroggs, *The New Testament and Homosexuality: Contextual Background for Contemporary Debate* (Philadelphia: Fortress Press, 1983); George R. Edwards, *Gay/Lesbian Liberation: A Biblical Perspective* (New York: The Pilgrim Press, 1984); and John Boswell, *Christianity, Social Tolerance, and Homosexuality* (Chicago: Univ. of Chicago Press, 1980).

52. *The Presbyterian Sexuality Report*, 118–19.

53. James R. Edwards, "Eros Deified," *Christianity Today* 35, no. 6 (27 May 1991): 15.

54. Rev. James Miller, Charlotte, North Carolina, quoted in "Sexuality Report Widely Condemned," *The Presbyterian Layman* 24, no. 3 (May/June 1991): 1, 3.

55. Edwards, "Eros Deified," 14.

56. The Rt. Rev. Edmond Browning, "Bridge-Building in a Divided Church," *The Witness* (January 1987): 2–3.

57. Statement by the Presiding Bishop and the Council of Advice, 20 February 1990. Emphasis mine.

58. House of Bishops statement, quoted in "Bishops 'Disassociate'

from Newark Ordination," *The Living Church,* 14 October 1990, 8, 15. Emphasis mine.

59. The Episcopal Synod of America (ESA) has threatened to leave the Episcopal Church over the issues of the ordination of women, inclusive language, homosexuality, and abortion. They are vehemently opposed to all four of those issues. For more on the conservative wing of the Episcopal Church, see Susan Erdey, "A Pre-Convention Rundown on the Right: Who's Who Among Traditionalists," *The Witness* 74, no. 6 (June 1991): 14–17.

60. "Bishops 'Disassociate' from Newark Ordination," 15.

61. Pastoral Statement of the House of Bishops as recorded in "Bishops Release Pastoral Statement," *The Living Church,* 28 (October 1990): 7.

62. The statement was signed by 3,600 lay and clergy people. Reported in *The Lutheran* (May 1994). Another statement, recently released by a second group of seminary faculty, is much more positive.

63. *The Lutheran* (January 1994): 37.

64. Rex Reed, "Church, State, and Sexuality," *The Lutheran* (January 1994): 63.

65. Jeff R. Johnson, "Chilstrom Meets with Alliance," *Voice and Vision* (February 1994): 4.

66. Edwards, "Eros Deified," 14.

67. Lewis, *Mere Christianity,* 92. See discussion in chapter 1.

68. Recorded in the *General Assembly Minutes,* 1991.

69. Excerpt from the interim report to the Episcopal House of Bishops by the Commission on Human Affairs and Health, 30 September 1987. See also the General Convention statements of 1979, 1988, and 1991.

70. See Fleming Rutledge, "Living Together Outside Marriage Is Selfish, Anti-Social, Individualistic," *The Episcopalian* (March 1987): 8–9, 11, 21. This is also the argument of traditionalist groups such as The Prayer Book Society, The Episcopal Synod of America, Episcopalians United, and *The Presbyterian Layman.*

71. April Allison, "Re-Imagining Backlash Hits Church Women," reprinted in *CLOUTreach* 3, no. 1 (spring 1994): 4. See also Robert R. Mills, "GA's ReImagining Report," 1, 4.

72. Episcopal House of Bishops statement on homosexual unions, 1977.

73. "Every ordinand is expected to lead a life which is a wholesome

example to all people." 1979 General Convention statement. This is also to be found in the Book of Common Prayer, 517, 532, 544.

74. Bailey, *Sex Offenders and Social Punishment*, 76.

75. Nygren, *Agape and Eros*, 222.

76. The feminist-womanist interpretations of the importance of self-love are elaborated upon in chapters 3 through 5. See Saiving, "The Human Situation: A Feminine View"; see also Barbara Hilkert Andolsen, "Agape in Feminist Ethics," *The Journal of Religious Ethics* 9, no. 1 (spring 1981): 69–83. In addition, mainstream critics of Nygren have challenged his insistence on the incompatibility of self-love and christian Agape. See, for example, D'Arcy, chapter 3, passim; Wallace Gray, "Human Inquiry into Divine Love," *Communio Viatorum: A Theological Quarterly*, 25, nos. 1–2 (1982): 25–34; Gene Outka, *Agape: An Ethical Analysis* (New Haven, Conn.: Yale Univ. Press, 1972), chapter 2; and Rist, 156–73.

77. The texts drawn from include Briggs, "Sexual Justice and the 'Righteousness of God'"; Rita Nakashima Brock, *Journeys by Heart: A Christology of Erotic Power* (New York: Crossroad, 1988); Tom F. Driver, *Christ in a Changing World: Toward an Ethical Christology* (New York: Crossroad, 1981); Marvin M. Ellison, "Common Decency: A New Christian Sexual Ethic," *Christianity and Crisis*, 50 (12 November 1990): 352–56 and *Sexual Justice: Reframing Christian Sexual Ethics* (forthcoming); Beverly W. Harrison, "Human Sexuality and Mutuality," *Christian Feminism: Visions of a New Humanity*, ed. Judith L. Weidman (San Francisco: Harper and Row, 1984), 141–57; Heyward, *Touching Our Strength*; Mary Hunt, *Fierce Tenderness: A Feminist Theology of Friendship* (New York: Crossroad, 1991); and James B. Nelson, *Embodiment: An Approach to Sexuality and Christian Theology* (Minneapolis: Augsburg Publishing House, 1978).

CHAPTER THREE

1. See Alice Echols, *Daring to Be Bad: Radical Feminism in America, 1967–1975* (Minneapolis: Univ. of Minnesota Press, 1989); Ferguson, *Blood at the Root*; Cherríe Moraga and Gloria Anzaldúa, eds., *This Bridge Called My Back: Writings of Radical*

Women of Color (Watertown, Mass.: Persephone Press, 1981); Barbara Smith, ed., *Home Girls: A Black Feminist Anthology* (New York: Kitchen Table, Women of Color Press, 1983).

2. This movement in feminist liberation theo-ethical analysis was rooted primarily on the East Coast at Union Theological Seminary in New York City and Episcopal Divinity School in Cambridge, Mass. To date, EDS is the only seminary that offers graduate degrees in feminist liberation theology.

3. Cheryl J. Sanders, Katie G. Cannon, Emilie M. Townes, Shawn M. Copeland, bell hooks, and Cheryl Townsend Gilkes, "Christian Ethics and Theology in Womanist Perspective," *Journal of Feminist Studies in Religion* 5, no. 2 (fall 1989): 83–112.

4. Ada María Isasi-Díaz, Elena Olazagasti-Segovia, Sandra Mangual-Rodriguez, Maria Antoinetta Berriozábal, Daisy L. Machado, Lordes Arguelles, and Raven-Anne Rivero, "*Mujeristas:* Who We Are and What We Are About," *Journal of Feminist Studies in Religion* 8, no. 1 (spring 1992): 105–26.

5. See, for example, The Boston Women's Health Book Collective, *Our Bodies, Ourselves: A Book by and for Women* (New York: Simon and Schuster, 1984); Moraga and Anzaldúa, *This Bridge Called My Back;* Carole S. Vance, ed., *Pleasure and Danger: Exploring Female Sexuality* (Boston: Routledge and Kegan Paul, 1984); and Ann Snitow, Christine Stansell, and Sharon Thompson, eds., *Powers of Desire: The Politics of Sexuality* (New York: Monthly Review Press, 1983). Theological literature includes Saiving, "The Human Situation: A Feminine View"; Penelope Washbourn, "Becoming Woman: Menstruation as Spiritual Experience," in *WomanSpirit Rising,* ed. Carol Christ and Judith Plaskow (San Francisco: Harper and Row, 1979. Originally published, 1960); and Carter Heyward, "Liberating the Body," in *Our Passion for Justice* (New York: The Pilgrim Press, 1984), 137–47.

6. Audre Lorde, "Uses of the Erotic: The Erotic as Power" in *Sister Outsider: Essays and Speeches by Audre Lorde* (Trumansburg, N.Y.: The Crossing Press, 1984): 53–59.

7. Ibid., 53–54.

8. Ibid., 54.

9. Ibid., 57.

10. Ibid., 53.

11. Ibid., 56.

12. Ibid., 54.
13. Nelle Morton, "The Goddess as Metaphoric Image," in *The Journey Is Home* (Boston: Beacon Press, 1985), 166.
14. Beverly W. Harrison, "Misogyny and Homophobia," 149.
15. See Saiving. Originally published in 1960, this was one of the earliest feminist theological pieces on the male definition and control of love.
16. Beverly W. Harrison, "The Power of Anger in the Work of Love: Christian Ethics for Women and Other Strangers," in *Making the Connections: Essays in Feminist Social Ethics*, ed. Carol Robb (Boston: Beacon Press, 1985), 12, 14, 18.
17. See Andolsen.
18. To the best of my knowledge, Sheila Briggs identifies herself not as a womanist theologian, but as a Black feminist. She currently teaches at the University of Southern California.
19. Rita Nakashima Brock currently teaches at Hamline University in Minneapolis.
20. Carter Heyward currently teaches theology at the Episcopal Divinity School in Cambridge, Mass. She was among the first eleven women irregularly ordained to the priesthood of the Episcopal Church in 1974.
21. Briggs, 251.
22. Ibid., 272.
23. Ibid.
24. The division of love into eros and agape encourages the exploitation of women in that the control of eros means the control of sexuality. The control of sexuality means that women are constrained into particular roles which maintain the complementarity theory. See, for example, Lewis's insistence on male headship in *Mere Christianity*, 102–3.
25. Briggs, 273.
26. Ibid.
27. Ibid., 272.
28. Ibid.
29. Ibid.
30. Ibid., 275.
31. Ibid., 274.
32. Ibid., 275.
33. Ibid., 274.
34. See discussion in chapter 1.
35. Brock, 46.

36. Ibid., 26.
37. Ibid., 25–26, 40.
38. Ibid., xiv.
39. Ibid.
40. Ibid., xv.
41. Ibid., 25. Brock draws heavily upon Haunani-Kay Trask's concept of the feminist eros in *Eros and Power: The Power of Feminist Theory* (Philadelphia: Univ. of Pennsylvania Press, 1986).
42. Brock, 26.
43. Ibid.
44. Ibid., 34.
45. Ibid., 39–40.
46. Ibid., 40.
47. Ibid., 41, 45.
48. Ibid., 46.
49. Ibid., 26.
50. Thielicke, 51, and Brock, 25–26.
51. Brock, 40.
52. Ibid., 39–40. See also chapter 1.
53. Heyward, *Touching Our Strength*, 98.
54. Ibid., 89, 94.
55. Ibid., 98.
56. Ibid., 95.
57. Ibid., 99.
58. Ibid.
59. Ibid., 93.
60. Ibid., 24.
61. Ibid., 94. See also Beverly W. Harrison, "The Power of Anger in the Work of Love," 3–21.
62. Heyward, *Touching Our Strength*, 105.
63. Ibid., 33.
64. Ibid., 191.
65. Ibid., 104–5, 191.
66. Ibid., 33.
67. Carter Heyward, "Sexuality, Love, and Justice" in *Our Passion for Justice: Images of Power, Sexuality, and Liberation* (New York: The Pilgrim Press, 1984): 86.
68. Heyward, *Touching Our Strength*, 95.
69. Ibid., 99.
70. Ibid., 33. See Nygren, 51–52.

71. Lewis, *The Four Loves*, 91, and Bailey, *Common Sense about Sexual Ethics*, 134.
72. Heyward, *Touching Our Strength*, 105.
73. Brock, 45.
74. Briggs, 272.
75. Heyward, *Touching Our Strength*, 34.
76. Ibid., 34, 129.
77. Judith Plaskow, *Standing Again at Sinai: Judaism from a Feminist Perspective* (San Francisco: Harper and Row, 1990), 203–4.
78. Brock, 107.
79. Ibid., 107–8.
80. Beverly W. Harrison, "The Power of Anger in the Work of Love," 11.
81. Ibid.
82. Plaskow, *Standing Again at Sinai*, 210.

CHAPTER FOUR

1. Kathleen Sands also makes this point in her article "Uses of the Thea(o)logian: Sex and Theodicy in Religious Feminism" in *Journal of Feminist Studies in Religion* 8, no. 1 (spring 1992): 9. One notable exception to this observation is an essay jointly authored by Beverly W. Harrison and Carter Heyward. See "Pain and Pleasure: Avoiding the Confusions of Christian Tradition in Feminist Theory," in *Christianity, Patriarchy, and Abuse: A Feminist Critique*, ed. Joanne Carlson Brown and Carole R. Bohn (New York: The Pilgrim Press, 1989), 148–73. In addition, Heyward addresses some of the contemporary secular feminist concerns in *Touching Our Strength*.

   Feminist liberation theo-ethicists have been slower to talk about sex and sexuality than secular feminists, I suspect, because of the repression of sex and sexuality in mainstream theology and churches.
2. Radical cultural feminist theorists include such thinkers as Kathleen Barry, Mary Daly, Andrea Dworkin, Susan Griffin, Audre Lorde, and Robin Morgan. Most radical cultural feminists understand the roots of women's oppression to be men. Furthermore, radical cultural feminists believe that the solution to sexism is the reassertion of the female principle. Biological explana-

tions of gender differences are commonly invoked, and male sexuality is characterized as "compulsive, violent, potentially lethal, and genitally oriented" while female sexuality is perceived as being "muted, diffuse, and interpersonally oriented. See Robin Morgan, "Lesbianism and Feminism: Synonyms or Contradictions?" *Going Too Far* (New York: Random House, 1977).

Libertarian feminist theory has developed primarily around the issue of sexuality. The expression of sexuality is celebrated and is connected to good health, individual happiness, and social progress. Libertarian feminism understands human sexuality as an exchange of pleasure and is organized around resisting sexual repression. Libertarian feminists urge women to reclaim control over their sexuality and demand the right to engage in whatever proffers pleasure, regardless of whether or not the particular sexual practices (sadomasochism, cruising, adult/child sexuality, and nonmonogamy) have been traditionally characterized as "male" pursuits. In short, those who identify with this stream of feminist theory support sexual relationships between consenting partners who seek sexual pleasure by any means. Among those theorists supporting this position are Amber Hollibaugh, Gayle Rubin, Carole S. Vance, and Ann Barr Snitow.

See also, Estelle B. Freedman and Barrie Thorne, "Introduction to 'The Feminist Sexuality Debates'"; Ann Ferguson, "Sex War: The Debate Between Radical and Libertarian Feminists"; Ilene Philipson, "The Repression of History and Gender: A Critical Perspective on the Feminist Sexuality Debate"; and Irene Diamond and Lee Quinby, "American Feminism in the Age of the Body." All are found in *Signs: Journal of Women in Culture and Society* 10, no. 1 (autumn 1984): 102–35.

3. See discussion in Steven Seidman, *Embattled Eros: Sexual Politics and Ethics in Contemporary America* (New York: Routledge, 1992), 104–6.

4. Heyward, *Touching Our Strength.*

5. Ferguson, *Blood at the Root,* 147.

6. This type of danger is elaborated upon to some extent in chapter 5.

7. See Sands for an elaboration, 22–23.

8. This refers to sex workers and women who stay married for purely economic reasons. This group includes women with varying degrees of privilege and marginalization. See Elizabeth M. Bounds, "Sexuality and Economic Reality: A First World and

Third World Comparison," in *Redefining Sexual Ethics: A Source-book of Essays, Stories, and Poems*, ed. Susan E. Davies and Elea-nor H. Haney (Cleveland: Pilgrim Press, 1991), 131–44.

9. Beverly W. Harrison, "The Power of Anger in the Work of Love," 11.

10. Brock, 26.

11. Briggs, 251.

12. Heyward, *Touching Our Strength*, 105.

13. Kathleen Sands also has challenged the feminist theological ide-alism regarding eros in "Powers, Pleasures, and Goods: An Invi-tation to Conversation on Lesbian Sex," a paper presented at the Lesbian Theology Group at the American Academy of Reli-gion (Kansas City, Mo., 1991).

14. I am primarily concerned about the cycles of eroticized violence generated by a distorted and controlled eros. What this means for the sexuality of white heterosexual men is important work and is being done by people like James Nelson, Paul Kivel, and Marvin Ellison. See, for example, James Nelson, *The Intimate Connection: Male Sexuality, Masculine Spirituality* (Philadelphia, Westminster Press, 1988); Paul Kivel, *Men's Work: How to Stop the Violence That Tears Our Lives Apart* (New York: Ballantine Books, 1992); and Marvin Ellison, "Men, Feminism, and Sexu-ality," *Christianity and Crisis* 48 (7 November 1988): 400–402, and *Sexual Justice: Reframing Christian Sexual Ethics* (forth-coming).

15. One of the problems with Nelson's earlier work was that he did not claim the male perspective from which he was offering de-scriptions of sexuality. This is important because as a white, het-erosexual man in a racist, heterosexist, and sexist society, the particularities of his social location influence how he under-stands and experiences sexuality. Since then, he has acknowl-edged the extent to which his maleness influences his theology. See *The Intimate Connection*.

16. James Nelson, *Embodiment*, 39–40.

17. Ibid., 40.

18. John Stoltenberg, "Gays and the Propornography Movement: Having the Hots for Sex Discrimination," in *Men Confront Pornography*, ed. Michael S. Kimmel (New York: Crown Pub-lishers, 1990), 254–55.

19. James Nelson, *The Intimate Connection*, 72–73. Marvin Ellison also connects warfare and sexual violence in "'Seeking a Now

That Can Breed Futures': Reflections on Male Sexuality, Nuclearism, and Sexual Violence," unpublished paper, 1987.

20. Paul Kivel, 77–132.
21. James Nelson, *The Intimate Connection,* 74. Emphasis mine.
22. Marie Marshall Fortune, *Sexual Violence: The Unmentionable Sin* (New York: The Pilgrim Press, 1983), 14–41.
23. Harrison and Heyward, "Pain and Pleasure," 150.
24. Intimate violence includes child, pet, partner, and elder abuse. Margaret A. Mayman uses this term in *Intimate Violence: Implications for Theories of Moral Agency* (New York: Union Theological Seminary, 1995). See also R. Emerson Dobash and Russell Dobash, *Violence Against Wives: A Case Against the Patriarchy* (New York: The Free Press, 1979); and Susan Schechter, *Women and Male Violence: The Visions and Struggles of the Battered Women's Movement* (Boston: South End Press, 1982).
25. For more on heterosexism and the limits of liberal theology, see Carter Heyward, "Heterosexist Theology: Being Above It All," *Journal of Feminist Studies in Religion* 3, no. 1 (spring 1987): 29–38. This article was developed further in Heyward's *Touching Our Strength.*
26. Thielicke, 51. C. S. Lewis argued that a man should be the dominant partner in a marriage. See *Mere Christianity,* 102–3.
27. R. Emerson Dobash and Russell Dobash, *Women, Violence, and Social Change* (London: Routledge, 1992), especially chapters 1 and 8.
28. Statistics on intimate violence in the United States include the following: a man beats a woman every twelve seconds; every day, at least four women die violently at the hands of men who profess to love them; and, in 1991, more than twenty-one thousand domestic assaults, rapes, and murders were reported to police *every week.* See the U.S. Senate Committee on the Judiciary, "Violence Against Women: A Week in the Life of America," Majority Staff Report (Washington: Government Printing Office, October 1992), 33. See also Marilyn French, *The War Against Women* (New York: Summit Press, 1992); and Ann Jones, *Next Time She'll Be Dead: Battering and How to Stop It* (Boston: Beacon Press, 1994).
29. Susan Schechter, 224.
30. Ellison, "'Seeking a Now That Can Breed Futures,'" 33–34.

31. It has also been documented that rapists experience a certain amount of elation in completing a rape. See Diana E. M. Russell, *The Politics of Rape: The Victim's Perspective* (New York: Stein and Day, 1975), 244–45.

32. For more on violence against lesbian women and gay men see The Anti-Violence Project, National Gay and Lesbian Task Force, "Statements on Anti-Gay Violence by Religious, Political, and Law Enforcement Leaders: An Organizing Resource" (Washington, D.C., 20 November 1989); Gary David Comstock, *Violence Against Lesbians and Gay Men* (New York: Columbia Univ. Press, 1991); John P. DeCecco, ed., *Bashers, Baiters and Bigots: Homophobia in American Society* (New York: Harrington Park Press, 1985); and Randy Shilts, *The Mayor of Castro Street: The Life and Times of Harvey Milk* (New York: St. Martin's Press, 1982).

33. Suzanne Pharr, *Homophobia: A Weapon of Sexism* (Inverness, Calif.: Chardon Press, 1988), 18.

34. Pharr, *Homophobia: A Weapon of Sexism,* 19.

35. Heyward, "Heterosexist Theology: Being Above It All," 30.

36. Thielicke, 282–83.

37. Lewis, *Mere Christianity,* 95–96.

38. Bailey, *Homosexuality and the Western Christian Tradition,* 166.

39. Beverly W. Harrison, "Misogyny and Homophobia," 136.

40. According to the Princeton Religion Research Center on Emerging Trends, September 1993, a July survey by Gallup found that 44 percent of U.S. adults believe AIDS is the result of God's punishment for immoral sexual behavior. Quoted in *The United Methodist Newscope,* 12 November 1993, 1. This reasoning is faulty, for if God is punishing "gays" by AIDS, God must really love lesbians, who have a much lower incidence of contracting AIDS than the general population. Furthermore, the logic breaks down when we are faced with those who are not gay who contract AIDS. For more on AIDS and violence, see Maine Civil Liberties Union, Maine Lesbian/Gay Political Alliance, and Univ. of Southern Maine, Department of Social Welfare, "Discrimination and Violence Survey of Gay People in Maine" (Portland: Univ. of Southern Maine, Department of Social Welfare, 1985). See also Kevin Gordon, "Religion, Moralizing, and AIDS: A Theological/Pastoral Essay," in *Homosexuality and Social Justice,* ed. Kevin Gordon (San Francisco:

The Consultation on Homosexuality, Social Justice, and Roman Catholic Theology, 1986), 206–32; and Cindy Patton, *Sex and Germs: The Politics of AIDS* (Boston: South End Press, 1985).

41. Violence against lesbian women and gay men is nearly a non-issue in the churches, although all four denominations include in their policies on homosexuality a denunciation of such violence. Slowly, over the last decade, mainline denominations have begun to realize the seriousness and extent of domestic and sexual violence. This awareness, however, has been excruciatingly slow in coming and equally as slow in generating a constructive response. See Mary D. Pellauer, Barbara Chester, and Jane Boyajian, eds., *Sexual Assault and Abuse: A Handbook for Clergy and Religious Professionals* (San Francisco: Harper and Row, 1987).

42. The "Women in Crisis" Committee of the Episcopal Diocese of Massachusetts is one example.

43. See Comstock; see also Kevin Gordon, ed., *Homosexuality and Social Justice.*

    It is important to note that many of the theological justifications discussed in what follows, as well as the strategies of ecclesiastical hierarchies, are present in both the issues affecting battered and sexually abused women and children and lesbian/gay survivors of physical and sexual violence.

44. See "Summary of General Convention Actions" in *The Daily of the General Convention of the Episcopal Church* (20 September 1979).

45. See chapter 2 above. This is similar to Bailey's distinctions between homosexual inverts and homosexual perverts. D. S. Bailey, *Homosexuality and the Western Christian Tradition,* xi.

46. For more on the effects of eroticized violence on spirituality, see Joanne Carlson Brown and Carole R. Bohn, eds., *Christianity, Patriarchy, and Abuse;* Marvin M. Ellison, "Sexuality and Spirituality: An Intimate—and Intimidating—Connection," *Church and Society* 80 (November–December 1989): 29; Fortune, *Sexual Violence: The Unmentionable Sin;* Heyward, *Touching Our Strength;* Annie Imbens and Ineke Jonker, *Christianity and Incest* (Minneapolis: Fortress Press, 1992); James Nelson, *The Intimate Connection;* and Pellauer, Chester, and Boyajian, eds., *Sexual Assault and Abuse.*

47. Heyward, *Touching Our Strength,* 105.

48. Dorothee Sölle with Shirley A. Cloyes, *To Work and to Love: A Theology of Creation* (Philadelphia: Fortress Press, 1984), 126.

49. Ethicist Margaret A. Mayman would characterize this as empowerment to be a moral agent. She maintains that moral agency is about resistance to violence. Conversation in March 1993.

50. For a description of the lesbian tendency to romanticize intimacy, see Lee Zevy with Sahli A. Cavallaro, "Invisibility, Fantasy, and Intimacy: Princess Charming Is Not a Prince," in *Lesbian Psychologies: Explorations and Challenges*, ed. The Boston Lesbian Psychologies Collective (Chicago: Univ. of Illinois Press, 1987), 83–94.

51. *Oxford English Dictionary*, 2d ed., s.v. *boundary*.

52. The following discussion of boundaries is based upon a series of conversations over the last several years with Marvin Ellison, Ann Franklin, Robin Gorsline, Kathleen Greider, Beverly Harrison, Carter Heyward, Margaret Craddock Huff, Margaret Mayman, Allison Mauel Moore, Diane Moore, Nancy Hamlin Soukup, Wilma Wake, and Ann Wetherilt.

53. Cited by Heyward, *Touching Our Strength*, 112.

54. Ellen Bass and Laura Davis, *The Courage to Heal: A Guide for Women Survivors of Child Sexual Abuse* (New York: Harper and Row, 1988), 182–84, 231–32, 276–79, and 444–45.

55. Feminist liberation psychologists and theologians Susan DeMattos, Carter Heyward, Margaret Craddock Huff, and Janet Surrey have been in conversation on this topic for several years. Surrey and Heyward have worked on this subject at the Stone Center at Wellesley College, Wellesley, Mass. See also Heyward, *Touching Our Strength*, and *When Boundaries Betray Us: Beyond Illusions of What Is Ethical in Therapy and Life* (San Francisco: Harper and Row, 1993).

CHAPTER FIVE

1. James Nelson, *Body Theology* (Louisville, Ky.: Westminster/John Knox Press, 1992), 186.

2. Ibid., 23.

3. Heyward, *Touching Our Strength*, 187.

4. Heyward and Harrison, "Pain and Pleasure," 149. See also Harrison, "Misogyny and Homophobia."

5. Brock, *Journey by Heart*, 25–26, 39–40.
6. Plaskow, *Standing Again at Sinai*, 201.
7. *The Presbyterian Sexuality Report*, 9.
8. Heyward, *Touching Our Strength*, 187.
9. Brock, 36.
10. Sands, 11. See also "Powers, Pleasures, and Goods: An Invitation to Conversation on Lesbian Sex," unpublished paper given at The American Academy of Religion in Kansas City, Mo., November 1991.
11. The charge of idealism is meant to imply that feminist liberation theo-ethical descriptions of eros are not grounded in the realities of people's lives. While that may, indeed, be an ongoing struggle in feminist liberation theo-ethics, a commitment to ongoing race and class analysis can continue to make descriptions of eros more concrete and eros much more relevant to and reflective of people's lives.
12. Sands, 7.
13. For an elaboration of this norm, see Ellison, "Common Decency."
14. For an elaboration of this, see Heyward, *Touching Our Strength*, 105 f.
15. "Christian" is meant to signify the imperialistic, male-dominated aspects of christianity.
16. Tom F. Driver has influenced my thought on this matter. Maintaining that "transcendence is radical immanence," he observes that to say so is to risk the heresy of panentheism, adding that "once one starts on the road of immanence, it is better to go all the way." See Driver, *Patterns of Grace: Human Experience as Word of God* (San Francisco: Harper and Row, 1977), 164.
17. See also Heyward, *Touching Our Strength*, 91.
18. Tom F. Driver has elaborated in some detail upon this theme. He maintains that "God is no more in a once-for-all incarnation in Jesus than in our present, fragile moment. . . . " See *Christ in a Changing World*, 76 ff. Carter Heyward has also developed this idea in her work. See *The Redemption of God* and *Speaking of Christ: A Lesbian Feminist Voice* (New York: The Pilgrim Press, 1989). See also James Nelson, *Body Theology*, 50–52.
19. Nygren, *Agape and Eros*, 217. This sentiment was also reflected in Thielicke, Bailey, and Lewis.
20. The majority report of *The Presbyterian Sexuality Report* refers to this as "justice-love."

21. Ellison, "Sexuality and Spirituality," 29.

22. Tom F. Driver, *Patterns of Grace: Human Experience as Word of God* (San Francisco: Harper and Row, 1977), especially chapter 7.

23. Heyward, *Touching Our Strength*, 99.

24. Conversation with Robin Gorsline, Cambridge, Mass., 1986.

25. Conversation with Tom F. Driver, New York City, May 1993.

26. Heyward, *Touching Our Strength*, 99.

27. Elie Wiesel, *Night* (New York: Avon, 1969), 76.

28. In using the term *choice*, I do not mean to imply a bourgeois or liberal theory of choice. However, what I do mean by the term is that we have the power to choose how, and sometimes whether, to be in relation to one another. What I am talking about here is conscious movement to intimate, nurturing relationships that enhance survival.

29. See, for example, Kendall Harmon, "Deeply Disturbing Document," *The Living Church*, 15 May 1988, 13. In his response to a sexuality curriculum in the Episcopal Church, he remarked that it was scandalous, "nearly identifying our sexuality with God."

30. In the mid 1960s, Tom Driver explored the question of the sexuality of Jesus. See "Sexuality and Jesus," in *Union Seminary Quarterly Review*, 20, no. 3 (March 1965): 235–46. He elaborated upon the subject further in *Christ in a Changing World*.

31. Ann Kirkus Wetherilt, *That They May Be Many: Voices of Women, Echoes of God* (New York: Continuum, 1994).

32. For sources on sexuality from a variety of perspectives, see Nancie Caraway, *Segregated Sisterhood: Racism and the Politics of American Feminism* (Knoxville: Univ. of Tennessee Press, 1991); The Combahee River Collective, "The Combahee River Collective Statement," in *Home Girls: A Black Feminist Anthology*, ed. Barbara Smith (Latham, N.Y.: Kitchen Table, Women of Color Press, 1983); Debra Connors, "Disability, Sexism, and the Social Order," in *Redefining Sexual Ethics: A Sourcebook of Essays, Stories, and Poems*, ed. Susan E. Davies and Eleanor H. Haney (Cleveland: Pilgrim Press, 1991), 189–202; Angela Y. Davis, "We Do Not Consent: Violence Against Women in a Racist Society," in *Women, Culture, and Politics* (New York: Random House, 1989), 35–52; Renée L. Hill, "Who Are We for Each Other?: Sexism, Sexuality, and Womanist Theology," in *Black Theology: A Documentary History, Vol. II, 1980–1992*, ed. James H. Cone and Gayraud S. Wilmore (Maryknoll, N.Y.: Orbis Books, 1993),

345–53; bell hooks, "Moved by Passion: Eros and Responsibility," in *Sisters of the Yam: Black Women and Self-Recovery* (Boston: South End Press, 1993), 113–28; Melanie Kaye, "Some Notes on Jewish Lesbian Identity," in *Nice Jewish Girls: A Lesbian Anthology*, ed. Evelyn Torton Beck (Trumansburg, N.Y.: Crossing Press, 1982), 28–44; Audre Lorde, "I Am Your Sister: Black Women Organizing Across Sexualities," in *Making Face, Making Soul— Haciendo Caras: Creative and Critical Perspectives by Feminists of Color*, ed. Gloria Anzaldúa (San Francisco: Aunt Lute Books, 1990), 321–25; Papusa Molina, "Recognizing, Accepting, and Celebrating Our Differences," in *Making Face, Making Soul*, 326–34; Cherríe Moraga, *Loving in the War Years* (Boston: South End Press, 1983); and Emilie Townes, "The Price of the Ticket: Racism, Sexism, Heterosexism, and the Church in Light of the AIDS Crisis," in *Redefining Sexual Ethics*, 67–74.

33. Delores S. Williams has advocated womanist/feminist dialogue and posed some issues that need attention. See *Sisters in the Wilderness* (Maryknoll, N.Y.: Orbis Books, 1993), 178–203, and "Womanist/Feminist Dialogue: Problems and Possibilities," *Journal of Feminist Studies in Religion* 9, nos. 1–2 (spring/fall 1993): 67–74.

34. Emilie M. Townes describes the patriarchal depiction of the sexuality of African American women in "Roundtable Discussion: Backlash," *Journal of Feminist Studies in Religion* 10, no. 1 (spring 1994): 98–103.

35. Margaret C. Huff, "The Interdependent Self: An Integrated Concept from Feminist Theology and Feminist Psychology," *Philosophy and Theology* 2, no. 2 (1989): 160–72.

36. Heyward, *Touching Our Strength*, 104–6. See also *The Redemption of God*.

37. Beverly W. Harrison, "The Power of Anger in the Work of Love," 3–21.

38. Nelle Morton was responsible for raising up the image of homecoming. See *The Journey Is Home*.

39. Carter Heyward writes at some length about the sadomasochistic fabric of society. See *Touching Our Strength*, 106–9.

40. Ferguson, "Sex War: The Debate Between Radical and Libertarian Feminists," 111–12. See also *Blood at the Root*.

41. For a detailed exploration of sex and survivors of incest, see Bass and Davis, *The Courage to Heal*, 239–69. For lesbian survivors of eroticized violence, see JoAnn Loulan, *Lesbian Sex* (San Fran-

cisco: Spinsters Ink, 1984) and *Lesbian Passion: Loving Ourselves and Each Other* (San Francisco: Spinsters/ Aunt Lute, 1987).

42. My thought on this subject has been shaped substantially by ongoing conversations with Kathleen Greider, Margaret Craddock Huff, and Ann Kirkus Wetherilt. My earlier reflection on this topic was presented in the Women and Religion Section at the American Academy of Religion (New Orleans, La., 1990).

43. Delores S. Williams, *Sisters in the Wilderness*, 175.

44. See Elizabeth M. Bounds, "Sexuality and Economic Reality," in *Redefining Sexual Ethics*, 131–44.

45. Ibid., 160.

46. Conversations with Beverly W. Harrison, Carter Heyward, Margaret Craddock Huff, Allison Mauel Moore, and Ann Kirkus Wetherilt.

47. In characterizing the position of some in various survivor movements, it is also important to insist that it is not appropriate for abusers to challenge survivors. Those who have committed acts of eroticized violence such as incest, battering, rape, or bashing have no say in whether or not the particular survivor will communicate with them. Nor do they have any right to interpret the experiences of the survivors and the effects of those experiences on the survivors' lives. Conversations with Robin Gorsline and Margaret Mayman, 1992–1994.

48. By *speciesism*, I mean the human species' determination of what other species will continue to survive and thrive in our ecosystems.

49. James Edwards, "Eros Deified," 14.

CHAPTER SIX

Note: The shape of this chapter was influenced by ongoing conversations with Marvin M. Ellison, Robin H. Gorsline, Carter Heyward, and Margaret Mayman.

1. Ellison, "Sexuality and Spirituality," 29.

2. *The Presbyterian Sexuality Report*, 4.

3. Isasi-Díaz, "Solidarity: Love of Neighbor in the 1980s," 32–33.

4. Conversation with Robin H. Gorsline, April 1993.

5. Conversation with Marvin M. Ellison, April 1993.

6. The Unitarian Universalist Association, the United Church of Christ, and the Metropolitan Community Church are three Protestant denominations that have progressive policies on sexuality and are inclusive and affirming of lesbian women and gay men.

SELECTED BIBLIOGRAPHY

Allison, April. "Re-Imagining Backlash Hits Church Women." *CLOUTreach* (spring 1994): 4.

Andolsen, Barbara Hilkert. "Agape in Feminist Ethics." *The Journal of Religious Ethics* 9 (spring 1981): 69–83.

Anti-Violence Project, National Gay and Lesbian Task Force. *Statements on Anti-Gay Violence by Religious, Political, and Law Enforcement Leaders: An Organizing Resource.* Washington, D.C.: 20 November 1989.

Aries, Philippe, and Andre Bejin, eds. *Western Sexuality: Practice and Precept in Past and Present Times.* Translated by Anthony Forster. Oxford: Basil Blackwell, 1985.

Avis, Paul. *Eros and the Sacred.* Harrisburg, Pa.: Morehouse Publishing, 1989.

Babinsky, Ellen L. "How Far Forbearance? The Authority of the Presbytery Regarding Ordination." *Insights* 106 (spring 1991): 37–48.

Bailey, D. S. *Common Sense About Sexual Ethics: A Christian View.* New York: The Macmillan Company, 1962.

———. "Homosexuality and Christian Morals." In *They Stand Apart,* ed. J. Tudor Rees and Harvey V. Usil. London: William Heinemann, 1955.

———. *Homosexuality and the Western Christian Tradition.* London: Longmans, Green, and Company, 1955.

———. "Love and Marriage." Theology 44 (April/May 1942).

———. *The Mystery of Love and Marriage: A Study in the Theology of Sexual Relation.* New York: Harper and Brothers, 1952.

———. "The Problem of Sexual Inversion." *Theology* 55 (February 1952): 47–52.

———. *Sexual Relation in Christian Thought.* New York: Harper and Brothers, 1959.

———. "Sexual Relationship and the Command of God." *The Churchman* 67 (June 1953).

———, comp. and ed. *Sexual Offenders and Social Punishment.* London: Church Information Office, 1956.

Barnette, Henlee H. "Review of the Mystery of Love and Marriage by D. S. Bailey." *The Review and Expositor: A Baptist Theological Journal* 50 (April 1953): 252–53.

Barnhouse, Ruth Tiffany. *Homosexuality: A Symbolic Confusion.* New York: Seabury Press, 1977.

———. "Homosexuality." *Anglican Theological Review,* Supplementary Series 6 (June 1976): 107–34.

———. "Lasting Heterosexual Marriage Is Still the Paradigm Despite Failures." *The Episcopalian* (April 1987): 14, 29.

———. "Response to My Critics." *Anglican Theological Review* 59 (April 1977): 194–97.

Barnwell, William. "Gays and the Divorced: Similar Scars." *The Christian Century* 95 (4–11 January 1978): 29–30.

Barrington, Judith, ed. *An Intimate Wilderness: Lesbian Writers on Sexuality.* Portland, Ore.: The Eighth Mountain Press, 1991.

Bass, Ellen, and Laura Davis. *The Courage to Heal: A Guide for Women Survivors of Child Sexual Abuse.* New York: Harper and Row, 1988.

Batchelor, Edward, Jr., ed. *Homosexuality and Ethics.* New York: The Pilgrim Press, 1980.

Benjamin, Jessica. *The Bonds of Love: Psychoanalysis, Feminism, and the Problem of Domination.* New York: Pantheon Books, 1988.

Berliner, Arthur K. "Sex, Sin, and the Church: The Dilemma of Homosexuality." *Journal of Religion and Health* 26 (summer 1987): 137–42.

Boswell, John. *Christianity, Social Tolerance, and Homosexuality.* Chicago: Univ. of Chicago Press, 1980.

Bounds, Elizabeth M. "Sexuality and Economic Reality: A First World and Third World Comparison." In *Redefining Sexual Ethics: A Sourcebook of Essays, Stories, and Poems,* ed. Susan E. Davies and Eleanor H. Haney, 131–44. Cleveland: The Pilgrim Press, 1991.

Briggs, Sheila. "Sexual Justice and the 'Righteousness of God.'" In *Sex and God: Some Varieties of Women's Religious Experience,* ed. Linda Hurcombe. New York: Routledge and Kegan Paul, 1987.

Brock, Rita Nakashima. *Journeys by Heart: A Christology of Erotic Power.* New York: Crossroad, 1988.

Brown, Joanne Carlson, and Carole R. Bohn, eds. *Christianity, Patriarchy, and Abuse: A Feminist Critique.* New York: The Pilgrim Press, 1989.

Browning, Edmond. "Bridge-Building in a Divided Church." *The Witness* (January 1987): 2–3.

Bunch, Charlotte, et al. *Building Feminist Theory: Essays from Quest.* New York: Longman, 1981.

Burch, Beverly. "Barriers to Intimacy: Conflicts over Power, Dependency, and Nurturing in Lesbian Relationships." In *Lesbian Psychologies: Explorations and Challenges*, ed. The Boston Lesbian Psychologies Collective. Chicago: Univ. of Illinois Press, 1987.

Burns, Maryviolet. *The Speaking That Profits Us: Violence in the Lives of Women of Color.* Seattle: Center for the Prevention of Sexual and Domestic Violence, 1986.

Butler, Judith. *Gender Trouble: Feminism and the Subversion of Identity.* New York: Routledge, 1990.

Byham, Kim. "And the Truth Shall Set You Free: The Rise and Fall of Robert Williams." *The Witness* 73 (April 1990): 10–12.

Caplan, Pat, ed. *The Cultural Construction of Sexuality.* London: Tavistock Publications Limited, 1987.

Caraway, Carol. "Romantic Love: Neither Sexist nor Heterosexist." *Philosophy and Theology* 1 (summer 1987): 361–68.

Caraway, Nancie. *Segregated Sisterhood: Racism and the Politics of American Feminism.* Knoxville: Univ. of Tennessee Press, 1991.

Carey, John J. "The Presbyterian Church and Sexuality: Why This? Why Now?" *Church and Society* 80 (November– December 1989): 1–5.

———. "Sexuality: What We Couldn't Say." *Christianity and Crisis* (19 August 1991): 258–59.

Carey, Jonathan Sinclair. "D. S. Bailey and 'The Name Forbidden among Christians'" *Anglican Theological Review* 70 (April 1988): 152–73.

Carnell, Corbin Scott. "C. S. Lewis on Eros as a Means of Grace." In *Imagination and the Spirit: Essays in Literature and the Christian Faith Presented to Clyde S. Kilby*, ed. Charles A. Huttar. Grand Rapids, Mich.: William B. Eerdmans Publishing Company, 1971.

The Church and Human Sexuality: A Lutheran Perspective, First Draft of a Social Statement. Chicago: Division for Church and Society of the Evangelical Lutheran Church in America, 1993.

The Church Studies Homosexuality: A Study for United Methodist Groups Using the Report of the Commission to Study Homosexuality. Nashville: Cokesbury, 1994.

Clark, David K. "Philosophical Reflections on Self-Worth and Self-Love." *Journal of Psychology and Theology* 13 (spring 1985): 3–11.

Clark, J. Michael. *A Defiant Celebration: Theological Ethics and Gay Sexuality.* Garland, Tex.: Tangelwüld Press, 1990.

Clark, Joan L. "Coming Out: The Process and Its Price." *Christianity and Crisis* 39 (11 June 1979): 149–53.

Clarke, Cheryl. "Lesbianism: An Act of Resistance." In *This Bridge Called My Back: Writings by Radical Women of Color*, ed. Cherríe Moraga and Gloria Anzaldúa. Watertown, Mass.: Persephone Press, 1981.

Clarke, Jennie, Ruth Ford, and Diana Nobbs, eds. *Unfinished Business: Confronting Issues of Christianity, Sexuality, and Politics*. Melbourne, Australia: ASCM Publications, 1985.

Clerk, N. W. *A Grief Observed*. Greenwich, Conn.: The Seabury Press, 1963.

Coats, William R. "Sex and the Mature Single Adult." *The Episcopalian* (May 1987): 24–25.

Cobb, John B. "Is the Church Ready to Legislate on Sex: Question for United Methodists." *Christianity and Crisis* 44 (14 May 1984): 182–85.

Coleman, Gerald D. "Homosexuality and the Churches: An Overview." *Ecumenical Trends* 13 (September 1984): 113–16.

Coleman, Peter. *Christian Attitudes to Homosexuality*. London: SPCK, 1980.

Collins, Patricia Hill. *Black Feminist Thought: Knowledge, Consciousness, and the Politics of Empowerment*. New York: Routledge, 1990.

Combahee River Collective, The. "The Combahee River Collective Statement." In *Home Girls: A Black Feminist Anthology*, ed. Barbara Smith. Latham, N.Y.: Kitchen Table, Women of Color Press, 1983.

Comstock, Gary. *Violence Against Lesbians and Gay Men*. New York: Columbia Univ. Press, 1991.

Connell, R. W. *Gender and Power*. Stanford, Calif.: Stanford Univ. Press, 1987.

Connors, Debra. "Disability, Sexism, and the Social Order." In *Redefining Sexual Ethics: A Sourcebook of Essays, Stories, and Poems*, ed. Susan E. Davies and Eleanor H. Haney, 167–80. Cleveland: The Pilgrim Press, 1991.

Cooey, Paula, Sharon A. Farmer, and Mary Ellen Ross, eds. *Embodied Love: Sensuality and Relationship as Feminist Values*. San Francisco: Harper and Row, 1988.

Cook, David E. "Homosexuality: A Review of the Debate." *Churchman: Journal of Anglican Theology* 94, no. 4 (1980): 297–313.

Coward, Rosalind. *Patriarchal Precedents: Sexuality and Social Relations*. London: Routledge and Kegan Paul, 1983.

Crew, Louie. "The Episcopal Church as Voyeur." *The Witness* 71 (June 1988): 14–16.

————. "Pabulum Is Pabulum Is Pabulum." *Christianity and Crisis* 48 (21 March 1988): 79–80.

Cuffe, Edwin D. "Insight and Common Sense." Review of *The Four Loves* by C. S. Lewis. *America (National Catholic Weekly Review,* 3 September 1960, 601–2.

D'Arcy, Martin. *The Mind and Heart of Love, Lion, and Unicorn: A Study in Eros and Agape.* Cleveland: World Publishing Company, 1962.

Davis, Angela Y. "We Do Not Consent: Violence Against Women in a Racist Society." In *Women, Culture, and Politics,* 35–52. New York: Random House, 1989.

DeCecco, John P., ed. *Bashers, Baiters, and Bigots: Homophobia in American Society.* New York: Harrington Park Press, 1985.

Denman, Rose Mary. "Looking Forward, Looking Back." *Christianity and Crisis* 48 (1 February 1988): 7–8.

Dennis, Walter D. "A Personal Preview of the Seventieth General Convention." *St. Luke's Journal of Theology* 34 (June 1991): 79–98.

DeWitt, Robert L. "Seeding Hope in Soil of Intolerance." *The Witness* 64 (February 1981): 3.

Diamond, Irene, and Lee Quinby. "American Feminism in the Age of the Body." *Signs: Journal of Women in Culture and Society* 10 (autumn 1984): 119–25.

Dietz, Donald. "The Christian Meaning of Love: A Study of the Thought of Anders Nygren." Dissertation, San Antonio, Tex.

Dixon, John W., Jr. "The Sacramentality of Sex." In *Male and Female: Christian Approaches to Sexuality,* ed. Ruth Barnhouse and Urban T. Holmes. New York: Seabury Press, 1976.

Dobash, R. Emerson, and Russell Dobash. *Violence against Wives: A Case against the Patriarchy.* New York: The Free Press, 1979.

————. *Women, Violence, and Social Change.* London: Routledge, 1992.

Donovan, Josephine. *Feminist Theory: The Intellectual Traditions of American Feminism.* New York: Frederick Ungar Publishing Co., 1985.

Driver, Tom F. *Christ in a Changing World: Toward an Ethical Christology.* New York: Crossroad, 1981.

————. *Patterns of Grace: Human Experience as Word of God.* San Francisco: Harper and Row, 1977.

————. "Presbyterians, Pagans, and Paglia." *Christianity and Crisis* 52 (3 February 1992): 19–20.

————. "Sexuality and Jesus." *Union Seminary Quarterly Review* 20 (March 1965): 235–46.

————. "On Taking Sex Seriously." *Christianity and Crisis* 23 (14 October 1963).

Driver, Tom F., and Herbert Richardson. *The Meaning of Orgasm: A Dialogue. The Collected Papers of the Glassborough Conference.* (n.d.).

Dworkin, Andrea. *Woman Hating.* New York: Dutton, 1974.

Echols, Alice. *Daring to Be Bad: Radical Feminism in America, 1967–1975.* Minneapolis: Univ. of Minnesota Press, 1989.

————. "The New Feminism of Yin and Yang." In *Powers of Desire: The Politics of Sexuality,* ed. Ann Snitow, Christine Stansell, and Sharon Thompson. New York: Monthly Review Press, 1983.

————. "The Taming of the Id: Feminist Sexual Politics, 1968–1983." In *Pleasure and Danger: Exploring Female Sexuality,* ed. Carole S. Vance. Boston: Routledge and Kegan Paul, 1984.

Edwards, Bruce. "Overdoing a Good Thing: Soon It Will Become Fashionable to Criticize Lewis." *Christianity Today* 23 (2 November 1979): 40.

Edwards, George R. *Gay/Lesbian Liberation: A Biblical Perspective.* New York: The Pilgrim Press, 1984.

Edwards, James R. "Eros Deified." *Christianity Today* 35 (27 May 1991): 14–15.

Ehrenreich, Barbara, Elizabeth Hess, and Gloria Jacobs. *Remaking Love: The Feminization of Sex.* Garden City, N.Y.: Anchor Press/Doubleday, 1987.

Eisenstein, Zillah. *The Radical Future of Liberal Feminism.* New York: Longman, 1981.

Eisenstein, Zillah, ed. *Capitalist Patriarchy and the Case for Socialist Feminism.* New York: Monthly Review Press, 1979.

Ellison, Marvin M. "Common Decency: A New Christian Sexual Ethic." *Christianity and Crisis* 50 (12 November 1990): 352–56.

————. "Faithfulness, Morality, and Vision: Questions for a Justice-Seeking Church." *Christianity and Crisis* 47 (9 November 1987): 381–83.

————. "Men, Feminism, and Sexuality." *Christianity and Crisis* 48 (7 November 1988): 400–402.

————. "Refusing to Be 'Good Soldiers': An Agenda for Men." In *Redefining Sexual Ethics: A Sourcebook of Essays, Stories, and Poems,* ed. Susan E. Davies and Eleanor H. Haney. Cleveland: The Pilgrim Press, 1991.

————. "Sexuality and Spirituality: An Intimate—and Intimidating—Connection." *Church and Society* 80 (November–December 1989): 26–34.

Elmer, Franklin D. "Review of *The Mystery of Love and Marriage* by D. S. Bailey." *The Journal of Religion* 33 (July 1953): 231–32.

Erdey, Susan. "Lots of Heat, Not Much Light: 1991 General Convention in Arizona." *The Witness* 74 (July/August 1991): 22–25.

————. "A Pre-Convention Rundown on the Right: Who's Who Among Traditionalists." *The Witness* 74 (June 1991): 14–17.

Eugene, Toinette. "While Love Is Unfashionable: An Exploration of Black Spirituality and Sexuality." In *Women's Consciousness, Women's Conscience: A Reader in Feminist Ethics*, ed. Barbara H. Andolsen, Christine Gudorf, and Mary D. Pellauer. Minneapolis: Winston Press, 1985.

Farley, Margaret A. "The Church and the Family: An Ethical Task." *Horizons* 10 (1983): 50–71.

Fenton, John Y., ed. *Theology and Body*. From Conference on Theology and Body, Emory Univ., 1973. Philadelphia: Westminster Press, 1974.

Ferguson, Ann. *Blood at the Root: Motherhood, Sexuality and Male Dominance*. Boston: Unwin Hyman/Pandora Press, 1989.

————. "Sex War: The Debate Between Radical and Libertarian Feminists." *Signs: Journal of Women in Culture and Society* 10 (autumn 1984): 106–12.

Ferre, Nels F. S. "Nygren's Theology of Agape." In *The Philosophy and Theology of Anders Nygren*, ed. Charles W. Kegley. Carbondale: Southern Illinois Univ. Press, 1970.

————. *Swedish Contributions to Modern Theology*. New York: Harper and Row, 1967.

Firestone, Shulamith. "Love in a Sexist Society." In *Eros, Agape, and Philia: Readings in the Philosophy of Love*, ed. Alan Soble. New York: Paragon House, 1989.

Fisher, David H. "The Homosexual Debate: A Critique of Some Critics." *Saint Luke's Journal of Theology* 22 (June 1979): 176–84.

Fortunato, John E. "The Last Committee on Sexuality (Ever)." *Christianity and Crisis* 51 (18 February 1991): 34–35.

————. "Should the Church Bless and Affirm Committed Gay Relationships?" *The Episcopalian*, April 1987, 14, 28.

Fortune, Marie Marshall. *Sexual Violence: The Unmentionable Sin*. New York: The Pilgrim Press, 1983.

Foster, Richard J. "God's Gift of Sexuality: Celebration and Warning in the Context of Faith." *Sojourners* 14 (July 1985): 15–19.

Frame, Randall L. "The Homosexual Lifestyle: Is There a Way Out?" *Christianity Today* 29 (9 August 1985): 32–34.

———. "Presbyterian Assembly Rejects Sexuality Report." *Christianity Today* 35 (22 July 1991): 37–38.

———. "Sexuality Report Draws Fire." *Christianity Today* 35 (29 April 1991): 37–38.

Fraser, Nancy. *Unruly Practices: Power, Discourse and Gender in Contemporary Social Theory.* Minneapolis: Univ. of Minnesota Press, 1989.

Frear, George Lewis, Jr. "Biblical Authority in Modern Christian Political Ethics: A Study Contrasting Karl Barth and Helmut Thielicke on the Subject." Ph. D. diss. 1969.

Freedman, Estelle B., and Barrie Thorne. "Introduction to 'The Feminist Sexuality Debates'" *Signs: Journal of Women in Culture and Society* 10 (autumn 1984): 102–5.

Fuchs, Eric. *Sexual Desire and Love: Origins and History of the Christian Ethic of Sexuality and Marriage,* trans. Marsha Daigle. New York: Seabury Press, 1983.

Fuerst, Wesley. "A Symposium on the LCA's Study of Issues Concerning Homosexuality." *Dialog* 26 (spring 1987): 142–48.

Fuss, Diana. *Essentially Speaking: Feminism, Nature and Difference.* New York: Routledge, 1989.

Gaiser, Frederick J., ed. "Sex, Intimacy, and Limits." *Word and World: Theology for Christian Ministry* 10 (spring 1990): 114–69.

Garcia, Norma, Cheryl Kennedy, Sarah F. Pearlman, and Julia Perez. "The Impact of Race and Culture Differences: Challenges to Intimacy in Lesbian Relationships." In *Lesbian Psychologies: Explorations and Challenges,* ed. The Boston Lesbian Psychologies Collective. Chicago: Univ. of Illinois Press, 1987.

Gay, Calvin [pseud]. "To the Presbyterians on Homosexuality: You Spoke from Ignorance." *Christianity and Crisis* 38 (30 October 1978): 254–59.

Gessell, John M. "Bishops Should 'Come Out' for Gays." *The Witness* 74 (February 1991): 18–19.

Gibbs, Lee W. "C. S. Lewis and the Anglican Via Media." *Restoration Quarterly* 32, no. 2 (1990): 105–19.

Gilson, Anne E. "Bringing God out of the Closet." *The Witness,* June 1990.

————. "Keeping Sex in Order: Heterosexism in Episcopal Church Policy." In *No Easy Peace: Liberating Anglicanism*, ed. Carter Heyward and Sue Phillips. Lanham, Md.: University Press of America, 1992.

————. "Therefore Choose Life." *The Witness* 68 (September 1985): 22.

Gittings, Jim. "A Bonfire in Baltimore: Presbyterian Task Force Reports on Sexuality." *Christianity and Crisis*, 27 May 1991, 172–77.

Glaser, Chris. *Uncommon Calling: A Gay Man's Struggle to Serve the Church*. San Francisco: Harper and Row, 1988.

Goldman, Ari L. "Highest Presbyterian Panel Bars Homosexual Minister." *The New York Times*, 5 November 1992, B21.

Gordon, Kevin. "Religion, Moralizing, and AIDS: A Theological/Pastoral Essay." In *Homosexuality and Social Justice*, ed. Kevin Gordon. San Francisco: The Consultation on Homosexuality, Social Justice, and Roman Catholic Theology, 1986.

Grant, Robert M. "Review of Homosexuality and the Western Christian Tradition by D. S. Bailey." *Anglican Theological Review* 38 (July 1956): 259–61.

————. "Review of Sexual Relation in Christian Thought by D. S. Bailey." *The Journal of Religion* 40 (July 1960): 212–13.

Gray, Wallace. "Human Inquiry into Divine Love." *Communio Viatorum: A Theological Quarterly* 25, nos. 1–2 (1982): 25–34.

Gudorf, Christine E. *Victimization: Examining Christian Complicity*. Philadelphia: Trinity Press International, 1992.

————. *Body, Sex, and Pleasure: Reconstructing Christian Sexual Ethics*. Cleveland: The Pilgrim Press, 1994.

Guitton, Jean. "Eros and Agape." In *Christian Married Love*, ed. Raymond Dennehy. San Francisco: Ignatius Press, 1981.

Haines, Denise G. "Should the Church Bless Committed but Not Married Sexually Active Relationships?" *The Episcopalian*, March 1987, 8–10.

Haines, Ronald. "Statement before Ordination of Elizabeth Carl." *Episcopal Life*, July 1991, 19.

Hall, Thor. *Anders Nygren*, ed. Bob E. Patterson. Makers of the Modern Theological Mind. Waco, Tex.: Word Books Publisher, 1978.

————. "The Nygren Corpus: Annotations to the Major Works of Anders Nygren of Lund." *Journal of the American Academy of Religion* 47 (June 1979): 269–89.

Haney, Eleanor H. *Vision and Struggle: Meditations on Feminist Spirituality and Politics*. Portland, Me.: Astarte Shell Press, 1989.

————. "Sexual Being—Burden and Possibility: A Feminist Reflection on Sexual Ethics." In *Redefining Sexual Ethics: A Sourcebook of Essays, Stories, and Poems,* ed. Susan E. Davies and Eleanor H. Haney. Cleveland: Pilgrim Press, 1991.

Haraway, Donna J. *Simians, Cyborgs, and Women: The Reinvention of Nature.* New York: Routledge, 1991.

Hard, Sheila A. "Agape and Eros: A Re-evaluation." *Dialog* 22 (winter 1983): 60–61.

Harris, Virginia R., and Trinity A. Ordoña. "Developing Unity Among Women of Color: Crossing the Barriers of Internalized Racism and Cross-Racial Hostility." In *Making Face, Making Soul— Haciendo Caras: Creative and Critical Perspectives by Feminists of Color,* ed. Gloria Anzaldúa. San Francisco: Aunt Lute Books, 1990.

Harrison, Beverly W. "Human Sexuality and Mutuality." In *Christian Feminism: Visions of a New Humanity,* ed. Judith L. Weidman. San Francisco: Harper and Row, 1984.

————. "Misogyny and Homophobia: The Unexplored Connections." In *Making the Connections: Essays in Feminist Social Ethics,* ed. Carol S. Robb. Boston: Beacon Press, 1985.

————. "The Power of Anger in the Work of Love: Christian Ethics for Women and Other Strangers." *In Making the Connections: Essays in Feminist Social Ethics,* ed. Carol S. Robb. Boston: Beacon Press, 1985.

Harrison, Beverly W., and Carter Heyward. "Pain and Pleasure: Avoiding the Confusions of Christian Tradition in Feminist Theory." In *Christianity, Patriarchy and Abuse,* ed. Joanne Carlson Brown and Carole R. Bohn. New York: The Pilgrim Press, 1989.

Harrison, James. "Building Bonds: The Church and Gays." *The Christian Century* 96 (2 May 1979): 500–504.

Hart, Nett. "Lesbian Desire as Social Action." In *Lesbian Philosophies and Cultures,* ed. Jeffner Allen. State Univ. of New York Press, 1990.

Hartsock, Nancy C. M. *Money, Sex and Power: Toward a Feminist Historical Materialism.* Boston: Northeastern Univ. Press, 1985.

Heath, Graham. *The Illusory Freedom: The Intellectual Origins and Social Consequences of the Sexual "Revolution".* London: Heinemann Medical, 1978.

Heikenen, J. W. "The Basic Principles of Anders Nygren's Theological Thought." *The Lutheran Quarterly* 1 (1949): 123–34.

Hencken, Joel D. "Homosexuals and Heterosexuals: We Are All Apologists." *Anglican Theological Review* 59 (April 1977): 191–93.

Hessel, Dieter T. "The General Assembly on Sexuality: Major Empha-
ses." *Church and Society: Body and Soul—A New Look at Human Sexuality and the Church,* November/December 1989.

Hewitt, Emily C., and Suzanne R. Hiatt. *Women Priests: Yes or No?*
New York: The Seabury Press, 1973.

Hewitt, Thomas Furman. *The American Church's Reaction to the Homo-
phile Movement, 1948–1978.* Ann Arbor, Mich.: University Micro-
films International, 1983.

Heyward, Carter. "Heterosexist Theology: Being Above It All." *Journal of Feminist Studies in Religion* 3 (spring 1987): 29–38.

———. "Liberating the Body." In *Our Passion for Justice,* 137–47.
New York: The Pilgrim Press, 1984.

———. *Our Passion for Justice: Images of Power, Sexuality, and Liberation.* New York: The Pilgrim Press, 1984.

———. *A Priest Forever: The Formation of a Woman and a Priest.* New
York: Harper and Row, 1976.

———. *The Redemption of God: A Theology of Mutual Relation.* Lanham, Md.: University Press of America, 1982.

———. *Speaking of Christ: A Lesbian Feminist Voice,* ed. Ellen C.
Davis. New York: The Pilgrim Press, 1989.

———. *Staying Power: Reflections on Gender, Justice, and Compassion.*
Cleveland: The Pilgrim Press, 1995.

———. *Touching Our Strength: The Erotic as Power and the Love of God.*
San Francisco: Harper and Row, 1989.

———. *When Boundaries Betray Us: Beyond Illusions of What Is Ethical
in Therapy and Life.* San Francisco: Harper and Row, 1993.

Heyward, Carter, and Mary Hunt. "Lesbianism and Feminist Theology." *Journal of Feminist Studies in Religion* 2 (fall 1986): 95–106.

Hill, Renée. "Who Are We for Each Other?: Sexism, Sexuality, and
Womanist Theology." In *Black Theology: A Documentary History,
Vol. II (1980–1992),* ed. James H. Cone and Gayraud S. Wilmore.
Maryknoll, N.Y.: Orbis Books, 1993.

Hoagland, Sarah Lucia. *Lesbian Ethics: Toward New Value.* Palo Alto,
Calif. Institute of Lesbian Studies, 1988.

Hollibaugh, Amber. "Desire for the Future: Radical Hope in Passion
and Pleasure." In *Pleasure and Danger: Exploring Female Sexuality,* ed.
Carole S. Vance. Boston: Routledge and Kegan Paul, 1984.

Hollibaugh, Amber, and Cherríe Moraga. "What We're Rollin Around
in Bed With: Sexual Silences in Feminism." In *Powers of Desire: The
Politics of Sexuality,* ed. Ann Snitow, Christine Stansell, and Sharon
Thompson. New York: Monthly Review Press, 1983.

hooks, bell. *Ain't I a Woman: Black Women and Feminism*. Boston: South End Press, 1981.

———. *Feminist Theory: From Margin to Center*. Boston: South End Press, 1984.

———. "Moved by Passion: Eros and Responsibility." In *Sisters of the Yam: Black Women and Self-Recovery*. Boston: South End Press, 1993.

———. *Talking Back: Thinking Feminist, Thinking Black*. Boston: South End Press, 1988.

———. *Yearning: Race, Gender, and Cultural Politics*. Boston: South End Press, 1990.

Hooper, Walter, ed. *They Stand Together: The Letters of C. S. Lewis to Arthur Greeves (1914–1963)*. New York: Macmillan Publishing Co., Inc., 1979.

Horton, Anne L., and Judith A. Williamson, eds. *Abuse and Religion: When Praying Isn't Enough*. Lexington, Mass.: D. C. Heath/Lexington Books, 1988.

Hovey, Gail. "Lesbian Minister's Life." *Christianity and Crisis* 50 (2 July 1990): 230–31.

———. "A March and a Trial." *Christianity and Crisis* 47 (9 November 1987): 371.

———. "In the Matter of Rose Mary Denman: Life and Times of a Minister." *Christianity and Crisis* 47 (9 November 1987): 379–80.

Howell, Leon. "Presbyterians and Sexuality: What Comes Next?" *Christianity and Crisis*, 15 July 1991, 212.

Huff, Margaret C. "The Interdependent Self: An Integrated Concept from Feminist Theology and Feminist Psychology." *Philosophy and Theology* 2, no. 2 (1989): 160–72.

Hulme, William E. "Review of 'The Ethics of Sex' by Helmut Thielicke." *Pastoral Psychology* 15 (February 1964): 63–65.

Hunt, Mary. *Fierce Tenderness: A Feminist Theology of Friendship*. New York: Crossroad, 1991.

Hyde, Clark, and Janet S. Hyde. "Homosexuality and the Theological Uses of Social Science: A Response to Ruth Tiffany Barnhouse." *Anglican Theological Review* 59 (April 1977): 187–90.

Imbens, Annie, and Ineke Jonker. *Christianity and Incest*. Minneapolis: Fortress Press, 1992.

Irwin, Alexander. *Eros Toward the World: Paul Tillich and the Theology of the Erotic*. Minneapolis: Fortress Press, 1991.

Isasi-Díaz, Ada María. "Solidarity: Love of Neighbor in the 1980s." In *Lift Every Voice: Constructing Christian Theologies from the Underside,* ed. Susan Brooks Thistlethwaite and Mary Potter Engel. San Francisco: Harper and Row, 1990.

————. "Viva la Diferencia!" *Journal of Feminist Studies in Religion* 8 (fall 1992): 98–102.

Isasi-Díaz, Ada María, Elena Olazagasti-Segovia, Sandra Mangual-Rodriguez, Maria Antoinetta Berriozábal, Daisy L. Machado, Lordes Arguelles, and Raven-Anne Rivero. "*Mujeristas*: Who We Are and What We Are About." *Journal of Feminist Studies in Religion* 8 (spring 1992): 105–26.

Jack, Dana Crowley. *Silencing the Self: Women and Depression*. New York: HarperCollins Publishers, 1991.

Jackson, Margaret. "'Facts of Life' or the Eroticization of Women's Oppression? Sexology and the Social Construction of Heterosexuality." In *The Cultural Construction of Sexuality*, ed. Pat Caplan. London: Tavistock Publications, 1987.

Jaggar, Alison M. *Feminist Politics and Human Nature*. Totowa, N.J.: Rowman and Allanheld, 1983.

Jaggar, Alison M., and Paula S. Rothenberg, eds. *Feminist Frameworks: Alternative Theoretical Accounts of the Relations Between Women and Men*. New York: McGraw-Hill Book Company, 1984.

Jaudon, Brian. "From Debate to Dialogue: Churches Struggle to Address Homosexuality and Sexual Ethics." *Sojourners* 20 (July 1991): 32–35.

Jones, H. Kimball. *Towards a Christian Understanding of the Homosexual*. New York: Association Press, 1966.

Jordan, June. "Where Is the Love?" In *Women's Consciousness, Women's Conscience: A Reader in Feminist Ethics*, ed. Barbara Hilkert Andolsen, Christine E. Gudorf, and Mary D. Pellauer. Minneapolis: Winston Press, 1985.

Kauffman, Linda, ed. *Feminism and Institutions: Dialogues on Feminist Theory*. Cambridge, Mass.: Basil Blackwell, 1989.

Kaye, Melanie. "Some Notes on Jewish Lesbian Identity." In *Nice Jewish Girls: A Lesbian Anthology*, ed. Evelyn Torton Beck. Trumansburg, N.Y.: Crossing Press, 1982.

Kegley, Charles W., ed. *The Philosophy and Theology of Anders Nygren*. Carbondale: Southern Illinois Univ. Press, 1970.

Keller, Catherine. *From a Broken Web: Separation, Sexism, and Self*. Boston: Beacon Press, 1986.

Kilby, C. S. "C. S. Lewis: Everyman's Theologian." *Christianity Today* 8 (1 January 1964): 11..

————. "Review of *The Four Loves* by C. S. Lewis." *Christianity Today* 5 (10 October 1960): 40.

King, Ynestra. "Healing the Wounds: Feminism, Ecology, and Nature/Culture Dualism." In *Gender/Body/Knowledge: Feminist Reconstructions of Being and Knowing*, ed. Alison M. Jaggar and Susan R. Bordo. New Brunswick, N.J.: Rutgers Univ. Press, 1989.

Kirk, Jerry R. *The Homosexual Crisis in the Mainline Church: A Presbyterian Minister Speaks Out*. Nashville: Thomas Nelson, Inc., 1978.

Kirkley, Charles F. "Fidelity in Marriage . . . Celibacy in Singleness." *Christianity and Crisis*, 14 May 1984, 186–88.

Kitzinger, Celia. *The Social Construction of Lesbianism*. London: Sage, 1987.

Kivel, Paul. *Men's Work: How to Stop the Violence That Tears Our Lives Apart*. New York: Ballantine Books, 1992.

Klann, Richard. "Helmut Thielicke Appraised." *Concordia Journal* 6 (July 1980): 155–63.

Kranz, Kirsten. "Bishops Face First Resolution Concerning Homosexuality." *The Living Church*, 28 July 1991, 6.

Kreeft, Peter. "How to Save Western Civilisation: C. S. Lewis as Prophet." In *A Man for All Christians: Essays in Honour of C. S. Lewis*, ed. Andrew Walker and James Patrick. London: Hodder and Stoughton, 1990.

Krook, Dorothea. *Three Traditions of Moral Thought*. Cambridge, U.K.: Cambridge Univ. Press, 1959

Lawlor, John, ed. *Patterns of Love and Courtesy: Essays in Memory of C. S. Lewis*. Evanston, Ill.: Northwestern Univ. Press, 1966.

Lebacqz, Karen. "Love Your Enemy: Sex, Power, and Christian Ethics." *Annual of the Society of Christian Ethics* (1990): 3–23.

————. "Sex: Justice in Church and Society." *Christianity and Crisis*, 27 May 1991, 174–77.

LeBlanc, Doug. "Conservatives Feel Betrayed by 'Affirmation Service,'" *United Voice* (November 1992): 1–2.

LeMoncheck, Linda. *Dehumanizing Women: Treating Persons as Sex Objects*. Totowa, N.J.: Rowman and Allanheld, 1985.

Lewis, C. S. *The Allegory of Love: A Study in Medieval Tradition*. 1936; repr. New York: Oxford Univ. Press, 1958.

————. *The Four Loves*. San Diego: Harcourt, Brace, Jovanovich, 1960.

————. *God in the Dock: Essays on Theology and Ethics*, ed. Walter Hooper. Grand Rapids, Mich.: William B. Eerdmans Publishing Company, 1970.

————. *Mere Christianity.* New York: Macmillan Publishing Company, 1943.

————. "Priestesses in the Church?" In *God in the Dock: Essays in Theology and Ethics,* ed. Walter Hooper. Grand Rapids, Mich.: William B. Eerdmans Publishing Company, 1970.

————. *Surprised by Joy: The Shape of My Early Life.* New York: Harcourt, Brace, and World, 1956.

————. "We Have No 'Right to Happiness'" In *God in the Dock. Essays in Theology and Ethics,* ed. Walter Hooper. Grand Rapids, Mich.: William B. Eerdmans Publishing Company, 1970.

Lewis, Dean H. "Homosexuality: Resources for Reflection." *Church and Society* 67 (May–June 1977): 3–40, 59–79.

Lillie, William. "The Christian Conception of Love." *Scottish Journal of Theology* 12 (1959): 225–42.

Linden, Robin Ruth, Darlene R. Pagano, Diana E. H. Russell, and Susan Leigh Star, eds. *Against Sadomasochism: A Radical Feminist Analysis.* San Francisco: Frog in the Well, 1982.

Livezey, Lois Gehr. "Sexual and Family Violence: A Growing Issue for the Churches." *Christian Century* 104 (28 October 1987): 941–42.

————. "Sexual and Family Violence: Breaking the Silence." In *Sexual Ethics and the Church: A Christian Century Symposium.* Chicago: The Christian Century Foundation, 1989.

Lobel, Kerry, ed. *Naming the Violence: Speaking Out About Lesbian Battering.* Seattle: Seal Press, 1986.

Lorde, Audre. "The Master's Tools Will Never Dismantle the Master's House." In *Sister Outsider: Essays and Speeches by Audre Lorde,* 110–13. Trumansburg, N.Y.: The Crossing Press, 1984.

————. "I Am Your Sister: Black Women Organizing Across Sexualities." In *Making Face, Making Soul—Haciendo Caras: Creative and Critical Perspectives by Feminists of Color,* ed. Gloria Anzaldúa. San Francisco: Aunt Lute Books, 1990.

————. "Scratching the Surface: Some Notes on Barriers to Women and Loving." In *Sister Outsider: Essays and Speeches by Audre Lorde,* 45–52. Trumansburg, N.Y.: The Crossing Press, 1984.

————. "Uses of the Erotic: The Erotic as Power." In *Sister Outsider: Essays and Speeches by Audre Lorde,* 53–59. Trumansburg, N.Y.: The Crossing Press, 1984.

Louden, R. Stuart. "Review of 'The Ethics of Sex' by Helmut Thielicke." *Reformed and Presbyterian World* 28 (spring 1965): 333–34.

Loulan, JoAnn. *Lesbian Passion: Loving Ourselves and Each Other.* San Francisco: Spinsters/Aunt Lute, 1987.

————. *Lesbian Sex.* San Francisco: Spinsters Ink, 1984.

Lovelace, Richard F. *Homosexuality and the Church.* Old Tappan, N.J.: Fleming H. Revell Company, 1978.

Maine Civil Liberties Union, Maine Lesbian/Gay Political Alliance, and Univ. of Southern Maine Department of Social Welfare, "Discrimination and Violence Survey of Gay People in Maine." Portland: Univ. of Southern Maine, Department of Social Welfare, 1985.

Malson, Micheline R., Jean F. O'Barr, Sarah Westphal-Wihl, and Mary Wyer, eds. *Feminist Theory in Practice and Process.* Chicago: Univ. of Chicago Press, 1986.

Mason, Raz. "The Price We Pay for Homophobia." *The Witness* 74 (May 1991): 26–27.

Mathers, James. "Homosexuality." *Theology* 83 (March 1980): 131–33.

Maurice, Frederic, ed., *The Life of Frederic Denison Maurice,* vol. 11. New York: 1884.

Mayman, Margaret A. *Intimate Violence: Implications for Theories of Moral Agency.* New York: Union Theological Seminary, 1995.

Meilaender, Gilbert. "The Singularity of Christian Ethics." *Journal of Religious Ethics* 17 (fall 1989): 95–119.

————. *The Taste for the Other: The Social and Ethical Thought of C. S. Lewis.* Grand Rapids, Mich.: William B. Eerdmans Publishing Company, 1978.

Miles, Margaret. *Augustine on the Body.* Missoula, Mont.: Scholar's Press, 1979.

Milhaven, John. "Conjugal Sexual Love." *Theological Studies* 35 (1974): 692–710.

Miller, Jean Baker. *Toward a New Psychology of Women.* Boston: Beacon Press, 1986.

Mills, Robert P. "GA's ReImagining Report Affirms Boundaries." *The Presbyterian Layman* 27, no. 4 (July/August 1994): 1, 4.

Molina, Papusa. "Recognizing, Accepting, and Celebrating Our Differences." In *Making Face, Making Soul—Haciendo Caras: Creative and Critical Perspectives by Feminists of Color,* ed. Gloria Anzaldúa. San Francisco: Aunt Lute Books, 1990.

Mollenkott, Virginia Ramey. "Human Rights and the Golden Rule: What the Bible Doesn't Say About Sexuality." *Christianity and Crisis* 47 (9 November 1987): 383–85.

Moody, Howard. "Pleasure, Too, Is a Gift from God: Sex, Sin, and the Judaeo-Christian Tradition." *Christianity and Crisis* 45 (10 June 1985): 227–31.

Moraga, Cherríe. *Loving in the War Years.* Boston: South End Press, 1983.

Moraga, Cherríe, and Gloria Anzaldúa, eds. *This Bridge Called My Back: Writings of Radical Women of Color.* Watertown, Mass.: Persephone Press, 1981.

Morgan, Robin. "Lesbianism and Feminism: Synonyms or Contradictions?" In *Going Too Far.* New York: Random House, 1977.

Morton, Nelle. *The Journey Is Home.* Boston: Beacon Press, 1985.

Mount, Eric, and Johanna W. H. Bos. "Scripture on Sexuality: Shifting Authority." *Journal of Presbyterian History* 59 (summer 1981): 219–42.

Naulty, R. A. "Christian Attitudes to Homosexuality." *St. Mark's Review* 137 (autumn 1989): 32–33.

Nelson, James. *Between Two Gardens: Reflections on Sexuality and Religious Experience.* New York: The Pilgrim Press, 1983.

———. *Embodiment: An Approach to Sexuality and Christian Theology.* Minneapolis: Augsburg Publishing House, 1978.

———. *The Intimate Connection: Male Sexuality, Masculine Spirituality.* Philadelphia: Westminster Press, 1988.

———. *Body Theology.* Louisville, Ky.: Westminster/John Knox Press, 1992.

———. "Review of The Ethics of Sex by Helmut Thielicke." *Theology and Life* 8 (winter 1965): 308–9.

Nelson, Randolph A. "Homosexuality and Social Ethics." *Word and World: Theology for Christian Ministry* 5 (fall 1985): 380–94.

Nelson, Susan Dunfee. "The Sin of Hiding: A Feminist Critique of Reinhold Niebuhr's Account of the Sin of Pride." *Soundings* 65 (February 1982).

Neuhaus, Richard John. "Homosexuality and the Churches." *First Things* 3 (May 1990): 64–70.

Newton, Esther, and Shirley Walton. "The Misunderstanding: Toward a More Precise Sexual Vocabulary." In *Pleasure and Danger: Exploring Female Sexuality,* ed. Carole S. Vance. Boston: Routledge and Kegan Paul, 1984.

Nicholson, Linda J., ed. *Feminism/Postmodernism.* New York: Routledge, 1990.

Niebuhr, Gustav. "Episcopalians Soften Stance on Sexuality." *New York Times,* 25 August 1994, A13.

Novak, Michael. "The Way Men Love." Review of *The Four Loves* by C. S. Lewis. *Commonweal* 72 (19 August 1960): 430.

Nunley, Jan. "Church Silence on Gay-Bashing Deadly." *The Witness* 73 (21 November 1990): 12–13.

Nygren, Anders. *Agape and Eros: A Study of the Christian Idea of Love.* London: SPCK, 1953.

————. "Intellectual Autobiography." In *The Philosophy and Theology of Anders Nygren,* ed. Charles W. Kegley. Carbondale: Southern Illinois Univ. Press, 1970.

————. *Meaning and Method: Prolegomena to a Scientific Philosophy of Religion and a Scientific Theology,* trans. Philip S. Watson. Philadelphia: Fortress Press, 1972.

Ortner, Sherry B., and Harriet Whitehead. *Sexual Meanings: The Cultural Construction of Gender and Sexuality.* Cambridge, U.K.: Cambridge Univ. Press, 1981.

Outka, Gene. *Agape: An Ethical Analysis.* New Haven: Yale Univ. Press, 1972.

Parker, Dorothy Mills. "Avowed Lesbian Ordained Priest in Washington." *The Living Church,* 30 June 1991, 6.

Pateman, Carole. *The Sexual Contract.* Stanford, Calif.: Stanford Univ. Press, 1988.

Patton, Cindy. *Sex and Germs: The Politics of AIDS.* Boston: South End Press, 1985.

Peevey, Debra. "Becoming Open and Affirming of Gay and Lesbian Christians, One Church's Story." *Chicago Theological Seminary Register* 81 (spring 1991): 32–38.

Pellauer, Mary, Barbara Chester, and Jane Boyajian, eds. *Sexual Assault and Abuse: A Handbook for Clergy and Religious Professionals.* San Francisco: Harper and Row, 1987.

Petersen, William J. *C. S. Lewis Had a Wife.* Wheaton, Ill.: Tyndale House Publishers, Inc., 1985.

Pharr, Suzanne. "The Connection Between Homophobia and Violence Against Women." *Aegis,* no. 41 (1986): 35–37.

————. *Homophobia: A Weapon of Sexism.* Inverness, Calif.: Chardon Press, 1988.

Phelan, Shane. *Identity Politics: Lesbian Feminism and the Limits of Community.* Philadelphia: Temple Univ. Press, 1989.

Philipson, Ilene. "The Repression of Sexuality and Gender: A Critical Perspective on the Feminist Sexuality Debate." *Signs: Journal of Women in Culture and Society* 10 (autumn 1984): 113–18.

Phillips, Jennifer M. "Gay Lives and Common Morality: In the Church, Tolerance Is Not Enough." *Christianity and Crisis* 50 (18 June 1990): 191–94.

Pierce, Susan E. "Anglican Church Launches Witch-Hunt against Gays." *The Witness* 71 (November 1988): 22–23.

————. "Church Needs New Sexual Ethic: An Interview with Carter Heyward and Virginia Ramey Mollenkott." *The Witness*, June 1991, 20–23.

————. "Same-Sex Marriage Is Nothing New." *The Witness* 71 (October 1988): 20–21.

Pittenger, Norman. "Apologist versus Apologist; A Critique of C. S. Lewis as 'Defender of the Faith.'" *Christian Century* 75 (1958): 1104–07.

————. "A Theological Approach to Understanding Homosexuality." *Religion and Life* 43 (winter 1974): 436–44.

Plaskow, Judith. *Standing Again at Sinai: Judaism from a Feminist Perspective.* San Francisco: Harper and Row, 1990.

————, *Sex, Sin and Grace: Women's Experience and the Theologies of Reinhold Niebuhr and Paul Tillich.* Lanham, Md.: Univ. Press of America, 1980.

Pogrebin, Letty Cottin. *Family Politics: Love and Power on an Intimate Frontier.* New York: McGraw-Hill Book Company, 1983.

Pollet, V. M. "Review of Agape and Eros by Anders Nygren." *Angelicum* 16 (1939): 367–69.

Post, Stephen G. *A Theory of Agape: On the Meaning of Christian Love.* London and Toronto: Associated University Presses, 1990.

Presbyterians and Human Sexuality. *Decisions of the 203rd General Assembly on Human Sexuality. The 203rd General Assembly (1991) Response to the Report of the Special Committee on Human Sexuality, Including a "Minority Report".* Louisville, Ky.: The Office of the General Assembly, Presbyterian Church (USA), 1991.

Quanbeck, Warren. "Anders Nygren." In *A Handbook of Christian Theologians,* ed. Dean G. Peerman and Martin E. Marty. Nashville: Abingdon, 1965.

Ramsey, Paul A. *One Flesh: A Christian View of Sex Within, Outside, and Before Marriage.* Bramcote, Notts.: Grove Books, 1975.

Ranck, Lee, ed. "Homosexuality." *Christian Social Action* 4 (February 1991): 6–31.

Raven, Charles E. "Towards a Wholesome Sex Ethic." Review. *The Expository Times* 66 (August 1955): 331.

Raymond, Janice. "Female Friendship and Feminist Ethics." In *Women's Consciousness, Women's Conscience: A Reader in Feminist Ethics,* ed. Barbara H. Andolsen, Christine Gudorf, and Mary D. Pellauer. Minneapolis: Winston Press, 1985.

Reed, Rex. "Church, State, and Sexuality." *The Lutheran,* January 1994, 63.

Rich, Adrienne. "Compulsory Heterosexuality and Lesbian Existence." In *Powers of Desire: The Politics of Sexuality*, ed. Ann Snitow, Christine Stansell, and Sharon Thompson. New York: Monthly Review Press, 1983.

———. "It Is the Lesbian in Us..." In *On Lies, Secrets, and Silence*, 199–202. New York: W.W. Norton and Company, 1979.

———. "The Meaning of Our Love for Women Is What We Have Constantly to Expand." In *On Lies, Secrets, and Silence*, 223–30. New York: W. W. Norton and Company, 1979.

Riggs, Marcia. "The Logic of Interstructured Oppression: A Black Womanist Perspective." In *Redefining Sexual Ethics: A Sourcebook of Essays, Stories, and Poems*, ed. Susan E. Davies and Eleanor H. Haney. Cleveland: Pilgrim Press, 1991.

Ringeling, Hermann. "Homosexualitaet; Pt 1: Zum Ansatz der Problemstellung in der Theologischen Ethik; Pt 2: Zur Ethischen Urteilsfindung." *Zeitschrift Fuer Evangelische Ethik* 31, no. 1 (1987): 6–35, 82–102.

Rist, John M. "Some Interpretations of Agape and Eros." In *The Philosophy and Theology of Anders Nygren*, ed. Charles W. Kegley. Carbondale: Southern Illinois Univ. Press, 1970.

Robinson, Patricia Murphy. "The Historical Repression of Women's Sexuality." In *Pleasure and Danger: Exploring Female Sexuality*, ed. Carole S. Vance. Boston: Routledge and Kegan Paul, 1984.

Rubin, Gayle. "Thinking Sex: Notes for a Radical Theory of the Politics of Sexuality." In *Pleasure and Danger: Exploring Female Sexuality*, ed. Carole S. Vance. Boston: Routledge and Kegan Paul, 1984.

Russell, Diana E. M. *The Politics of Rape: The Victim's Perspective*. New York: Stein and Day, 1975.

Russell, Letty M. *Household of Freedom: Authority in Feminist Theology*. Philadelphia: The Westminster Press, 1987.

Rutledge, Fleming. "Living Together Outside Marriage Is Selfish, Anti-social, Individualistic." *The Episcopalian*, March 1987, 8–9, 11, 21.

Saiving, Valerie. "The Human Situation: A Feminine View." In *WomanSpirit Rising*, ed. Carol Christ and Judith Plaskow. San Francisco: Harper and Row, 1979 1960 .

Sanders, Cheryl J., Katie G. Cannon, Emilie M. Townes, M. Shawn Copeland, bell hooks, and Cheryl Townsend Gilkes. "Christian Ethics and Theology in Womanist Perspective." *Journal of Feminist Studies in Religion* 5 (fall 1989): 83–112.

Sands, Kathleen M. "Uses of the Thea(o)logian: Sex and Theodicy in

Religious Feminism." *Journal of Feminist Studies in Religion* 8 (spring 1992): 7–34.

Saver, George. *C. S. Lewis and His Times.* London: Macmillan, 1988.

Scarry, Elaine. *The Body in Pain: The Making and Unmaking of the World.* New York: Oxford Univ. Press, 1985.

Schechter, Susan. *Women and Male Violence: The Visions and Struggles of the Battered Women's Movement.* Boston: South End Press, 1982.

Schott, Robin May. *Cognition and Eros: A Critique of the Kantian Paradigm.* Boston: Beacon Press, 1988.

Schrotenboer, Paul G. "Review of the Ethics of Sex by Helmut Thielicke." *Westminster Theological Journal* 29 (November 1966): 107–10.

Scott, David A. "Trinity and Ethics: The Thought of Helmut Thielicke." *Lutheran Quarterly* 29 (February 1977): 3–12.

Scroggs, Robin. *The New Testament and Homosexuality: Contextual Background for Contemporary Debate.* Philadelphia: Fortress Press, 1983.

Seidman, Steven. *Embattled Eros: Sexual Politics and Ethics in Contemporary America.* New York: Routledge, 1992.

Shafer, Byron. "The Problem of Homophobia." *Church and Society* 73 (November–December 1982): 42–48.

Sherrard, Philip. *Christianity and Eros: Essays on the Theme of Sexual Love.* London: SPCK, 1976.

Sherwood, Zalmon. "On Being a Gay Priest." *The Witness* 68 (September 1985): 20–21.

Shinn, Roger L. "Review of *The Ethics of Sex* by Helmut Thielicke." *Union Seminary Quarterly Review* 20 (January 1965): 203–5.

Sims, Bennett J. "Sex and Homosexuality." *Christianity Today* 22 (24 February 1978): 23–30.

Simson, Rennie. "The Afro-American Female: The Historical Context of the Construction of Sexual Identity." In *Powers of Desire: The Politics of Sexuality,* ed. Ann Snitow, Christine Stansell, and Sharon Thompson. New York: Monthly Review Press, 1983.

Singer, Irving. *The Nature of Love.* In 3 vols. Chicago: Univ. of Chicago Press, 1984–87.

Smedes, Lewis. *Sex for Christians.* Grand Rapids, Mich.: William B. Eerdmans Publishing Company, 1976.

Smith, Barbara, ed. *Home Girls: A Black Feminist Anthology.* New York: Kitchen Table, Women of Color Press, 1983.

Smith, Barbara, and Beverly Smith. "Across the Kitchen Table: A Sister-to-Sister Dialogue." In *This Bridge Called My Back: Writings by Radical Women of Color,* ed. Cherríe Moraga and Gloria Anzaldúa. Watertown, Mass.: Persephone Press, 1981.

Smith, Dwight C., Jr. "Presbyterians on Homosexuality: Studying 'Others,' Finding Self." *Christianity and Crisis* 38 (February 20, 1978): 22–27.

Smith, Robert Houston. *Patches of Godlight: The Pattern of Thought of C. S. Lewis.* Athens, Ga.: Univ. of Georgia Press, 1981.

Snitow, Ann, Christine Stansell, and Sharon Thompson, eds. *Powers of Desire: The Politics of Sexuality.* New York: Monthly Review Press, 1983.

Soble, Alan. *The Structure of Love.* New Haven: Yale Univ. Press, 1990.

Sölle, Dorothee, with Shirley A. Cloyes. *To Work and to Love: A Theology of Creation.* Philadelphia: Fortress Press, 1984, 126.

Spelman, Elizabeth V. *Inessential Woman: Problems of Exclusion in Feminist Thought.* Boston: Beacon Press, 1988.

Spong, John S. "Sexual Ethics: No Longer a Matter of Black and White." *The Episcopalian,* February 1987, 6–7.

———. *Living in Sin?: A Bishop Rethinks Human Sexuality.* San Francisco: Harper and Row, 1988.

———. "Understanding the Gay Reality." *The Christian Century* 103 (22 January 1986): 62–63.

———. "A Call to Confront Homophobia." *The Witness* 73 (November 1990): 22–25.

Stackhouse, Max L. "Thirty-Eight Theses on Christian Social Ethics and Sexuality." *This World* 25 (spring 1989): 119–25.

Steinfels, Peter. "Cries of Heresy After Feminists Meet." *The New York Times,* 14 May 1994, 28.

Stemmeler, Michael L., and J. Michael Clark, eds. *Homophobia and the Judaeo-Christian Tradition.* Gay Men's Issues in Religious Studies Series. Dallas: Monument Press, 1990.

Stettner, John W. "Review of The Ethics of Sex by Helmut Thielicke." *Journal of Religion and Health* 4 (July 1965): 376–77.

Stimpson, Catherine R., and Ethel Spector Person. *Women: Sex and Sexuality.* Chicago: Univ. of Chicago Press, 1980.

Stine, Esther, C., ed. "Homophobia: The Overlooked Sin." *Church and Society* 73 (November–December 1982): 3–71.

Stinnette, Charles R. "Review of Sexual Relation in Christian Thought by D.S. Bailey." *The Anglican Theological Review* 42 (October 1960): 366–68.

Stoltenberg, John. "Gays and the Propornography Movement: Having the Hots for Sex Discrimination." In *Men Confront Pornography,* ed. Michael S. Kimmell. New York: Crown Publishers, 1990.

————. *Refusing to Be a Man: Essays on Sex and Justice.* Portland, Ore.: Breitenbush Books, 1989.

Stott, John R. W. "Homosexual 'Marriage': Why Same-Sex Partnerships Are Not a Christian Option." *Christianity Today* 29 (22 April 1985): 21–28.

Stowe, W. McFerrin, Bp. "The Church and Homosexuals." *Christianity and Crisis* 39 (20 August 1979): 206–8.

Suhor, Mary Lou. "In the Matter of Sherwood and Gilson." *The Witness* 69 (January 1986): 4.

Swerdlow, Amy, and Hanna Lessinger, eds. *Class, Race, and Sex: The Dynamics of Control.* Boston: G. K. Hall and Company, 1983.

Sys, Jacques. "'Look Out! It's Alive!': C. S. Lewis on Doctrine." In *A Christian for All Christians: Essays in Honour of C. S. Lewis,* ed. Andrew Walker and James Patrick. London: Hodder and Stoughton, 1990.

The Consultation on Homosexuality, Social Justice, and Roman Catholic Theology. *Homosexuality and Social Justice.* Reissue of the *Report of the Task Force on Gay/Lesbian Issues, San Francisco,* ed. Kevin Gordon. San Francisco: The Consultation on Homosexuality, Social Justice, and Roman Catholic Theology, 1986.

Thielicke, Helmut. *The Ethics of Sex.* New York: Harper and Row, 1964.

Thorson-Smith, Sylvia. *Reconciling the Broken Silence: The Church in Dialogue on Gay and Lesbian Issues.* Louisville, Ky.: The Christian Education Program Area of the Congregational Ministry Division, Presbyterian Church (U.S.A.), 1993.

Thrall, M. E. "Review of The Man-Woman Relation in Christian Thought by D. S. Bailey." *The Journal of Theological Studies* 12 (October 1961): 412–14.

Throckmorton, Burton H. "One Summer Day in New Hampshire: Bright Sun, Dappled Shade, Secret Trial." *Christianity and Crisis* 47 (9 November 1987): 380–81.

Townes, Emilie M. "The Price of the Ticket: Racism, Sexism, Heterosexism, and the Church in Light of the AIDS Crisis." In *Redefining Sexual Ethics: A Sourcebook of Essays, Stories, and Poems,* ed. Susan E. Davies and Eleanor H. Haney. Cleveland: The Pilgrim Press, 1991.

Trask, Haunani-Kay. *Eros and Power: The Promise of Feminist Theory.* Philadelphia: Univ. of Pennsylvania Press, 1986.

Traycik, Auburn Faber. "From Fanfare to Fiasco: Newark's New Gay Priest." *Christian Challenge* 29 (March 1990): 14–20.

Valverde, Mariana. *Sex, Power, and Pleasure.* Toronto: The Women's Press, 1985.

Vance, Carole S. "Gender Systems, Ideology, and Sex Research." In *Powers of Desire: The Politics of Sexuality,* ed. Ann Snitow, Christine Stansell, and Sharon Thompson. New York: Monthly Review Press, 1983.

———. "Pleasure and Danger: Toward a Politics of Sexuality." In *Pleasure and Danger: Exploring Female Sexuality,* ed. Carole S. Vance. Boston: Routledge and Kegan Paul, 1984.

Vance, Carole S., and Ann Barr Snitow. "Toward a Conversation About Sex in Feminism: A Modest Proposal." *Signs: Journal of Women in Culture and Society* 10 (autumn 1984): 126–35.

Vincinus, Martha. "Sexuality and Power." *Feminist Studies* 8, no. 1 (1982).

Wallis, Jim. "Is Anyone Listening: The Need for a Better Dialogue in the Churches on Gay and Lesbian Sexuality." *Sojourners* 20 (July 1991): 10–28.

Wantland, William C. "The Bible and Sexual Ethics." *The Living Church,* 31 May 1987, 8–11.

———. "Changing Patterns of Sexuality." *The Living Church,* 26 April 1987, 10–13.

Warnach, Victor. "Agape in the New Testament." In *The Philosophy and Theology of Anders Nygren,* ed. Charles W. Kegley. Carbondale: Southern Illinois Univ. Press, 1970.

Washbourn, Penelope. "Becoming Woman: Menstruation as Spiritual Experience." In *WomanSpirit Rising,* ed. Carole Christ and Judith Plaskow. San Francisco: Harper and Row, 1979.

Webster, Paula. "The Forbidden: Eroticism and Taboo." In *Pleasure and Danger: Exploring Female Sexuality,* ed. Carole S. Vance. Boston: Routledge and Kegan Paul, 1984.

Weeks, Jeffrey. *Sex, Politics and Society: The Regulation of Sexuality Since 1800.* London: Longman, 1981.

———. *Sexuality and Its Discontents: Meanings, Myths, and Modern Sexuality.* London: Routlege and Kegan Paul, 1985.

———. *Sexuality.* London: Tavistock Publications, 1986.

Wetherilt, Ann Kirkus. *That They May Be Many: Voices of Women, Echoes of God.* New York: Continuum, 1994.

White, William Luther. "A Critique of Some C. S. Lewis Critics." *Religion and Life* 38 (winter 1969): 535–47.

Wilcox, John R. "Conflict Over Sexuality: The Family." In *The Public Vocation of Christian Ethics,* ed. Beverly W. Harrison, Robert L. Stivers, and Ronald H. Stone. New York: The Pilgrim Press, 1986.

Williams, Daniel Day. *The Spirit and the Forms of Love.* New York: Harper and Row, 1968.

Williams, Delores S. "Kairos Time: Challenge of the Centrisms." *Christianity and Crisis* 52 (3 February 1992): 16–18.

———. *Sisters in the Wilderness: The Challenge of Womanist God-Talk.* Maryknoll, N.Y.: Orbis Books, 1993.

———. "Womanist/Feminist Dialogue: Problems and Possibilities." *Journal of Feminist Studies in Religion* 9, nos. 1–2 (spring/fall 1993): 67–74.

Williams, Robert J. *Just as I Am: A Practical Guide to Being Out, Proud, and Christian.* New York: Crown Publishers, 1992.

———. "Toward a Theology for Lesbian and Gay Marriage." *Anglican Theological Review* 72 (spring 1990): 134–57.

Willis, John Randolph. *Pleasures Forevermore: The Theology of C. S. Lewis.* Chicago: Loyola Univ. Press.

Wilson, A. N. *C. S. Lewis: A Biography.* New York: W. W. Norton and Company, 1990.

Wingren, Gustaf. "Swedish Theology Since 1900." *Scottish Journal of Theology* 9 (June 1956): 113–34.

———. *Theology in Conflict: Barth—Bultmann—Nygren,* trans. Eric H. Walstrom. Philadelphia: Muhlenberg Press, 1958.

Wynn, John Charles, ed. *Sexual Ethics and Christian Responsibility.* New York: Association Press, 1970.

Yarnold, G. D. "Review of The Man-Woman Relation in Christian Thought by D. S. Bailey." *The Journal of Ecclesiastical History* 11 (October 1960): 259.

Yates, John W. "Sex and Older Singles." *The Episcopalian,* May 1987, 24–25.

Young, Iris Marion. *Justice and the Politics of Difference.* Princeton, N.J.: Princeton Univ. Press, 1990.

Zevy, Lee. "Invisibility, Fantasy, and Intimacy: Princess Charming Is Not a Prince." In *Lesbian Psychologies: Explorations and Challenges,* ed. The Boston Lesbian Psychologies Collective. Chicago: Univ. of Illinois Press, 1987.

INDEX